'Mr Riddell does a masterly job of capturing the ins and outs of Mr Blair's remarkably close relationship with an American president who is in so many ways his complete opposite . . . [this] immensely readable book may not be the last word on Tony Blair's war and his relationship with George Bush, but it will surely long stand as one of the best.'

Ivo H. Daalder, *New York Times*

'Writing contemporary history while events are still unfolding is an increasingly popular art form. *Hug Them Close* confirms Riddell as the leading exponent. He has a powerful sense of history. This is not just a chronicle of current events but a penetrating analysis of them set in a historical perspective.'

Richard Wilson, *Times Literary Supplement*

'Riddell is authoritative and insightful in describing how successive British prime ministers from Churchill onwards, with the possible exception of the avidly pro-European Ted Heath, had tried to tame the US tendency towards isolationism by hugging the Americans close.'

Alan Milburn, *The Times*

'An impeccably sourced and revelatory book.'

Steve Richards, *Independent*

D0054756

To my lovely and adorable girls, Avril and Emily.

Hug
Them
Close

Blair, Clinton, Bush
and the 'Special Relationship'

Peter Riddell

POLITICO'S

First published in Great Britain 2003 by
Politico's Publishing, an imprint of
Methuen Publishing Limited
215 Vauxhall Bridge Road
London SW1V 1EJ

This revised edition published 2004

10 9 8 7 6 5 4 3 2 1

A CIP catalogue record for this book is available from the British Library.

ISBN 1 84275 118 2

Printed and bound in Great Britain by Cox and Wyman.

Contents

Preface

This book is the result of frustration and annoyance. These may seem strange motives for authorship, but during the early months of 2003 I became increasingly frustrated and annoyed about how Tony Blair's relations with George W. Bush were portrayed in the media and in Parliament. Much of what was said and written struck me then, and even more now, as ill-informed and superficial. Jibes about Blair being 'Bush's poodle' or charges about Blair and Bush being war criminals were matched by one-sided partisanship. Condemnations of the 'axis of weasel' and 'cheese-eating surrender monkeys' were common, and not just in the more xeonophobic tabloids. The demonisation of France and Germany, and the celebration of 'Rummy' as if the American Defense Secretary was some kind of cartoon hero, reflected the debasement of journalism in Britain. President Chirac made several errors during the early months of 2003, but both he and Chancellor Schröder had legitimate reasons of their own for acting as they did, widely shared by their own voters. These need to be understood rather than just abusively dismissed. Similarly, Tony Blair's relations with Washington are much more complicated than implied by the crude anti-American placards of the anti-war demonstrators. I wanted to redress the balance by trying to explain what happened and what motivated the main players on both sides of the Atlantic.

The following pages are about the politics and personalities of transatlantic relations, not about the war in Iraq. The war was the occasion for writing the book, and is its climax, though we are far from the end of the story. But as important is what happened over the preceding months and years. You cannot appreciate why Tony Blair backed the US in 2003 unless you take into account not only the 11 September attacks, but also, much earlier, his attitude towards newly elected President George W. Bush, and his relations with President Bill Clinton. To understand these events, and his decision to adopt his 'hug them close' approach to the White House, you have to look back at the relations between prime ministers and presidents since the 1940s. Only then is it possible to appreciate why Tony Blair has been, in many ways, a traditional British prime minister in his approach to Washington, and in his desire to avoid choosing between Europe and America.

Hug Them Close combines reporting and analysis, based on my own experience as a journalist, on the *Financial Times* and, since 1991, *The Times*. I first visited Washington in 1975 and have been back virtually every year since, spending nearly three years there as Washington Bureau Chief of the *FT* in the days of the first President Bush. I covered many of the events described, observing prime ministers and presidents at first hand since the early 1980s.

I feel as much at home in Washington as in any European capital, more so in many ways since I both lived there and met my wife there. I despise the patronising anti-Americanism of some on both the left and right in Britain, and many more in the rest of Europe. America is a second home, where I have enjoyed the warm friendship of many thoughtful and intelligent people. I never fail to be thrilled each time I approach Washington from Dulles Airport and catch a first glimpse of the Lincoln Memorial across the Potomac, or see the Manhattan skyline for the first time coming in from JFK airport. That is why, on my first visit to the US after the 11 September attacks, my initial sight of the Manhattan skyline without the twin towers was so poignant. That is also why I regard the 'America had it coming' attitude of some on the European left as contemptible and morally bankrupt. I understand why, for many Americans, something fundamental did change on 11 September.

Yet the United States is still a foreign country. Terrorism is a real and urgent threat, but it is not the only serious global problem. I do not share the belief of American neo-conservatives – a diverse group anyway – that what works in the United States is, by definition, best, and should be transplanted around the world. This attitude has stimulated much of the anti-Americanism seen in the Middle East and Europe. America is the most powerful nation on earth, and is mainly a force for good. But it cannot ensure security and peace on its own. The US needs allies and partners, to whom it listens, rather than dictates.

Also, when I lived in Washington, I became more of a pro-European – or, rather, I realised that Britain's future is primarily as part of Europe, rather than as a 51st state. The visits of Jacques Delors, then President of the European Commission, mattered far more than those of virtually all British ministers, apart from Margaret Thatcher. For all the close bilateral ties of so many kinds, ultimately in the eyes of Washington Britain is a European power, albeit one usually closer to America than either France or Germany. Thus any attempt to separate ourselves from the rest of Europe is a damaging delusion.

While writing this book, I spoke to many involved in the Downing Street–White House relationship over the past decade.

Some conversations date back several years to the time of the events described. Most were after the end of the Iraq war. As often with works of contemporary history, much of the information has been on an off-the-record basis, as well as on-the-record via public statements, interviews and, most recently, the revelations in the Hutton inquiry. This presents any author with an awkward dilemma. References to 'private information' in the footnotes of many books understandably irritate readers who wonder about the reliability of the unattributable quotations. The sources are unwilling to be named because they are still working for the government, in London, Washington, Paris and Berlin. Not using such unattributable quotations would deprive readers of information which would otherwise not be available and which, I believe, enriches the book.

In the following chapters, I have tried to be open and transparent. Where possible I have attributed quotations. References to major speeches, articles and books are given in the bibliography. In other cases, where a statement is attributed to someone, I either heard it directly from them or had it reliably reported to me by someone who was present when, say, Tony Blair, Bill Clinton or George W. Bush made the reported remarks. That applies, for example, to the account of Blair and Clinton's conversation at Chequers in December 2000, which was reported to me by one of the participants the following day. Similarly, my accounts of Blair's response on 11 September and his meetings with Bush are based on reports by those who were there. Definitions of who is a senior or close Blair adviser or official tend to be elastic in the British press, just as a senior backbencher tends to be anyone who has been re-elected for a second parliament. But when I use the terms 'senior' or 'close', I mean people who would be recognised as such, not least by Tony Blair himself, if their identities were revealed.

Most of this book comes from conversations with still-serving senior politicians, civil servants, diplomats and advisers since the events described are so recent. Few are willing to be quoted by name. However, the handful of senior officials who were closely involved in these events who have now retired have been willing to have their comments attributed. For instance, Sir Christopher Meyer, who served as British Ambassador to Washington from November 1997 until the end of February 2003, has been very candid about his memories of these years in television interviews, and in talking with me while I was writing this book. I am very grateful to him for his generosity in giving me time during many conversations over the years, both in Washington and since his return to London. His insights have been invaluable. Lord Wilson of Dinton, Cabinet Secretary from January 1998 until July 2002, also allowed me to quote him attributably, for which I would like to thank him. Even though my thanks to still serving senior officials and advisers are anonymous, they are nonetheless considerable. Those in 10 Downing Street, the Foreign Office, the Bush administration, the State Department and the French and German Governments who helped me know who they are. I hope they will think I have done justice to their assistance in the following pages. Of course, all interpretations, and inevitable misinterpretations, are entirely my own.

Much of what I learned about transatlantic relations has come from former colleagues on the *Financial Times*, both in London and particularly during my happy period in Washington, as well from my current colleagues on *The Times*, especially in the political team at

Westminster who make my working life so much fun and so stimu-lating. I also owe a considerable debt to many American and British friends who are part of my transatlantic world.

This book has been produced, very quickly, by Politico's, whose publishing arm is now part of Methuen. My good friend Sean Magee has now had a hand in bringing out most of my books in various publishing houses over nearly two decades and I am, as ever, grateful to him for his humour and gentle editing. The irrepressible Iain Dale of Politico's accepted and backed my idea for this book on the spot, and John Schwartz was his usual efficient self in seeing the book through. (Two stylistic points. I have generally adopted English spellings except in direct quotations and about the World Trade Center, where I thought the American version was more appropriate. I have also referred to George W. Bush's father, the 41st, as opposed to the current 43rd, US President as Bush senior or the elder Bush, for convenience as opposed to correctness.)

My wife Avril and my daughter Emily have, as always, offered advice, encouragement and love. They have been very patient and supportive during the self-absorbed few months while I have been writing this book. Their unique contribution is recognised in the dedication. I hope they, and all those others who have helped me, believe the effort has been worthwhile.

Peter Riddell
August 2003

Preface to the Revised Edition

Much has happened since I finished writing the first edition, so I have made many changes, particularly in the last four chapters of the book, to take account of new developments. Iraq has remained unstable and violent, with daily attacks on American troops and Iraqi security forces. There have been many more deaths since President Bush declared the main military operation over on 1 May 2003 than during the previous six weeks of the 'war'. There have also been highly damaging charges about the abuse of Iraqi prisoners by coalition, and particularly American, forces. The capture of Saddam Hussein in December 2003 has made little difference. However, there is evidence of improvements in public services, and, even though the Pentagon greatly under-estimated the task of creating a free, pluralist society, an interim Iraqi administration of sorts has emerged.

But no weapons of mass destruction have been found in Iraq, fuelling the debate in the US and Britain over the legality of and justification for going to war. These doubts have been underlined by some of the many books which appeared during the autumn and winter of 2003–4, particularly those by Robin Cook, Hans Blix, the former chief weapons inspector, Richard Clarke, the former White House counter-terrorism chief and Bob Woodward, the indefatigable chronicler of Washington power. Terrorism has continued elsewhere, notably with the explosions in Madrid in March 2004. A breakthrough in the Israel–Palestine dispute has been as elusive as ever, with the hopes of early summer 2003 dashed by a renewal of violence, and by President Bush's one-sided backing of the Sharon Government's imposed solution. Although formal civilities have returned to transatlantic relations, the underlying tensions and disagreements remain.

In Britain, the long-awaited report in late January 2004 of the inquiry by Lord Hutton into the death of David Kelly cleared the Government of bad faith and misconduct, while damning the BBC, leading to the resignation of both the chairman and director-general of the corporation. But what was widely seen as the one-sided nature of the Hutton report failed to end the controversy, and Tony Blair was forced to set up an inquiry under Lord Butler of Brockwell, the former Cabinet Secretary, into the intelligence issues involved with weapons of mass destruction. Not only have Iraq and his close relations with President Bush continued to undermine public support and trust in Tony Blair, but the political costs of the war have also become more apparent. Labour MPs have been more willing to rebel against key items of his domestic programme, while Blair's European policy has been undermined, with euro entry postponed indefinitely. The bungled announcement of a u-turn over a referendum on any European constitution merely underlined Blair's weakness.

These developments have reinforced, rather than altered, the main conclusions of the first edition of this book. In many ways, the central dilemma has become even starker. Mr Blair exaggerated the immediate threat from Iraq, but he genuinely believed – as did British and other intelligence agencies – that Saddam Hussein possessed weapons of mass destruction and the intention to develop more. That is why he wanted the return of the UN inspectors in late 2002, in the hope that either their discovery of Iraqi WMD would prevent a war or would, if Iraq failed to co-operate, provide a clearcut justification for military action which would be widely backed internationally. Even as late as January and February 2003, he hoped to avoid war, albeit that this involved more than a touch of his familiar self-delusion. But his calculations failed on both counts. The UN inspectors did not find WMD, nor did the Americans afterwards. Unlike many comentators, I do not question Mr Blair's sincerity in believing in the existence of WMD in Iraq. That has still left the puzzle – as much to the intelligence world as to outsiders – about why WMD have not been found. So Mr Blair has had to deal with the consequences of his underlying strategy – which he could never fully acknowledge in public – of going along with whatever President Bush decided. This was the inevitable result of the 'hug them close' approach.

None of these events has, however, shaken Mr Blair's belief in the rightness of what he did over the winter of 2002–3, or in the wisdom and necessity of 'hug them close'. However, my overall verdict is harsher than when I completed the first edition in August 2003. The gamble that Mr Blair took – on WMD and on being able to influence Washington's thinking and policy towards the Israel–Palestine dispute and the shape of post-war Iraq – has so far failed. He realised the risks. However genuine his motives, Mr Blair has to be judged by the results. Iraq is now a shadow not only over his second term, but also over his whole premiership.

Peter Riddell
April 2004

1. Hug Them Close

My view is that the Prime Minister, far from lacking conviction, has almost too much, particularly when dealing with the world beyond Britain. He is a little Manichean for my perhaps now jaded taste, seeing matters in stark terms of good and evil, black and white, contending with each other.

Lord Jenkins of Hillhead, speaking in the
House of Lords, 24 September 2002

The price of influence is that we do not leave the US to face the tricky issues alone. By tricky, I mean the ones which people wish weren't there, don't want to deal with, and, if I can put it a little pejoratively, know the US should confront, but want the luxury of criticising them for it. So if the US act alone, they are unilateralist; but if they want allies, people shuffle to the back. International terrorism is one such issue.

Tony Blair, speech to British Ambassadors and diplomats,
London, 7 January 2003

People say that you are doing this because the Americans are telling you to do it. I keep telling them that it's worse than that. I believe in it.

Tony Blair in remarks to the Parliamentary
Labour Party, February 2003

Tony Blair's visitor at Chequers on the evening of Wednesday 13 December 2000 stayed up late, as usual, and was loquacious, as usual. Bill Clinton was on his presidential farewell tour to Britain and Northern Ireland. He was visiting the Prime Minister just after the US Supreme Court had finally decided in favour of George W. Bush, rather than Vice President Al Gore, after the six-week long saga of the disputed Florida election. Bill Clinton had three pieces of advice to what he had always regarded as his younger protégé. First, 'Don't screw up your election like Al [Gore] did.' Second, 'Get as close to George Bush as you have been to me.' Third, 'Don't underestimate George W. He's a shrewd, tough politician and absolutely ruthless.' Blair listened and agreed. Labour's re-election campaign in Britain six months later avoided the mistakes which cost Al Gore the presidency. Blair quickly sought to get on the inside track with the new President and his administration. And he soon learnt not to underestimate Bush.

Yet Blair hardly needed Clinton's advice. He had already decided to get close to the new president. Long before December 2000, he had adopted what one senior Blair adviser describes as the 'hug them close' approach to the White House. But in many ways, this late night Chequers conversation – related to me the following day – epitomises the Blair approach, by focusing on personal relations, not on ideology. And it reflects a very traditional British attitude towards working with Washington, whoever is in the White House.

This book seeks to explain Tony Blair's transatlantic strategy, to examine his relations with Presidents Clinton and Bush, and to look at what these links have meant for Britain's European policy. Blair's relations with the United States are one of the most misunderstood aspects of his premiership. During the war with Iraq in spring 2003, he was widely attacked on the left in Britain and by many in the rest of Europe as merely 'Bush's poodle', obediently following Washington's orders. Meanwhile, on the right, and among American conservatives, Tony Blair has been seen, and praised, as a loyal and brave champion of Atlanticism within 'new' Europe against the weak appeasers of 'old' Europe. Both views are caricatures, and misread Blair's personality, objectives and policies. In particular, the critics underestimate how much Blair himself was worried about Iraq and weapons of mass destruction. But it is easy to see why these misapprehensions have occurred in view of the strongly pro-American tone of Blair's public comments. Later chapters show why and how the Prime Minister gradually became committed during the course of 2002 to President Bush's policy of getting rid of Saddam Hussein. The process was more complicated and less sudden than is commonly believed.

A recurrent question is how far Blair's determination to be close to the White House – the 'hug them close' approach – has been justified when set against other foreign policy objectives. Blair's closeness to Bush has had significant costs, and has undermined Britain's aspirations to take a leading role in Europe. The book highlights major failings in British diplomacy over the winter of 2002–3 as 10 Downing Street and the Foreign Office were slow to detect the signs of a revival in the Franco–German alliance and consistently misread French intentions, particularly President Chirac's determination to block a further United Nations resolution in March 2003. The result was both to leave Blair politically vulnerable at the start of the Iraq war and to undermine his aim of detaching Germany from its long-standing close alliance with France.

A central theme is that the arguments and splits of early 2003 over the war with Iraq had their origins in attitudes formed by Blair much earlier, notably during the Clinton presidency. Blair's concern about Saddam Hussein and weapons of mass destruction was not some new discovery post-11 September, or a response to American pressure. Before 11 September, Blair was in some respects more worried about the threat from Iraq than Bush himself. The dangers of weapons of mass destruction had regularly appeared in Blair's public statements going back to 1997. The language he used in February and March 2003 was strikingly similar to what he was saying more than five years earlier. The reasons why he became interested in weapons of mass destruction so early in his premiership, discussed in detail in Chapter 4, were one of the main revelations while writing this book. They not only explain much of what happened later over Iraq, but also provide insights into Blair's character and approach to politics.

Blair is more of an instinctive than an intellectual politician. He relies heavily on his intuition. One of his closest advisers said that he possessed more than any other contemporary British politician 'an instinct to see the coming issue. This political instinct puts him a jump ahead of other people.' The adviser was referring specifically to Blair's early worries about weapons of mass destruction. Blair is stronger on big strategic themes than on details. Reflecting his training as a barrister in absorbing a brief, he can, and often does, quickly read up on a subject, and forcefully express its essence. He can focus on whatever is the big issue of the day, talking about this or that new initiative. But he prefers the big picture. He is not a pointillist. He does not have a vast storehouse of political or policy knowledge. And he is not really 'a policy wonk', unlike the earnest young Blairite men, and a few women, who go to think-tank seminars and to Third Way or Progressive Governance conferences.

Blair differs both from Bill Clinton and from Gordon Brown, his closest international and domestic political associates. Clinton is both an intuitive politician and a policy intellectual, while Brown is a pre-eminent policy intellectual. But Blair is essentially an instinctive politician, and not a policy intellectual. Ahead of the Iraq war, for example, Brown had read Henry Kissinger's *Does America Need a Foreign Policy?* while Blair prefers books on religion, and biographies. That partly reflects another key difference between Blair and Brown. Whereas Brown is very much in the democratic socialist tradition, particularly as influenced by the discipline and hard work ethic of Scottish Presbyterianism, Blair is not part of any Labour class or intellectual tradition. As he often says, he chose Labour, and was not born into the party. His roots are as much in the Liberal Party of Gladstone and Asquith as in the Labour Party of Attlee and Wilson. That is why he has often lamented the division in the progressive/centre-left forces in Britain in the 1900s between Labour and the Liberals. In other respects, Blair has more in common with Continental Christian Democrats than with the neo-Marxist origins of many European socialist parties.

This absence of deep ideological roots has misled many people into thinking that he does not have deep views at all, and is merely a successful electoral operator. Blair arouses strong feelings. He is admired by many for his leadership qualities, for his strength in a crisis, while many others loathe him. They see him as a smiling chameleon, an insincere actor with presidential ambitions, who adopts whatever approach his 'spin doctors' tell him will play best

with the public. Hence all the 'phoney Tony' jibes and his vulnerability on questions of personal trust shown by opinion polls. Yet this
public image – so vividly conveyed by Rory Bremner's impressions –
is misleading and one-sided. Blair undoubtedly has the skills of an
actor and public performer, going back to his participation in school
plays at Fettes and to his undergraduate phase as an imitation Rolling
Stones type of rock musician. This theatrical side is displayed
nowadays in his speeches. He also has the ability to understand and
articulate the public mood. He practises the empathetic conversa-
tional political style – 'I feel your pain' – perfected by Bill Clinton.
That was seen most memorably in his public reaction on the day of
Princess Diana's death in August 1997 and, more cloyingly, later that
autumn in toasting the Queen as 'the Best of British'.

However, these theatrical skills are combined with a strong moral
outlook. Blair relies heavily on his personal moral compass – his sense
of right and wrong. This goes back a long time, to his discussions as
an undergraduate about ethical Christianity and the work of the
Scottish moral philosopher John Macmurray. His interest in the
Koran and Islam long pre-date the 11 September attacks and formed
part of his summer holiday reading in 2000. Yet his religious interest,
while open and occasionally discussed, is very different from the bible
studies and public prayer meetings of the 'born-again' Christians
around George W. Bush. Blair was embarrassed, and annoyed, when
asked in a television interview whether he prayed with the president.
For Blair, a religious commitment is reflected less in public religious
devotions and more in his approach to politics. This first surfaced in
the early 1990s, when he was Labour's Shadow Home Secretary and
talked about the moral and social causes of crime. The international

side first appeared after he became Prime Minister, particularly in 1998 when he talked about the threat from Saddam Hussein, and, the following year, when he attacked Serbian ethnic cleansing in Kosovo. This was reflected in his speech of April 1999 in Chicago on the 'doctrine of international community', justifying intervention in what had previously been seen as the internal affairs of nation states on humanitarian grounds. This had conscious echoes of Gladstone's protests over the Bulgarian atrocities in the late 1870s.

Blair's critics, both within his own party and in the Conservative opposition and the press, have disliked his moralising tone. They argue that it is false and sounds hypocritical. At its worst, his approach can grate and appear sermonising. But Blair's abilities as an actor do not mean he is insincere. The opposite criticism is more valid. Blair means exactly what he says about addressing the ills of the world in 'right and wrong' terms, almost regardless of the strategic implications. This has put him, and Britain, in some very risky positions, as later chapters discuss. But Blair believes that his moral outlook not only should, but will, prevail.

Roy Jenkins – Lord Jenkins of Hillhead – was one of the most acute observers of political character, both during his own long career and as a distinguished biographer. During his last years, he became a historical mentor and dinner companion for Tony Blair, who respected his knowledge, wisdom and insights. In return, Jenkins formed a shrewd view of Blair, though became more critical of him after the 2001 election over his failure to take the lead in pressing for British entry into the euro. During a debate on Iraq in the House of Lords in September 2002, his last big speech before his death the following January, Jenkins gave an acute character sketch of Blair:

7

> *I have a high regard for the Prime Minister. I have been*
> *repelled by attempts to portray him as a vacuous man with*
> *an artificial smile and no convictions. I am reminded of*
> *similar attempts by a frustrated Right to suggest that*
> *Gladstone was mad, Asquith was corrupt and Attlee was*
> *negligible. My view is that the Prime Minister, far from*
> *lacking conviction, has almost too much, particularly*
> *when dealing with the world beyond Britain. He is a little*
> *too Manichean for my perhaps now jaded taste, seeing*
> *matters in stark terms of good and evil, black and white,*
> *contending with each other, and with a consequent belief*
> *that if evil is cast down, good will inevitably follow. I am*
> *more inclined to see the world and the regimes in it in*
> *varying shades of grey. The experience of the past year, not*
> *least in Afghanistan, has given more support to that view*
> *than to the more Utopian one that a quick 'change of*
> *regime' can make us all live happily ever after.*

Blair's subsequent behaviour during the run-up to the Iraq war confirms the Jenkins view: the absolute conviction of moral rightness in seeing Saddam Hussein as a threat to the world and the need, therefore, urgently to remove the threat from him. And, as Jenkins argued, there are dangers in too stark a view, of not acknowledging the messiness of all the options.

Moreover, a subsidiary clause in the Jenkins speech reveals one of the paradoxes of the Blair premiership: the contrast between his conviction approach to foreign affairs and his more cautious approach domestically. In this context, the euro counts as a domestic issue. One former senior civil servant who closely observed the inner workings of Downing Street sees two explanations. First, Blair would rather have liked to have been a president, above the battles of Congress, and able to be a major figure on the world stage. In that sense, however subliminally, or even partly intentionally, Blair and his political team in 10 Downing Street have copied the American television series *The West Wing*, especially as they had no prior experience of working as ministers and advisers in a Cabinet and parliamentary system. Blair saw Clinton perform as President and believed he could do better. So the presidentialism of Blair's style and foreign policy can be seen, in part, as acting out this role. Second, Blair saw foreign affairs as an arena in which he could operate largely free of the constraints imposed by Gordon Brown's dominance of the domestic agenda. The Chancellor had an effective veto over large areas of economic, social and industrial policy, and over the euro entry tests after October 1997. But Brown had no role on the international stage, at least in military and security matters. (Brown did, however, have distinct, and influential, views on the international financial system and how to tackle global poverty.)

But Blair flourished in the absence of Brown in his dealings with other world leaders. Looked at another way, this official also says that Brown may have thought that 'Tony may exhaust himself internationally or, given enough rope, may hang himself on foreign ventures.' This view has proved wrong so far, but is not entirely misplaced. On the view of one close adviser: 'Blair's stamina is his weak point.' Blair does not have the physical staying power of, say, a Margaret Thatcher at the height of her powers. He can exhaust himself on big projects. For instance, after all the lengthy negotiations and late nights leading up to the Good Friday agreement in Northern Ireland in spring 1998, Blair was 'nearly out of action in June and July', appearing listless and not giving a lead. Subsequently, Blair has shown more resilience but, at times since the 11 September attacks, he has understandably appeared exhausted after several long flights. Moreover, Blair has clearly taken big risks internationally: in Kosovo, Sierra Leone, Afghanistan and, above all, Iraq. He played for high political stakes in the run-up to the Iraq war, and the risks did not end with the fall of Baghdad. Brown took a back seat during both the Kosovo and the Afghanistan conflicts. James Naughtie records (2001, p. 228) how during Kosovo, 'it had become especially obvious that Brown was not prepared to connect himself to the military crisis in the Balkans. Around Blair it was asked if the Chancellor's silence was the action of a minister concerned to preserve diplomatic propriety or a minister saying, once again, you're on your own.' By contrast, Brown decided very publicly to back Blair over Iraq in February and March 2003, going out of his way to seek interviews and other opportunities to support the Prime Minister over the war.

The strands of the instinctive/intuitive politician, the theatrical skills as an actor and the strong moral compass come together in Blair's emphasis on personal relations with other leaders. He has seen other leaders in personal, not ideological, terms: as people with whom he can, or cannot, do business. Hence, there was no problem for him – though there was for some of his advisers – in switching from the fellow Third Wayer Bill Clinton to the conservative Republican George W. Bush. Blair devotes enormous amounts of time to meeting with, and talking to, other leaders: not just Clinton and Bush, but also, particularly, fellow European heads of government. Critics argue that Blair, like, say, Thatcher in the late 1980s, exaggerates personal bonds between leaders. Thatcher's warm relationship with Mikhail Gorbachev – not least their liking for a good argument – blinded her to some of the flaws in the Soviet leader's approach, and to the growing weaknesses in his political position. Similarly, now, Blair and Bush have put too much emphasis on their personal relations with Vladimir Putin, the Russian leader.

Blair has considerable personal charm and believes that, if only he can talk to this or that person, they will be won over to his viewpoint. He is a natural conciliator. He hates people to leave a meeting with him feeling angry or disagreeing. He can appear to say whatever his guest or audience wants to hear. Blair does have a tendency towards self-deception. Lord Jenkins drew comparisons between Blair and Franklin Delano Roosevelt. In an interview with the *Independent* in September 2002, Jenkins said of the two:

> First, they both have a great ability to enthuse those who come to see them for half an hour. They go out thinking the world is a better place and they are a more important person than they were when they went in. Both have been brilliant at that. Second, sometimes people misinterpret them because they seem to give more agreement to the proposition of the other person than is really the case.

Blair's opacity can lead to misunderstandings. Two examples stand out. First, Blair's dinner with Brown at the Granita restaurant in Islington in June 1994 created the belief among the Brown camp that their man had been promised the succession, fuelling resentment during the second term when this still appeared to be a long way off. In reality, I doubt if a specific promise was made, apart from Brown being given control over the main economic agenda. Rather, Blair did not want his old friend to leave feeling more let down than he was bound already to be, and talked in warm, though unspecific, terms about the future. Second, the long courtship, both before and after the 1997 election, between Blair and Paddy Ashdown over bringing the Liberal Democrats into closer alliance with New Labour came to nothing. To some extent, Ashdown's own eagerness created false hopes, as his two volumes of diaries (2000 and 2001) show. But how far was he deliberately deceived by Blair? Ashdown's reply is enigmatic: 'He always meant it when he said it.'

Blair generally believes that he can manoeuvre round problems. Either his personal skills will persuade other leaders, or his strong convictions will be vindicated since they are self-evidently right. Because he believes he is right, then events will justify him. That can smack of self-delusion and lead him to take risky positions, as during the Kosovo conflict in spring 1999, and again over Iraq in 2002–3. Blair's approach in these cases has been neither opportunistic nor focus-group-driven. The driving force has been his moral conviction about the need to act to prevent, respectively, ethnic cleansing and attacks by weapons of mass destruction. These convictions are sincere. The question is more whether they have always been wise. However, throughout his premiership, his moral convictions have been balanced by his determination to keep as close as possible to Washington.

In opposition, before the 1997 election, Blair repeated the conventional wisdom of the time that Britain's influence with, and value to,

America lay in its role in Europe and its ability to keep the EU outward-looking and firmly linked to the US on economic and defence matters. He rejected the view that Britain had to choose between Europe and America. That is still Blair's view, but it has developed over time into something more specific and deeply felt. This reflects Blair's experience both during the Clinton years and particularly after the 11 September attacks.

The Clinton years were crucial for Blair. This is both because Clinton's relationship with Blair was partly one of older brother to younger brother, or master to pupil, as it is described by one senior Downing Street adviser who has attended virtually all the meetings between the two men. Blair admired, and admires, Clinton's political skills and learnt a lot directly from him. Clinton continued to see himself in the master role well after Blair did not, and that produced tension on both sides. Working with the White House also educated Blair in how to handle the transatlantic relationship. The Kosovo conflict of March to June 1999 was a coming of age for Blair. He learnt a brutal lesson both in what he could expect from Clinton personally and in how, and how not, to exercise influence in Washington. In particular, domestic political factors always come first in Washington and no president likes being upstaged on his home patch, as Blair temporarily did when winning the praise of the American media during a visit in April 1999. Blair applied both lessons in his relations with George W. Bush, particularly after the 11 September attacks. He has played the role of candid friend in private, but loyal ally in public.

But the high priority put on relations with Washington is not just personal. It also reflects his belief that, for all its military power,

America should not be left to act alone: that its allies have a duty and a responsibility to act with it. Implicit in this view is that a unilateralist America is more likely to act against the interests of its allies than a multilateralist Washington. This view has been reinforced by the American reaction to the 11 September attacks. Blair stood out from other European leaders in understanding how Americans felt more vulnerable after 11 September, and therefore took a different view of national security. Blair spelt out his fears about leaving America alone in January 2003 in addressing British Ambassadors and senior diplomats in London:

> *We should remain the closest ally of the US, and as allies influence them to continue broadening their agenda. The price of influence is that we do not leave the US to face the tricky issues alone. By tricky, I mean the ones which people wish weren't there, don't want to deal with, and, if I can put it a little pejoratively, know the US should confront, but want the luxury of criticising them for it. So if the US act alone, they are unilateralist; but if they want allies, people shuffle to the back. International terrorism is one such issue . . . America should not be forced to take this issue on alone. We should all be part of it . . . So when the US confront these issues, we should be with them; and we should, in return, expect these issues to be confronted with the international community, proportionately, sensibly and in a way that delivers a better prospect of long-term peace, security and justice.*

Blair presented this support as part of a bargain. In return, America should 'listen back' on issues such as the Middle East peace process, global poverty, global warming, and the United Nations.

The problem is that the bargain is lop-sided. The president still takes the decisions and American interests come first. A British prime minister earns his right to have his say, to be consulted by an American president, but that influence is seldom crucial. At one level, British ministers and diplomats have traditionally become players in the open and often bitter inter-agency debates in Washington. The current rivalries between Colin Powell and the State Department and Donald Rumsfeld and the Pentagon have been unusual only in the importance of the issues they are debating, not in the existence of open disagreements. These are permanent. Similar rivalries have existed in previous administrations. However, British prime ministers and ambassadors in Washington have always sought not to become too identified with one faction or another. Colin Powell has been seen as closest to the British position on many issues, such as the Middle East and favouring multilateralist solutions. But British politicians and diplomats have been careful to keep close contacts with both the Pentagon and Vice President Dick Cheney's office. The British aim, in the view of one of Blair's advisers with long knowledge of Washington, is to be 'above the battle: to stand to one side and not to be associated with either faction.' The British Government must not be seen as 'another agency'.

Above all, the key link is with the White House, trying to influence the President – conducted on a day-to-day basis between the President's National Security Adviser (Condoleezza Rice) and the Prime Minister's foreign affairs adviser (Sir David Manning between the 11 September attacks and July 2003). Their contacts, via phone calls at least once each day and often more, have become the core of the White House–Downing Street relationship – to a large extent supplanting the previously central role of the Foreign Secretary and the British Ambassador in Washington. Both now have different roles. Jack Straw, Foreign Secretary since June 2001, has focussed on diplomacy at the United Nations, in the European Union, and in sustaining the international coalition, while the British Ambassador has operated more to maintain contacts across Washington's agencies and in trying to influence opinion in Congress. Normally, the maximum that a prime minister can claim is to have reinforced a president's instincts. For instance, Blair's calls after the 11 September attacks for the immediate focus to be on dealing with the Taliban and al-Qa'eda in Afghanistan, leaving Iraq to be addressed separately, were not decisive. That is what Bush quickly decided to do anyway, though Blair's views were a reassurance. Blair can claim more influence over the President's decision to seek a United Nations resolution in autumn 2002, and in keeping up the pressure over the Middle East peace process, despite all the disappointments.

The insider 'hug them' approach also ties a British prime minister into a president's decisions. Blair had more sympathy than many in the Foreign Office and the intelligence agencies in London over Bush's desire to tackle Saddam Hussein as a matter of urgency after the end of the main Afghanistan operations in early 2002. Blair believed that Saddam was both an evil dictator and a danger to his own people and the Middle East region, as he had been in the past. Now there was an opportunity to get rid of him. Yet the American and British tactics differed. For the Bush team, getting rid of Saddam was a priority from spring 2002 onwards. Most of his administration believed that military action was inevitable. Many on the British side saw such action as a probability. But Blair was constrained by domestic and Labour Party hostility to war in Iraq. Moreover, Blair was advised that he could only legally go to war on the basis of the threat of weapons of mass destruction, and breaches of past UN resolutions, not just to get rid of Saddam. He could therefore not explicitly endorse regime change as a goal, however much he privately agreed. He also insisted upon going through the UN route.

Yet these differences of priority and tactics, and ambiguities in the interpretation of UN resolution 1441 (agreed in early November 2002) put Blair in an increasingly exposed political position as the American determination to go to war became more evident. This led to an emphasis by Blair on weapons of mass destruction, rather than on regime change. This concern was only partially shared in Washington. But Blair knew that America was determined to get rid of Saddam so to justify military action he had to stress the threat from Saddam's weapons of mass destruction. This emphasis – and the exaggeration of the immediate threat from Saddam's weapons – later caused serious political trouble and recriminations for Blair, especially when weapons of mass destruction were not found in the weeks after the fall of Baghdad. A further tragic dimension was added after the suicide in late July 2003 of Dr David Kelly, a leading Government expert on biological weapons. The arguments over the use of intelligence material, both in the September 2002 dossier prepared by the Joint Intelligence Committee and the 'dodgy' dossier of February 2003, reflected Blair's need to highlight the threat from weapons of mass destruction. Almost everyone in the main western intelligence agencies believed that

Saddam had supplies of chemical and biological stocks, and an intention to develop a WMD programme. This was also the view of Hans Blix, the executive chairman of the UN weapons inspectors, UNMOVIC, before his team return to Iraq in late 2002 (as he discusses in his book, 2004). The question was, rather, whether such weapons of mass destruction could be delivered and therefore amounted to such an imminent threat as to justify pre-emptive military action. Or did Blair go along with the US, and an American military timetable because he did not want to split from Washington and because of the desirable long-term goal of getting rid of Saddam?

Blair had claimed that Saddam could always avoid war, even as late as early March 2003, if he was completely open with the UN inspectors and surrendered any weapons of mass destruction. But this was not how it looked in Washington, where the search for a further UN resolution was seen as an optional political device to help Blair, not as necessary in itself. Blair was being indulged as a close and loyal ally, but, ultimately, he was expected to fall into line and to commit British forces. That did not make Blair just a 'poodle' of Bush. After all, Blair agreed about the threat from Saddam and the desirability of removing him. But nor was he operating entirely independently. Blair's conviction about the evils of Saddam and his weapons was matched by his overriding determination to see that America was not left alone to face terrorism. For Blair, the risks of a unilateral America outweighed the risks of going to war in the face of domestic and European hostility. And the Americans knew that. Bush always expected Blair to be with him at the crunch.

Blair has always insisted – and still insists – that there is no contradiction in being both a strong supporter of the United States and an advocate of a leading role for Britain in Europe. He has consistently argued that Britain should never allow itself to get into a position where it has to choose between America and Europe. Yet that was the choice he faced in spring 2003, not only because of British errors but also as a result of a series of major diplomatic mistakes by all the main players. Blair believes in co-operation rather than competition across the Atlantic. He rejects talk of a multipolar world put forward by the French and some European centralists in which a united Europe is a counterweight to the United States. That, in the Blair view, risks destabilising the world by encouraging unilateralist tendencies in America and by undermining joint influence on problems such as the Middle East peace process and the fight against terrorism. Rather, European countries, by agreement if possible, should seek to work with and influence the US. In practice, relations are more complicated: a mixture of competition over economic issues and partnership (usually) on security matters.

On the Blair view, Britain should be a bridge across the Atlantic, between Europe and the United States. As one of Blair's senior advisers puts it, 'sometimes we will be at one end of the bridge and sometimes at the other': at the European end over global warming and the Kyoto treaty, and at the American end over the campaign against terrorism. But the 'bridge' – as a metaphor and diplomatic strategy – has never been fully accepted on either side of the Atlantic, and especially not by other European leaders, particularly the French, who have resented British claims to a special role as transatlantic interlocutor. Now the central spans of the bridge have been severely damaged, as a result of fire from both sides of the Atlantic before and during the Iraq war. Europe was, of course, divided about the war, with many of the new entrants to the EU in central and eastern Europe publicly backing the US, along with Britain, Italy and Spain. Yet, more important, was the division between Britain, on the one hand, and France and Germany, on the other hand. Euro-sceptics, both in London and Washington, argue that the European divisions show that Britain should have nothing to do with the EU's desire for a common foreign and defence policy, and should, instead, throw in its lot with the US. The counter-view is that, by being so close to President Bush, Tony Blair has undermined his hopes of taking a leading role in Europe, confirming all the long-standing doubts about Britain's ambivalent relationship with the EU. Blair himself has been at his most Panglossian, or perhaps self-deluding, in believing that the damage to the 'bridge' has been repaired – that America wants to work with Europe again and those European countries who opposed the war do not want to repeat the divisions and arguments of spring 2003. The strategic dilemma remains for Britain of how to balance Europe and America.

In his relations with both Presidents Clinton and Bush, and in the strains and arguments of early 2003, Tony Blair has behaved very much in the traditional British pattern. Getting to know, and getting close to, the American president has been a top priority for almost all prime ministers since the days of Winston Churchill. Even in his final premiership from 1951 to 1955, when he was approaching eighty, Churchill was forever wanting to get on a plane to Washington to talk to the president. The two Harolds, Macmillan and Wilson, and Margaret Thatcher were also eager to be invited as guests by the president of the day, whether welcome or not. The main exception was Edward Heath in the early 1970s. Heath is so far the only British prime minister since the 1940s to put consultations with European allies ahead of talks with Washington and not to want to have a close relationship with the American president. Nixon wanted to be close to Heath, but this was not reciprocated.

Otherwise, what Washington is thinking – and, as important, 'Can we influence what the Americans do?' – has been at the forefront of the minds of British prime ministers and their advisers. In this respect, Blair has been in the Churchill, Macmillan and Thatcher pattern rather than the Heath one. This desire to work closely with the Americans has generally mattered far more than any identity, or divergence, of ideological views between prime minister and president. Common views and approach have, from time to time, been an important cement in the relationship, notably between Margaret Thatcher and Ronald Reagan in the 1980s. But they have not been essential, partly because the leader of the smaller and weaker power, Britain, has recognised that he or she has to work with whomever is elected as American president. Blair took a particularly hard-headed and realist view of the arrival of George W. Bush in the White House.

By contrast, relations with the leaders of the rest of Europe – particularly the French President and the German Chancellor – have had a lower priority in 10 Downing Street, while obviously still being very important. A British prime minister meets the main European heads of government more often than the American president, especially as there are now at least four, and often more, summits of European Union leaders each year, leaving aside many bilateral meetings. Blair is particularly assiduous in keeping up his contacts with Gerhard Schröder and, at least up to March 2003, with Jacques

Chirac, as well as with allies such as José María Aznar. Yet contacts with Washington still seem to matter more. The phones between Downing Street and the White House have rung much more often – especially at times of international crisis – than those between the Prime Minister's office and the French President's office in the Élysée Palace in Paris or the German Chancellery in Bonn (and, recently, Berlin). The question addressed later is whether Blair could have done more in the autumn of 2002 to build a common European approach on Iraq, so avoiding the later transatlantic divisions.

British prime ministers have generally wanted to avoid at all costs any substantial or lasting public differences with Washington. Where disagreements have occurred – and they have been frequent – successive British Governments have had a policy of playing them down – stressing, rather, the underlying harmony and general unity of values and objectives. The transatlantic alliance has come first. While prime ministers, and particularly diplomats, have usually tried to avoid that misleading term, 'special relationship', these two words have often been an underlying theme of their contacts with presidents, at least on the British side.

However, the British attitude to relations with other European leaders has often been the opposite. Prime ministers have seen political advantages at home in having a row with Europe. 'Blaming the French' was a convenient political expedient for the Blair Government in March 2003 to defend the case for going to war when a further UN resolution could not be passed in the Security Council. 'Blaming the Americans' would have been inconceivable. The regular summits of leaders, known as European Councils, have often been depicted by Government spokesmen as adversarial contests between rivals, rather than collaborative meetings of friends, as when the Prime Minister meets the American President. The 'us' versus 'them' image was epitomised by the 'game, set and match' claim by John Major's spokesman after the Maastricht summit in December 1991. Differences have been reinforced by the prejudices of the media, particularly the tabloids, with their crude anti-French, and occasionally anti-German, campaigns.

The next chapter sets out the historical context of the relations of American presidents and British prime ministers since the 1940s – putting the strategic dilemmas faced by Blair and his style of diplomacy in context. Later chapters discuss the record of Blair's relations with, Bill Clinton and George W. Bush. Two points stand out. First, Blair's consistent emphasis on the threat from weapons of mass destruction; and, second, his concern to work closely with the United States, and the American President. As Tony Blair told questioning MPs at a meeting of the Parliamentary Labour Party in February 2003 in the run-up to the war with Iraq: 'People say that you are doing this because the Americans are telling you to do it. I keep telling them that it's worse than that. I believe in it.'

2. Honorary Consultants

Each time we have to choose between Europe and the open sea, we shall always choose the open sea. Each time I have to choose between you and Roosevelt, I shall always choose Roosevelt.

Winston Churchill to Charles de Gaulle in spring 1944, cited in de Gaulle's *War Memoirs: Unity, 1942–44*

We should never again find ourselves on the opposite side to the United States in a major international crisis affecting Britain's interests.

Margaret Thatcher on the lessons of Suez in *The Path to Power*

British statesmen were content to act as honorary consultants to our deliberations.

Henry Kissinger on the 'special relationship' in *White House Years*

The 'special relationship' is an irritatingly misleading, though remarkably persistent, term. It is misleading not because it is wrong, but because it is partly right. Yet its use almost always obscures more than it clarifies. As Henry Kissinger remarked of the time when he arrived in the White House in 1969 as National Security Adviser (1979, p. 90), 'the special relationship with Britain was peculiarly impervious to abstract theories.' The term's elusiveness is one reason for its survival. It is easy to dismiss 'hands across the sea' sentiments, repeated ritualistically at Anglo–American meetings, and redolent of the wartime alliance. But they are not devoid of all meaning – as was seen in the deep expressions of British sympathy and support for America after the 11 September attacks. However, such expressions of esteem and affection have little influence over how the two countries decide on their foreign policies.

Yet the term is still often used. Raymond Seitz, one of the most respected US ambassadors in Britain since the days of David Bruce in the 1960s, referred in his memoirs (1998, p. 325) to his vow not to use the phrase 'special relationship':

> *Like a brass plate, on a church floor, the words seemed a little worn from years of hard rubbing. By the beginning of the 1990s, I also thought the formula was misleading, especially with the rapid unravelling of the Cold War. In Britain, however, 'special relationship' remained a kind of knee-jerk catch-phrase, almost like an advertising jingle, and it overlooked that the official partnership was a relatively recent state of affairs, and a pragmatic one.*

Britain's relations with the United States are unusually close, and have been since the Second World War. Yet the relationship is inherently asymmetrical as London has a far greater interest in affecting what Washington does and says, than vice versa. As Sir Percy Cradock, Margaret Thatcher's Foreign Policy Adviser from 1984, wrote in his headmasterly 'First Thoughts' paper for her on his arrival in Downing Street (1997, p. 26): 'Our capacity to influence events was limited

and the Americans held the preponderant power and responsibility.'
Anglo–American relations since the late 1940s have been the story of
how Britain has adjusted to that asymmetry, and how successive
British prime ministers have balanced the transatlantic link with
Britain's role in Europe. This is not a linear progression, of a gradual
movement from an Atlanticist emphasis to a European one. Far from
it. Of course, Britain's entry into the European Economic
Community in January 1973 marked a sharp change in Britain's
foreign commitments. But it was less decisive than Edward Heath,
the main architect of entry, intended, or hoped. The pull of
Washington remained, and remains. Tony Blair has been in a long
line of prime ministers in often putting the claims of transatlantic
solidarity ahead of those of European unity.

The most consistent feature of transatlantic relations – again with
the significant exception of Edward Heath – has been the desire of
other prime ministers to be insiders in the Washington policy debate.
This has been both a substitute for, and a way of prolonging, global
aspirations. British politicians, and diplomats, always want to be the
first to be phoned when a crisis erupts, or preferably beforehand. The
Blair–Bush relationship has been a classic illustration of this approach.
As in the quotation at the beginning of this chapter, Kissinger (1979,
p. 90) captures the British approach well in referring to

> *the superb self-discipline by which Britain had succeeded*
> *in maintaining political influence after its physical power*
> *had waned. When Britain emerged from the Second World*
> *War too enfeebled to insist upon its views, it wasted no*
> *time in mourning an irretrievable past. British leaders*

> *instead tenaciously elaborated the 'special relationship'*
> *with us. This was, in effect, a pattern of consultation so*
> *matter-of-factly intimate that it became psychologically*
> *impossible to ignore British views. They evolved a habit of*
> *meetings so regular that autonomous American action*
> *somehow came to seem to violate club rules.*

Kissinger underrates the pain of adjustment, and relations were not always as smooth as he implies in his phrase about diplomatic subtlety overcoming substantive disagreement. But close working relationships – particularly between diplomats and military planners and intelligence agencies – have limited the fall-out and damage from any disagreements. The overwhelming power of the United States, particularly after the end of the Cold War, has meant that the prizes of defence and intelligence co-operation are far too great to put at risk. As Vice-Admiral Sir Alan West, then Chief of Defence Intelligence, told MPs on the Defence Select Committee looking at the lessons of Kosovo (Fourteenth Report, 1999–2000. lxxvii), 'America's intelligence capability is amazing. We are extremely lucky that we have got such a good ally.'

A close relationship has also had attractions for the Americans. Despite recurrent unilateralist rhetoric, the US has seldom liked operating alone. It has wanted to lead and to determine policy, but not to take action on its own. Sir Percy Cradock writes (1997, p. 52) how 'close British association had its benefits for the Americans who generally did not wish to act in isolation.' On several occasions this has involved a desire for British military involvement, not just because of admiration for the quality of British forces but as a symbol that America is not on its own. In his fascinating series of essays *On Specialness* (1998), Alex Danchev quotes an internal State Department memorandum of March 1950:

> *Certainly the UK is our closest friend and strongest and most dependable ally. The British and ourselves have far more worldwide interests than any other nation and are the only two in a position to fight anywhere in the world in the event of war or to wield much influence all over the world in peacetime.*

A few months later, Oliver Franks, the epitome of the post-war 'great and the good', reported to London from the British Embassy in Washington at the start of the Korean War (as quoted in Danchev, 1993, p. 126): 'The Americans will to some extent – I know this to be true of the Defense Department – test the quality of the partnership by our attitude to the notion of a token ground force.' Despite the initial opposition of the chiefs of staff in London, Britain agreed. Fifteen years later, Harold Wilson would not agree to Lyndon Johnson's request for a token British presence in Vietnam. Tony Blair has been much more willing to commit British forces, both on their own and with the Americans. Britain's military contribution has been central both to its usefulness to Washington and to the ambiguities of its relations with the rest of Europe. Having sizeable and effective armed forces which are regularly used in this way is to a large extent what has made Britain a nation apart in Europe, the perpetual awkward partner.

The 'insider' strategy has also had dangers for Britain. Maintaining close relations has at times seemed almost an end in itself in that

British prime ministers generally suppressed, or publicly played down their differences with Washington. Seldom have they asked 'what do we get out of the "special relationship"?' Were necessary, and often overdue, foreign policy choices avoided, or deferred, because of a belief in the 'special relationship'? Were the generally unsentimental policymakers in Washington manipulating the British almost to act as their defenders and proxies in Europe on the basis of the attractions to Britain of close access to American policy thinking? These dilemmas were addressed early on by Pierson Dixon, later to be Britain's United Nations Ambassador at the time of Suez, in a Foreign Office minute in 1951 (quoted in Danchev, 1993, p. 129):

> *If we cannot entirely change American policy, then we must, it seems to me, resign ourselves to a role of counsellor and moderator. We have already had considerable effect in this role. But we should accept the disagreeable conclusion, in the end, that we must allow the United States to take the lead and follow, or at least not break with them. It is difficult for us, after centuries of leading others, to resign ourselves to the position of allowing another and greater power to lead us.*

These questions recur again and again. Few at the time, or for some years afterwards, addressed the question with Dixon's clarity. Writing nearly half a century later about his experience in the 1980s, Sir Percy Cradock warns (1997, p. 209):

> *The American connection was too readily over-valued. The ease of communication, the successes achieved in part-*

> *nership with the US, nurtured the delusion that Britain*
> *could manage with a good line to Washington, and little*
> *else. What this overlooked was the hard-headed, unsenti-*
> *mental nature of America's appraisal of its allies. We*
> *would be valued for what we could provide, especially in*
> *Europe.*

Cosy relations with American opposite numbers also fed British delusions of grandeur, or, almost as bad, feelings of superiority. President Woodrow Wilson was the first to reject the British embrace when he spoke in London in December 1918 at the start of his triumphant post-war visit to Europe: 'You must not speak of us who come over here as cousins, still less as brothers – we are neither.' A later formulation, much favoured by Harold Macmillan, but even more irritating to American policymakers, was his Greeks and Romans comparison – with its patronising implication that the wise and experienced British could guide and educate the crude, though powerful, Americans. While not expressed publicly after the 1960s, this thought still persisted in the minds of some British politicians and diplomats for a long time afterwards.

Moreover, talk of a 'special relationship' confuses values and interests. For most of the past sixty years, Britain and the United States have shared a common outlook, a belief in freedom and democracy, in an open international financial and economic system. This reflects a common language, overlapping popular and elite cultures, many shared historical traditions, the joint wartime experience and, for forty years, a common enemy in the Soviet Union. None of these links should be dismissed. They do matter. But if these have provided the framework, then interests, and policies have often diverged significantly. The history of Anglo–American relations could be written as much about British suspicion of American motives and intentions as about agreement, and of successive presidents putting American interests ahead of the concerns of their ally.

Even in the heyday of the wartime alliance, Churchill and Roosevelt often clashed, particularly from early 1943 onwards. These differences were initially over the timing of the invasion of North-West Europe (the Second Front), over the Prime Minister's various madcap schemes for new offensives in the Mediterranean and, then, over post-war plans. The balance of power tilted more and more in America's favour. The stark implications were brought home well before the war ended when the Americans sought to impose their own view of post-war financial arrangements and were suspicious of, and hostile to, Britain's imperial links. Reflecting both their own anti-colonialist history and instincts and their own commercial interests, the Americans wanted to dismantle the remaining imperial preferences and exchange controls. Despite all the earlier help for Britain, the American negotiators had little sympathy for Britain's financial plight after six years of war, as Robert Skidelsky tellingly records in the third volume of his masterly biography of Keynes, who led the British side. The termination of Lend Lease in August 1945 inaugurated a period when Anglo–American relations were cool. This phase only lasted for two or three years until the start of the Cold War, with the confrontation over Greece, the Berlin blockade, the Marshall Plan and the inauguration of a wider Atlantic Alliance and NATO.

Politicians in London still saw Britain as a power with global responsibilities, even after the withdrawal from Palestine, and from

India and the new Pakistan. It was Britain's role to work alongside the US, but in its own right and not as part of any European federation and union. The prevailing attitude was that closer European co-operation was all right, within bounds, for the defeated and conquered powers, but need not, and should not, affect a global power like Britain with its transatlantic and particularly Commonwealth ties. The British took a dismissive attitude in May 1950 towards the Schuman Plan for creating the European Coal and Steel Community. Roy Denman (1996, p. 187) vividly records the alarm in London towards the French proposal and, particularly, over the political implications. He quotes the minutes of a ministerial meeting chaired by Attlee:

> *It looked like a challenge to the United States and the United Kingdom. It was agreed that it showed a regrettable tendency to move away from the concept of the Atlantic Community and in the direction of a European Federation. There was general agreement that the French Government had behaved extremely badly in springing this proposal on the world at this juncture without any attempt at consultation with His Majesty's Government or the US Government.*

This was an over-optimistic view of the American attitude. To the alarm of many in London who cherished the 'special relationship', Washington turned out to be quick to realise the importance, and desirability, of closer European integration – and to regret Britain's decision to stand aside.

The Korean War, like subsequent wars, fostered illusions about Britain's role. As Danchev reports (1993, p. 127), Attlee told Bevin how throughout the talks with the Truman administration, 'the UK was lifted out of the "European queue" and we were treated as partners, unequal no doubt in power, but still equal in counsel.' When Churchill returned to power in October 1951, he was eager for summit meetings with either Truman or Eisenhower (after January 1953), as well as with Soviet leaders, especially after Stalin's death in 1953. But Eisenhower took an unsentimental view of his old wartime comrade in arms.

British politicians talked then, and for at least another decade, of foreign policy involving three circles – the transatlantic relationship, Europe and the Commonwealth, with the former implicitly, and often explicitly, the most important. In one crucial respect, however, uncertainty about the United States fuelled a British determination to maintain its ability to act independently of Washington. The Attlee Government's decision to develop a British atomic bomb reflected both suspicion of, and a desire to be independent of, the United States. The passage of the McMahon Act by Congress in 1946 had banned collaboration with any other country on the development of atomic weapons, including Britain and Canada, the two wartime collaborators in the Manhattan Project to develop the A-Bomb. This produced an anguished debate in Whitehall with the Treasury arguing against the acquisition of nuclear weapons on grounds of cost and possible strains to the economy. Peter Hennessy (2003, pp. 47–8) records the contrast between the dry official minutes of the key Cabinet committee meeting in October 1946 and the more vivid memories of participants. Sir Michael Perrin of the Ministry of

Supply remembered the colourful intervention by Bevin, who had arrived late after a heavy lunch:

> *We've got to have this. I don't mind for myself, but I don't want any other Foreign Secretary of this country to be talked at, or to, by the Secretary of State in the United States as I just have in my discussions with Mr Byrnes. We've got to have this thing over here, whatever it costs. We've got to have the bloody Union Jack on top of it.*

Less bluntly expressed, this has remained an entrenched doctrine for British politicians of both main parties ever since. Always, there were doubts about whether the Americans would defend Britain if faced with the ultimate nuclear choice, and a belief that possession of nuclear weapons would ensure that Britain retained a seat at the 'top table'.

For all his frequent references to the 'special relationship', Churchill had doubts about the reliability of the Americans. Indeed, the very awfulness of thermonuclear destruction led the nearly octogenarian Churchill to press both for a summit meeting to agree controls and for a British H-bomb (in succession to the A-Bomb), partly to influence the two superpowers. Hennessy reports on the Cabinet minutes for July 1954 and a contribution (almost certainly by Churchill):

> *No country could claim to be a leading military power unless it possessed the most up-to-date weapons; and the fact must be faced that, unless we possessed thermo-nuclear*

> *weapons, we should lose our influence and standing in*
> *world affairs.*

The Suez crisis of autumn 1956 is generally seen as the great dividing line in post-war British history since the débâcle highlighted the need to adjust to a reduced role in the world. But it was a not a clear line and the adjustment was only partial. Suez was unquestionably a brutal lesson in the limitations in Britain's ability to act without American support. The hostility of Washington, and its refusal to support the pound, forced the Eden Government to halt the operation – though Conservative ministers blamed the Americans for having misled Britain. Around 120 Conservative backbenchers signed a motion accusing America of 'gravely endangering the Atlantic alliances.'

The shocks throughout the world of Whitehall were profound. The minutes of a Cabinet discussion on the eve of Macmillan's succession to the premiership in January 1957 are revealing. A Foreign Office suggestion about a possible pooling of Britain's nuclear resources with European allies to create a third nuclear power went too far for the Cabinet. But the minutes (quoted in Dimbleby and Reynolds, p. 220) go on to record the view of ministers that:

> *There must be a sea change in the basis of Anglo–American*
> *relations. It was doubtful whether the US would now be*
> *willing to accord to us alone the special position which we had*
> *held as their principal ally during the war. We might therefore*
> *be better able to influence them if we were part of an associ-*

> *ation of powers which had greater political, economic and*
> *military strength than we alone could command.*

Several reviews were set up to consider Britain's place in the world. The withdrawal from the colonies of the tropical empire, notably in Africa and the Caribbean, accelerated, and over the next few years there were the hesitant, and often ambivalent, beginnings of the movement towards closer involvement in Europe. Yet the main, and urgent, response of Harold Macmillan after he became Prime Minister in January 1957 was to repair relations with Washington. By contrast, the reaction of France, the joint participant in the Suez operation, was the opposite, even before de Gaulle's return in spring 1958. French politicians decided to become closer to Germany, rather than to what they saw as an unreliable United States. This strengthened the momentum towards setting up the European Economic Community under the Treaty of Rome in 1957, a process from which Britain excluded itself. Alistair Horne, Macmillan's official biographer, records (1989, p. 22) how:

> *Macmillan clearly and consciously gave the*
> *London–Washington entente priority over relations with*
> *Europe. Axiomatic with this, on the one hand, was that*
> *Britain should never again permit a basic policy conflict*
> *with the US; on the other hand, that it should at the same*
> *time go all out for the independent nuclear deterrent.*

By being close to Washington, Macmillan hoped to prolong Britain's global role. But, like Attlee and Churchill, he wanted an independent nuclear capability in part 'to secure United States co-operation in a situation in which their interests were less immediately threatened than our own.' To an American observer like Henry Kissinger (1994, p. 598): 'It was under Macmillan that Great Britain completed the transition from power to influence. He decided to embed British policy in American policy and to expand the range of British options by skilfully handling relations with Washington . . . He readily conceded the centre stage to Washington while seeking to shape the drama from behind the curtains.'

However, influence was at times as elusive as power. For all his outwardly close personal relations with Eisenhower and then Kennedy, Macmillan's desire to retain a seat at the 'top table' was increasingly hard to sustain. The release of the private papers for the early 1960s makes his role in both the Berlin crisis of 1961 and the Cuban missile confrontation of 1962 much less central, or consistent, than the impression he conveyed at the time. Sir Percy Cradock concludes in his history of the Joint Intelligence Committee (2002, pp. 159–60) that British policy over Berlin was

> *showy and ultimately ineffective . . . Fundamentally, it was confused: it reflected a wish to go on playing an independent role at a time when Britain no longer had the power to do so; and a continuing failure to see the strength of the European idea . . . It exaggerated the value of continuous summitry, particularly when there was little chance of anything fruitful emerging from such meetings. It also underrated the influence Federal Germany already exerted in Europe and in Washington.*

During the Cuban missile crisis of October 1962, Kennedy and Macmillan communicated regularly, certainly more than the President did with any other European leader. But the Prime Minister did not affect Washington's decisions. He was less influential than David Ormsby-Gore, Britain's Ambassador in Washington, a long-standing close friend of Kennedy, who was frequently in the White House during the 'Thirteen Days.' Macmillan was more the trusted and liked adviser, and reassuring confidant to the younger President. Cradock concludes unsentimentally (2002, p. 185) that 'the relationship [established by Ormsby-Gore] was only complicated by Macmillan's constant and unsuccessful search for a larger role for himself in what was an exclusively US–Soviet struggle.'

At the same time, after a number of missteps, the Macmillan Government applied to join the Common Market, with the strong support of the Kennedy administration. In a 1962 pamphlet specifically aimed at reassuring the many critics of the British application, Macmillan argued: 'If we remain outside the European Community, it seems to me inevitable that the realities of power would compel our American friends to attach increasing weight to the views and interests of the Community, and to pay less attention to our own.' Despite the enthusiasm of Edward Heath, the chief British negotiator, the application was full of ambiguities, reflecting the unresolved conflicts of interest and policy over Britain's global, Commonwealth and transatlantic ties.

These tensions reached their climax over the winter of 1962–3, when the Kennedy administration abandoned the Skybolt stand-off missile system, intended to be the heart of the future British nuclear deterrent. This decision posed a fundamental challenge to

Macmillan's defence and political strategy by threatening Britain's role as a separate nuclear power. Many in the State Department saw this as a desirable outcome. But Kennedy responded to the pleas of Macmillan at the Nassau summit in December 1962 – based as much on the Prime Minister's domestic political vulnerability as on defence strategy. The President agreed that Britain could have the Polaris-submarine-based system. This appeared a very favourable deal for Britain, which ensured a continuing nuclear defence role over the following decades. However, for all Macmillan's obvious relief at being rescued from an acute political predicament, the agreement, in practice, represented the end of an independent British deterrent and confirmation of Britain's dependence on the United States. Over the following decades, the Royal Navy became more and more reliant on US facilities for the maintenance and operation of the Polaris submarines, and, from the 1990s, the Trident submarines.

Kennedy worried about how and why such a serious problem with the US's closest ally suddenly emerged. He commissioned a private report by political scientist Richard Neustadt, which was delivered to the President, and read by him, just before his final, fatal trip to Dallas in November 1963. Based on conversations with senior officials on both sides of the Atlantic, the report was only published 36 years later. It shows that the Skybolt crisis arose in part because senior officials in Washington took insufficient account of British concerns. American interests came first. But as Neustadt (1999, p. 118) speculates:

> *Had Britain seemed more 'enemy' than 'friend' a likely question in November [before Skybolt was formally*

> *cancelled] would have been: if we hurt them what harm can they do us? Had Britain been both hostile and powerful – as Russia – no doubt we then would have pursued that question carefully; the possibilities of harm become immense and obvious. But Britain being Britain nobody pursued that question, carefully or otherwise.*

The Nassau agreement was seen in a very different light in Paris. As the quotation at the beginning of the chapter underlines, Charles de Gaulle always had reasons to be suspicious of Britain's true instincts. He turned round Churchill's words in delivering his veto in January 1963 on Britain's application to join the Common Market. On 14 January, at a news conference at the Élysée Palace, de Gaulle disdainfully looked at Britain's position:

> *England is insular. The nature and structure and economic context of England differ profoundly from those of the other states of the Continent . . . There would appear a colossal Atlantic community under American dependence and leadership which would soon swallow up the European Community.*

De Gaulle went on to reject the Nassau agreement and the American offer of involvement in Polaris. In retrospect, as Alistair Horne argues (1989, pp. 446–7), Nassau looks more like the pretext for the veto than its cause. But the Polaris agreement unquestionably highlighted all de Gaulle's long-standing reasons for doubting Britain's European commitment. The sequel was equally significant. Only a week after de Gaulle's imperious veto, Adenauer, the German Chancellor who did not get on with Macmillan, travelled to Paris to sign the Franco–German Treaty of Friendship. This formalised the alliance which was the heart of European developments for most of the rest of the century, much to the frustration of British diplomats who often sought, unsuccessfully, to detach one or other partner.

Nassau and the de Gaulle veto exposed the ambiguities and frailties of British foreign policy. Just before Nassau, Dean Acheson, one of the main architects of the Cold War alliance, delivered his famous remark that 'Great Britain has lost an Empire and has not yet found a role.' These words created a furore in Britain, particularly among the jingo press. Less often quoted is what Acheson said after that famous sentence:

> *The attempt to play a separate power role – that is, a role apart from Europe, a role based on the 'special relationship' with the US, a role based on being head of a 'Commonwealth' which has no political structure, or unity, or strength and enjoys a fragile and precarious economic relationship – this role is about played out.*

Acheson was right, but few in Britain were then willing to admit that. After the de Gaulle veto, Macmillan despairingly confided to his diary: 'de Gaulle is trying to dominate Europe . . . It is the end – or at least a temporary bar – to everything for which I have worked for many years . . . All our policies at home and abroad are in ruins.' Yet for some later historians, the veto was inevitable. At the end of his thought-provoking official history of Britain's relations with Europe up to 1963, Alan Milward (2002, p. 483) concludes that:

> *Britain's weakness in the negotiations did not spring from its tactics but from direct conflict between its own worldwide strategy, which in the Conservative Party still had powerful adherents, and that of France. It was not a part of the United Kingdom's strategy to base its economic or political future on European preferences. France, however, would accept nothing less and the outcome was de Gaulle's veto.*

The Wilson years continued the ambivalence in attitudes towards Washington and Europe. After taking office in October 1964, Wilson dropped pre-election pledges to cancel Polaris – in retrospect (Hennessy, 2003, p. 71) using very similar arguments to his predecessors about not wanting to be subordinate to Washington and being in a position to restrain the Americans. Wilson sought, never wholly satisfactorily, to have close relations with Lyndon Johnson and then Richard Nixon. Yet, during this period, the retreat from East of Suez commitments was decided and a second abortive application to join the European Community was made. Even before Heath took office, Britain had run out of alternative foreign policy approaches, especially as the economy faced continuing acute economic troubles.

In June 1970 Edward Heath became Prime Minister, with the overriding priority of joining the European Community. To achieve this, he decided to distance Britain from the United States. Heath wanted harmonious relations with the Nixon administration, but not a special or privileged relationship. On his visit to Washington in December 1970, Heath left no doubt that his main aim was to secure Britain's entry into the European Community. Henry Kissinger, then Nixon's National Security Adviser in the White House, vividly records (1979, p. 937) the surprise and shock in Washington at this new approach by America's closest ally. Heath told Nixon that:

> *Once in, Britain would play a constructive role with regard to our concerns. But he could not risk making any concessions to us in advance: he wished neither to negotiate Common Market issues bilaterally with us nor to appear as – or, for that matter, to be – America's Trojan Horse in Europe. No previous British Prime Minister would have considered making such a statement to an American President. Neither the amiable context nor Nixon's understanding reply could obscure the fact that we were witnessing a revolution in Britain's post-war foreign policy.*

Kissinger then admitted there might be benefits to the United States in having European policies influenced by 'Britain's global experience and pragmatic style'. Heath, he noted, 'was a new experience for American leaders: a British Prime Minister who based his policies towards the US not on sentimental attachments but on a cool calculation of interests.' The Americans were unsettled to face a British leader who talked of a united Europe in competition, but not confrontation, with the United States. This implied a marked shift from the long-established pattern where American and British officials consulted together before alliance meetings. Instead, Heath talked about Britain working with its European Community allies to develop a common policy on any foreign policy issue and only then to co-ordinate with Washington. So prior consultation was now to mean across the Channel rather than across the Atlantic. Unlike his predecessors or successors up to and including Blair, Heath did not want to be the bridge or go-between across the Atlantic.

A bemused Kissinger admitted (1979, p. 961) that: 'We faced in Heath the curiosity of a more benign British version of de Gaulle.' This did not last long since Britain was only in the European Community for fourteen months before Heath fell. Moreover, the then Sir Alec Douglas Home, the former Prime Minister and Heath's Foreign Secretary, was much more of an Atlanticist, seeking to keep up close ties as far as possible. Kissinger also kept open channels with senior British officials and the nuclear relationship was unaffected. But the conflict between the American and Heath view emerged when Kissinger, now as Secretary of State, launched his 'Year of Europe.' This was brusquely dismissed by Heath and other European leaders. Later that year, when the Yom Kippur War broke out, Heath privately made it clear that a request by Washington to use NATO bases in Britain for planes carrying supplies to Israel would not be welcome. And there were further tensions when America put its forces on a high state of readiness in order to warn off the Soviet Union from intervening. Dimbleby and Reynolds conclude (1988, p. 266) that 'By 1973, there were many signs that America and Britain were drifting apart diplomatically. The special relationship seemed to be a thing of the past.'

The Heath period, however, proved to be an exception. James Callaghan, who became Foreign Secretary in March 1974 after the defeat of the Heath Government, was an Atlanticist in his bones. Within days of taking office, he told MPs: 'I must emphasise that we repudiate the view that a united Europe will emerge only out of a process of struggle against America.' He quickly sought to repair relations with Washington, despite differences later that year over Cyprus. Both as Foreign Secretary and as Prime Minister from 1976 until 1979, Callaghan had good relations with Kissinger and then with President Jimmy Carter, as well as with European leaders like Helmut Schmidt and Valery Giscard d'Estaing. Callaghan sought to revive the intermediary or bridge role. But as John Dumbrell notes in his balanced history of Anglo–American relations in the post-war era (2001, p. 82) that this policy raised

> *some acute difficulties. At one level, there was the problem of being taken for granted by the US. With Britain following a clear 'Atlantic intermediary strategy', Washington might be tempted to concentrate its favours and attention either on France (NATO bad boy) or, more likely, on West Germany (key to NATO modernisation and security, and probable leader of an integrated Europe).*

Even more damaging was the simple issue of Britain's credibility in Europe.

Yet the Callaghan years were marked by an economic, rather than a political, crisis which – in clear parallels with the 1940s disputes – underlined how dependent Britain was on American support and goodwill. The IMF crisis of autumn 1976 has entered Labour folklore as the time when the leadership abandoned the party's ideals, and its public spending plans, in order to secure the backing of international bankers. In reality, the beginnings of the check to the rapid growth in public spending of the mid-1970s came earlier, in late 1975. Moreover, the alleged 'cuts' in spending, generally reductions in planned growth, to secure the standby loan from the International Monetary Fund, were small. But the myth mattered, and the discussions in the Callaghan Cabinet were long and anguished. The US Treasury in the Ford administration took a tough line, believing that the spendthrift 'socialists' in Britain needed to face up to economic reality. In particular, both William Simon, Treasury Secretary, and Arthur Burns, Chairman of the Federal Reserve, wanted to ensure that Britain did not adopt a siege economy, with import controls and other restrictions. But President Ford and Henry Kissinger were worried that the Treasury and the Fed were applying too much pressure and might, in Kissinger's words, 'have destroyed Britain's ability to go on playing a major role in world affairs.' Burk and Cairncross (1992, p. 227) conclude in their fascinating study of the IMF crisis that

> *There were those in America, Germany and elsewhere who hoped that a changed Britain would emerge, phoenix-like, from the crisis, free from past illusions and able to hold to a steady line of policy. They wanted to see, not just the measures that would put an end to the crisis but a change of heart, a forswearing of what they regarded as economic heresies such as deficit financing and over-expansion of the money supply. They wanted, and ultimately got, Thatcherism.*

The Thatcher years are conventionally seen as the post-war high point of close relations between London and Washington, particularly after Ronald Reagan became President in January 1981. They were fellow crusaders against Soviet Communism. As Sir Percy Cradock, her Foreign Policy Adviser for the second half of her premiership, notes (1997, p. 51): 'Solidarity with the US as a cardinal principle of foreign policy acquired a special sanctity under Margaret Thatcher, but as a working rule it had been in place for many British Governments over many years.' It was the passion and the personal warmth that were unusual, though this has tended to produce exaggerated impressions of both the harmony and the unusualness of the Thatcher period. But the Prime Minister was not naive about the President. As Sir Percy dryly points out (1997, p. 54): 'For her part, the Prime Minister when dealing with him exercised charm and tact in unusual measure. She had no illusions about her friend's intellectual capacity, but she was well aware of the power of his office and the strength of his personal beliefs.'

Margaret Thatcher generally played the Washington political game with skill, using her direct access when it counted, notably in acting as a restraining voice over some of Reagan's more adventurous nuclear disarmament initiatives. She supported the principle of the Star Wars anti-missile defence project (the Strategic Defence Initiative), despite deep misgivings in the Foreign Office and in contrast to French opposition. But she used her personal influence with Reagan to obtain a written commitment to the doctrine of nuclear deterrence. Moreover, like other European leaders, she feared a 'decoupling' of American and European security interests, making Europe more vulnerable to Soviet threats. These worries surfaced particularly after the abortive Reykjavik summit in October 1986 when President Reagan had proposed sweeping cuts in strategic nuclear weapons. As she writes in her memoirs (1993, p. 471): 'My own reaction when I heard how far the Americans had been prepared to go was as if there had been an earthquake beneath my feet.' The proposal would have killed off the Trident missile. She arranged to fly over to Washington a month later and, after initially securing agreement from then Vice-President Bush, Secretary of State George Schultz and Defense Secretary Casper Weinberger, she agreed a reassuring statement at a Camp David summit with Reagan which fully met her concerns.

Thatcher, however, could never take American support for granted. While the Reagan administration eventually came out in public support of Britain over its decision to recapture the Falkland Islands in spring 1982 after the Argentine invasion, it was not automatic or immediate. Many in the State Department favoured a neutral stance, to the fury of Thatcher who believed that the US should unconditionally support its closest ally in the face of unprovoked aggression. This again showed that American interests (in this case maintaining good terms with Latin America and deep-seated anti-colonialism) came before helping the closest ally. Sir Nicholas Henderson, Britain's Ambassador in Washington at the time, records (1994, p. 465) how he was engaged 'in the delicate diplomatic task of trying to bridge the widening gulf between the non-negotiating mood in London and the growing feeling in Washington that we ought not to insist on a humiliating surrender on the part of the Argentines.' Mrs Thatcher, he recalls, 'was openly critical of the USA's inadequate support.' Sir Nicholas replied that the US decision to come down on the British side at the end of April 'was not a decision that was self-evident or should be taken for granted.' In fact, well before this formal decision, the Pentagon, under the lead of Casper Weinberger, had been operating its own 'special relationship' with the British armed forces by supplying vital equipment, and intelligence, without which the Falklands could probably not have been retaken.

One of the little appreciated paradoxes of the Thatcher years is how she was at times more outspoken in criticising American actions than some other British prime ministers. Her personal link to Reagan and her commitment to the 'special relationship' meant that no one could doubt her pro-American credentials when she spoke out, when others might have been more nervous. For instance, Thatcher strongly criticised Washington's attempted cancellation of the Siberian pipeline project in response to the Soviet invasion of Afghanistan. This dispute was eventually settled, but Thatcher took a European view. Similarly, Thatcher was very upset by the American invasion of Grenada, a Commonwealth country, in October 1983 without consultation with London. British ministers had been misled about US intentions, and as she writes in her memoirs (1993, p. 331): 'At the time, I felt dismayed by what had happened. At best, the British Government had been made to look impotent; at worst, we looked deceitful.' This row came at a particularly sensitive time in the controversy over the siting of American cruise missiles in Britain. But American interests again came first. Harsh words were said, but the wounds quickly healed.

Two and half years later, Reagan was careful to consult Thatcher over his decision to bomb Libya in retaliation for an attack on a Berlin night club which had killed an American serviceman and injured several dozen more. The US wanted to use its bases in Britain for the bombing. Thatcher agreed, but only after an agonised debate within her Cabinet, where ministers were worried about the legal justification under the United Nations Charter for such a raid. She also faced considerable opposition in the Commons and in the country. She believed that British interests lay in supporting Washington, though both France and Spain refused to allow US planes to fly over their countries. Critics argued that this decision showed the 'special relationship' was now one-way.

After the end of the Reagan years, two developments began to reshape the Atlantic relationship. First came the end of the Cold War in 1989, as in a few months all the strains of the preceding decade led to the sudden collapse of Communist dominance of the former Soviet satellites in central and eastern Europe. The pace was dizzying that autumn: too fast, it turned out, for Margaret Thatcher who tried unsuccessfully to delay German unification. She antagonised not only the Bush administration but also the Kohl Government in Bonn – in the process, losing the support of the two central pillars of British foreign policy, the United States and Europe. This was the low point of her foreign policy, both in influence and public standing.

The second development was a renewed drive towards European integration, led chiefly by Jacques Delors as President of the commission. The creation of the single European market and, then, the Delors proposals for economic and monetary union leading up to the Maastricht agreement of December 1991 had awkward implications for both the US and Britain. US officials, unsuccessfully, sought a seat at the table in discussions over the single market. And, as later chapters underline, there was growing anxiety in Washington about talk of closer European co-operation on foreign policy and defence, ineffective though it mainly was during the 1990s.

Moreover, these moves towards integration led to a profound shift of opinion within the Conservative Party over Europe. Margaret Thatcher's Bruges speech of September 1988 signalled the growth of deep hostility among a growing minority, and then majority, of Conservative MPs towards further European integration. As Cradock notes (1997, p. 125), 'she did not like the Europeans; she did not speak their languages; and she had little time for their traditions.' This growing hostility led to increasing conflicts with her Cabinet colleagues, as well as marginalisation in Europe. Her increasingly strident tone over Europe – her 'no, no, no' comments in the Commons after the Rome summit in autumn 1990 – precipitated the resignation of Geoffrey Howe. This triggered the leadership contest of November 1990 which led to her departure from Downing Street. After the deep divisions of the Major premiership, this anti-European shift produced a growing interest in a closer relationship with the United States, particularly after the strongly Atlanticist Iain Duncan Smith became Conservative leader in September 2001. This was encouraged by the increasingly euro-sceptic press.

These changes were uncomfortable for the Thatcher and Major administrations. The long-dependable ally was no longer quite so important in Washington as during the Cold War. That was brought home to Margaret Thatcher when George Bush senior, '41' in Washington parlance, took over in January 1989 from Ronald Reagan. Bush and particularly James Baker, his Secretary of State, were no longer willing to indulge Mrs Thatcher as much as Reagan had done. There was a period of coolness, as she candidly records in her memoirs (1993, p. 783): 'as President, George Bush felt the need to distance himself from his predecessor: turning his back fairly publicly on the special position I had enjoyed in the Reagan administration's counsels and confidences was a way of doing that.' Her main target in her memoirs is James Baker and the State Department, who 'put the relationship with Germany – rather than "special relationship" with Britain – at the centre.' She challenged this German focus, arguing (1993, p. 784) that 'the ties of blood, language, culture and values which bound Britain and America were the only firm basis for US policy in the West; only a very clever person could fail to appreciate something so obvious.' To Thatcher's evident relief, the familiar close relationship with the United States was restored following Iraq's invasion of Kuwait in August 1990. And, despite initial alarm in Washington over the ousting of Margaret Thatcher by her Cabinet and parliamentary colleagues that November, John Major, her successor, soon developed a close relationship with George Bush.

The arrival of Bill Clinton in the White House in January 1993 created problems – partly because of self-inflicted errors by the British Conservatives during the 1992 election campaign. Not only did the Tories offer help to the Bush campaign – in itself by no means unusual – but the Major Government was accused of looking through Home Office files to see if anything damaging could be found about then candidate Clinton from his days in Oxford in the late 1960s. Nothing was found, possibly the only time a skeleton was not discovered about his past. Hillary Clinton notes in her memoirs (2003, p. 320) how

> *Bill's relations with Prime Minister Major had gotten off*
> *to a rocky start when we learned that Major's Government*
> *co-operated with the first Bush administration by*
> *attempting to unearth records of Bill's activities in*
> *England during the student protests against the Vietnam*
> *War. No such records existed, but overt meddling in*
> *American politics by the Tories was disconcerting.*

John Major has denied that this happened (1999, p. 498): 'I was assured that this was nonsense, but it was widely believed to be true, and Clinton's staffers resented it and made no secret of their feelings.' Major dismisses it as a 'staffers' feud'. Raymond Seitz (1998, p. 322) says that when Major visited Washington a few weeks after Clinton took office:

> *I preceded him by a couple of days in order to scout out the*
> *tricky political terrain . . . The British press was almost*
> *ghoulish in its anticipation of rancour at the high levels.*
> *Just before the Prime Minister arrived at the White House,*
> *Clinton was sitting with a few aides in the Oval Office.*
> *'Don't forget to say "special relationship" when the press*
> *comes in,' one of them joked – a little like 'don't forget to*
> *put out the cat.' 'Oh yes, Clinton said, 'How could I*
> *forget? The "special relationship".' And he threw back his*
> *head and laughed.*

The next two years were a period of particular strain, partly because of disagreements about Bosnia but also, particularly for John Major, over Northern Ireland. In the longer run, the differences over Bosnia were more significant in pointing to a divergence of views between America and Europe over post-Cold War security and defence. The British and the French felt that the Americans did not understand what was happening in the Balkans, while many in Washington thought that the effect of European policies was to connive in Serbian aggression and ethnic cleansing. Paddy Ashdown notes in his diaries (2000, p. 293) how John Major said his chief concern was 'the widening gulf between the US and European members of NATO. The Clinton administration is more hostile to Europe than Bush's was. The PM fears that failure to provide Clinton with support for whatever action he favours could accelerate the withdrawal of US troops from Europe and mark the beginning of the end for NATO.' Richard Holbrooke, who brokered the Dayton agreement of 1995, records (1998, p. 333) how 'When I returned to Washington in September 1994, the strains in the Anglo–American alliance had been at a level that was nearly intolerable, and rebuilding the relationship, which I still believed was "special" – a once-standard phrase that had been banned by the Major Government – had been a high priority.' Northern Ireland had soured personal relations.

The Major Government felt that the Clinton White House ran roughshod over British interests, taking a one-sided view, particularly over the granting of a visa to Gerry Adams of Sinn Fein to visit the US in March 1994. This was in direct defiance of the wishes of Major and the advice of the State Department. Major writes (1999, p. 474) that he 'warned the President in a letter of 10 March that, on Sinn Fein's track record, Adams would pocket American concessions, play them against the British Government, and fail to deliver anything in return. That turned out to be the case.' Seitz, who became increasingly estranged from his masters in Washington, had a 'formal dressing down' in 10 Downing Street. But the Ambassador, now seen as a 'honorary Brit' by some White House officials, was scathing about the failure of Adams to deliver:

> *The quid for the Adams visa never produced its quo. Throughout the following months, the Clinton White House made one concession after another (fund-raising, official recognition, high-level meetings, presidential photos and so forth, and again and again it backed away from its own conditions, usually over the furious objections of the British. In this fractious atmosphere, London even stopped passing sensitive intelligence to the White House because it often seemed to find its way back to the IRA.*

This account of the ups and downs of transatlantic relations since the late 1940s shows that because of a decline in military or 'hard' power on a global scale, British Governments have consistently sought a close, insider relationship with successive American presidents – with the striking, partial, exception of the Heath years. The approach was well summed up by Kathleen Burk (1996):

> *During the twentieth century, the US waxed while the UK waned; the US was increasingly confident and then triumphalist, while the UK was by turns co-operative, defensive or defiant; the UK attempted to co-opt American power for British goals, which it presented – and*

> *frequently believed to be – joint goals. And this was all*
> *encased, at least from 1940 on, in the jewel box of a*
> *'special relationship'.*

This approach has made Britain the indispensable ally, reversing the direction of the 'Greeks and Romans' argument, so that it is the British who tend to be patronised rather than the Americans: 'We can always rely on Harold, Jim, Margaret or Tony . . .' Therefore, have British prime ministers sacrificed British national interests by being so close to Washington? Or, would they have done better to follow the French example of robust, and often prickly, independence of Washington? At a purely tactical level, Henry Kissinger noted (1994, p. 598) how forty years ago 'de Gaulle frequently behaved obstreperously in order to make ignoring him painful: Macmillan made it so easy for the United States to solicit Britain's views that ignoring him would have been embarrassing.' Embarrassment is, however, an insecure basis for foreign policy. At a strategic level, for most of the period, Britain agreed with the United States about the challenge from the Soviet bloc, while France could be seen as a free-rider, hiding beneath American nuclear protection. Yet it is abundantly clear that successive administrations in Washington have always put US interests first, and that, while Britain has usually, though not invariably, had the chance to have its say, the junior partner has been expected to agree, or has been ignored.

Nonetheless, British politicians, and diplomats, have found it natural to work with their American opposite numbers, whatever the immediate differences of policy and interest. Relations have been closer, and more candid, than with European leaders and officials.

These instincts and habits, as well as then recent memories of the 1940s, held back British support for closer involvement with the European Community. Moreover, from the days of Macmillan onwards, British prime ministers have believed there is no conflict between Atlantic ties and membership of the European Community/Union. Indeed, they argue that the two reinforce each other: that by being closely involved in Europe, the British voice will be more influential in Washington. Until the George W. Bush administration, American policymakers encouraged this British approach. James Steinberg from the Clinton National Security Council staff argued in the mid-1990s that 'the future importance of the Anglo–American relationship will depend in large measure on the extent to which the UK accepts an integrated role in the EU's development.'

However, neither Washington nor London has seen Britain merely as part of a common or even joint EU approach. Rather, the Americans have regarded the UK as an ally arguing a common US–British line within Community institutions on everything from security and defence to trade. This is the 'Trojan Horse' view that has always aroused so much suspicion in Paris and was specifically rejected by Edward Heath in 1970. Apart from Heath, British prime ministers have seen themselves as interlocutors or bridges between America and Europe, interpreting one to the other. The assumption of that role has seldom gone down well with either German chancellors, from Adenauer to Kohl, or French presidents, from de Gaulle to Chirac. Yet even Margaret Thatcher, the least sympathetic of British prime ministers towards the European Community in her later years, was seen by other leaders as a useful means of influencing

Washington, particularly over nuclear defence, because of her special access to Ronald Reagan.

But this Atlantic–European balancing act has been dependent both on a shared view of the world and on mutual restraint by Europeans and Americans. So, while there have often been differences, they have generally been containable. Until 1989, the main constraint was the Cold War. In the following decade, though differences were increasingly apparent over security and defence policy, they were contained because both sides still wanted to work together. The Americans were often irritated by European attitudes and divisions, but the administrations of George Bush senior and Bill Clinton still sought to work with European institutions and leaders. Washington still paid lip service, and usually more, to Europe's desire to have a more collective voice and role. Bill Clinton was a natural multilateralist by temperament, even if sometimes a unilateralist in his actions, like most American presidents.

These constraints enabled British prime ministers to continue to have it both ways, to favour closer European integration – though only up to the point of not surrendering national control over foreign, defence and tax policies – and to remain close to Washington. Many of these assumptions were already being challenged before Tony Blair became Prime Minister in May 1997 and before George W. Bush became President in January 2001. Yet the following chapters show how long-familiar attitudes and habits of working persisted in London, despite a more unilateralist approach in Washington – and how they produced growing strains on the transatlantic bridge.

3. Bill Clinton's Younger Brother

I see Britain as in some ways a bridge between the US and Europe, not in any sense of any special relationship, so-called and all the rest of it, but just that it is important to say to America, 'You know we value your friendship, your contribution and we want you thoroughly engaged with Europe'; and to say to people in Europe, 'You know, thank goodness there is America there because America plays a vital role and strong leadership role in the world which is to the benefit of all the world.'

Tony Blair, in a briefing to American journalists,
10 Downing Street, 2 February 1998

I've worked with President Clinton now for some nine months as British Prime Minister. I have found him throughout someone I could trust, someone I could rely upon, someone I am proud to call not just a colleague, but a friend.

Tony Blair, speaking at a White House
press conference, 6 February 1998

Tony Blair often looked like Bill Clinton's younger brother when the two of them were together during the 1990s. Blair was the slightly prim, hard-working, well-behaved one, respecting Clinton's greater talents as a public performer, learning from him about the arts and skills of politics, while avoiding his self-indulgence and personal flaws. An acute, and occasionally acid observer, Joe Klein noted (2002, p. 74) how: 'Clinton was pre-eminent in gatherings of world leaders: and older brother to Britain's Tony Blair.' Initially, Blair seemed over-awed by Clinton's pyrotechnics, the unstoppable flow of energy and words. Yet for all its public closeness, their relationship always had 'an edge', in the words of one of Blair's closest advisers who was present at virtually all their meetings. The assumption of worldly-wise superiority on the part of Clinton as the elder brother was tested after May 1997 when Blair the younger brother demonstrated success and began to assert himself. Blair – recognising the superior political skills of Clinton – was, for his part, never entirely at ease with Clinton while they were both in office.

Even when Clinton was most in trouble – as in February 1998 shortly after the first allegations about the Monica Lewinsky affair became public – it was Blair who appeared rattled. By chance, Blair happened to be in Washington then on his first official visit as Prime Minister. On the way over, and during the visit, he privately admitted to uncertainty about how to handle the allegations, especially given his own reputation for morality and marital fidelity. Blair consulted one of his closest political advisers: 'Where should I be?' The response was, 'Stick by your friend.' That was Blair's instinct and he decided not to distance himself from the President, not least because, as Paddy Ashdown recorded in his diaries the previous month (2001, p. 159): 'Tony Blair reckoned that Clinton has a 60/40 chance of surviving.' Blair wanted Clinton's support over Northern Ireland and did not want to antagonise the President. Blair's private line then was that Clinton had done nothing to wrong him and he was willing to take him at face value. Blair said he liked and trusted Clinton, regarding him as both thoughtful and intellectually impressive. (Blair adopted a similar approach four years later in saying that he found George W. Bush personally trustworthy and reasonable in private when public comments by members of the administration were alarming many in Britain.) At the joint press conference in the White House on 6 February, Blair's body language revealed his nervousness about making a slip and creating unfavourable headlines. By contrast, Clinton was his usual self-confident self, brushing aside questions about Lewinsky. Later that day Blair admitted to me that the experience had been uncomfortable.

Blair quickly, however, became his own man. He developed a distinctive international viewpoint and image well before George W. Bush became President in January 2001. This was largely as a result of working with Clinton over the previous two and a half years. Blair became partly disillusioned with Clinton's inability to deliver on his promises, especially after the Kosovo conflict (as discussed in the next chapter). But Blair retained a warm affection for Clinton personally, seeing him often after he left office, as well as retaining an enormous respect for his political skills and shrewd advice.

Blair's foreign policy ideas before he became Labour leader in 1994 were less the result of deep thinking about Britain's place in the world than his personal response to his early, frustrating years as a politician. His election addresses in the Beaconsfield by-election in 1982, and a year later when he was elected for Sedgefield, expressed support for the then official Labour policy of withdrawal, if necessary, from the European Community. Along with his membership of the Campaign for Nuclear Disarmament – much stressed later by Conservative

politicians – these stances appear to have been no more than opportunistic flags of convenience when he was trying to get into the
Commons, rather than deep ideological commitments. His later
conversions were on the way to the ballot box rather than on the road
to Damascus. Both his pro-Americanism and its counterpart, his pro-
Europeanism, were originally a reaction to Labour's electoral failures
in the 1980s and early 1990s. They were both parts of a self-
conscious 'modernisation' strategy which Blair, Brown and Peter
Mandelson developed in this period. Yet, in contrast to his earlier
lightly worn positions, Blair developed a much deeper, personal
commitment both to the American alliance and to closer relations
with the rest of Europe. These views were, characteristically, the result
of his direct, personal experience.

Hostility to both the United States and to the European Union
were the hallmarks of Labour's approach in the early 1980s and
featured strongly in Labour's manifesto for the 1983 general election
– 'the longest-suicide note in history', as it was called by Gerald
Kaufman, later Labour's Foreign Affairs Spokesman. These attitudes
– and the associated commitments to unilateral nuclear disarmament
and withdrawal from the EU – were only gradually abandoned
during the rest of the 1980s by Neil Kinnock, with the active support
of his protégés, Blair, Brown and Mandelson.

Labour's 'modernisers' embraced Europe both because a policy of
withdrawal was electorally disastrous and because support for active
involvement in Europe seemed to be part of a forward-looking
progressive approach. The turning point was less the dropping of the
pledge to leave the then European Community than a speech by
Jacques Delors, then President of the European Commission, to the

TUC annual congress in September 1988. He offered the unions, and Labour, a role in a Europe that was not a capitalist club, the erroneous left-wing caricature of the 1970s and early 1980s, but one which had an increasing emphasis on social and employment policies. 'Social' Europe, with new rights for workers, and statutory consultation with social partners such as trade unions, had an obvious appeal on the left. This was reinforced by the expansion of the community budget going to regions of high unemployment and with serious problems of deprivation. These were all Labour strongholds, held even in the bleak years for the party in the 1980s. The unions and Labour-controlled local councils were ignored, or treated as the enemy, by the Thatcher Government in London. So they were naturally receptive to Delors' appeal and turned to Brussels, which was prepared to treat them seriously. The attractions of the European route were underlined by Labour's success at the 1989 elections for the European Parliament when the party gained 13 seats to win 45, against 32 for the Conservatives. This was Labour's best performance in a nationwide election for more than a decade.

But if Delors came before Clinton, it was the success of the Arkansas man in the November 1992 elections that was central both to the development of New Labour and to Blair's own emergence as a potential Labour leader. Philip Gould, Labour's mercurial public opinion adviser and strategist, had gone to Little Rock and been based in the 'war room' there for the last five weeks of the campaign. His message about the success of Clinton and the New Democrats found a ready audience in the Blair–Brown camp, who were disillusioned and searching for a new approach after Labour's fourth successive defeat in April 1992. However, Gould later recorded

(1998, p. 175) that a long document summarising the Clinton campaign and Labour's strategic position went down 'like a lead balloon' with the party leadership. A decade later, its analysis looks obvious, but not then. Gould argued that Labour was seen to be looking 'downwards, not upwards' and 'backwards, not forwards'; it was for 'minorities and not the mainstream', and it was 'not trusted to run the economy properly.' His conclusion was that 'Labour needs a proper connection with the aspirations of ordinary working people.' Under the theme of the 'new populism', Gould argued that Labour would only build up a new relationship of trust with the British people once the party had changed itself. That is what the Democrats had done by calling themselves the 'New Democrats'. The American experience was particularly appealing for Blair, Brown and Mandelson and the 'modernisers' since there were few successful socialist or social democrat parties in Europe to provide inspiring examples – particularly in view of the repeated defeats of the SPD in Germany by Helmut Kohl's Christian Democrats.

Blair and Brown visited Washington in January 1993 as the Clinton team was taking office and they talked to his advisers. Sidney Blumenthal records in his self-justificatory, though revealing, defence of Clinton (2003, p. 301) how Jonathan Powell, then a diplomat at the British Embassy in Washington, before later becoming Blair's Chief of Staff, organised a small lunch for the two visitors. Leading Clintonites explained how the new President had won. 'On every point the British visitors drew instant analogies. The two were eager and incredulous. They could barely believe that someone like Clinton had been elected, and they seemed slightly humbled by the news. It was a very American story with a happy ending.'

The main lessons drawn from the visit and Philip Gould's earlier analysis were electoral: both strategic in positioning and tactical in how to campaign. The first involved shedding past unfavourable tax and spending images and, instead, conveying an image of fiscal responsibility. Instead of sectional appeals to interest groups, the emphasis should, rather, be as wide as possible, to include what were characteristically described as 'hard-working' families, or in Clinton's American phraseology, 'the forgotten middle class.' There was also a tough edge: no hand-outs, help only to those prepared to help themselves. Or, 'responsibility in exchange for opportunity'. The second, tactical, lessons were about the need for tight discipline, a finely honed and repeated message and a highly professional operation fighting the media war twenty-four hours a day.

But the Labour leadership did not immediately embrace this message of hope from the New World. Far from it. 'Clintonisation' quickly became a term of suspicion and abuse on the Labour left. The critics included John Prescott, long before he became Blair's loyal deputy. The left suspected that the 'modernisers' like Blair and Brown had a hidden agenda to turn Labour into a social democrat party (they were largely right in Blair's case). John Rentoul, an acute biographer of Blair, records (2001, p. 196) how Peter Mandelson was summoned by John Smith, the Labour leader, as Blair and Brown's joint adjutant while they were away. Mandelson's version of Smith's dressing-down was: 'All this Clintonisation business, it's just upsetting everyone. Stop boat-rocking with all this talk of change and modernisation. It will just divide the party. If we remain united we'll win. Do just shut up.'

Yet if the Clinton example was not followed by Labour while John Smith was leader, it influenced the 'modernisers'. Blair saw both a strategy and a style that could bring success to a centre-left party, appealing both to the middle ground (what came to be known as Middle England) and to Labour's traditional supporters. Rentoul argues (2001, p. 198) that Blair 'had at last found a populist language in which to express the ethical socialist ideas which had formed his political convictions.' In a reference to a discussion in December 1993, Paddy Ashdown records (2000, p. 223) how Blair is 'much influenced by Clinton's new contract between the citizen and the state'. Blair's famous slogan, 'tough on crime, tough on the causes of crime' (in fact devised by Brown) is a classic expression of this approach. There are direct parallels in the language used by Clinton and the New Democrats and by Blair and New Labour during this period.

After Blair became Labour leader in July 1994, the Clinton influences came more to the fore. These were primarily electoral – in the organisation of campaigning – rather than in policy thinking. The lessons of spin were applied more than those of substance. This was partly because of the different policy background in the US, and partly because Clinton's freedom of manoeuvre was severely curtailed after the Republican capture of the Senate and the House of Representatives in the November 1994 mid-term elections. The relative significance of the electoral lessons was brought home a week before the May 1997 election when I was part of a team from *The Times* who interviewed Blair, and the other party leaders, during the campaign. We went to his Islington home where the normally calm and friendly Blair was, for once, slightly tetchy. He was obviously tired and he had nothing to gain from doing yet another media interview. So when I suggested that Clinton had not achieved much during more than four years in office, Blair snapped back: 'Well, he got re-elected, didn't he?' This answer revealed a lot about Blair's attitudes and thinking, not just then, but also over his whole first term.

Nonetheless, New Labour did examine in detail, and partially adopt, some policies developed in the United States and debated by the New Democrats. Gordon Brown closely followed the American political scene, regularly taking his summer holidays on Cape Cod. And Ed Balls, his Economic Adviser, had links to the Clinton Treasury via Larry Summers, who had taught him at Harvard. The two looked at a wide range of American policies, rather than simply at the experience of the Clinton administration. For instance, the record of the independent Federal Reserve was influential in the preparation of Brown's first, and most important, policy announcement after the May 1997 election when the Bank of England was made responsible for setting interest rates. The Brown–Balls team also drew from a series of initiatives in different US states both on welfare-to-work schemes to get people out of unemployment into jobs and on using tax credits to provide incentives for the working poor.

These examples are entirely domestic. There were very few references to American foreign policy in either Blair's pre-election speeches or the Labour manifesto in 1997. When Blair visited Washington in April 1996, he was given a warm welcome by Clinton. This was a very different reception from when Neil Kinnock was publicly and deliberately undermined on a comparable visit to Ronald Reagan in March 1987 (on that occasion with the connivance of Mrs Thatcher's advisers in Downing Street, including Charles, now Lord, Powell, then Thatcher's Foreign Affairs Private Secretary, and elder brother of Jonathan Powell). It was during the 1996 visit that Sidney Blumenthal acted as matchmaker by hosting a party where Blair met and had a long discussion with Hillary Clinton. As she records (2003, p. 422): "'You and the Blairs are political soul mates", Sid told me. "You have to meet each other.'" And the First Lady quickly saw a 'connection' and a shared political vision.

President Clinton was careful not to cause offence to John Major – with whom he was by then on workmanlike, if hardly cordial, relations. But Clinton treated his visitor as a potential prime minister. Apart from boosting Blair's image at home as leader taken seriously in Washington, a 'Prime Minister in waiting', the visit was more about the parallel political and electoral approach of the New Democrats and New Labour than any specific foreign policy issues. According to one British participant in the hour-long meeting in the Oval Office, who had regularly sat in on conversations between the President and John Major, the refreshing feature was how much Clinton and Blair 'talked politics'. Apart from obligatory references to Northern Ireland – where Blair stressed his broad support for Major's approach – and to Bosnia, most of the discussion was about political strategy. Clinton and Blair talked about how to deal with insecurity, voters' anxieties about their jobs, homes and pensions in face of rapid technological and economic change. These discussions were aptly described by Mike McCurry, the White House spokesman, as a 'wonkathon', But there was no sense then of a distinctive 'Blair' approach to international affairs. In a speech to businessmen of the British-American Chamber of Commerce in New York, before flying down to Washington, Blair for the first time highlighted what became his familiar mantra:

It is absurd to imagine that, for Britain, there is a choice between the relationship with Europe and that with America. On the contrary, the real value to the US of the British role in Europe lies in the influence we can and will exert to keep Europe firmly linked to the US in defence, outward-looking, open to trade and investment, and open also to the inclusion of the new democracies in Central and Eastern Europe.

The Blair visit came when a fundamental debate was under way in the United States about relations with Europe after the Cold War. Many of the familiar assumptions about common threats and interests binding the two sides of the Atlantic together had disappeared. Yet the Clinton years were marked by incoherence and inconsistency. Bill Clinton may have been the most travelled president, but there was little sense of a long-term strategy. Clinton's defenders point to his involvement in the Middle East and Northern Ireland peace processes; brokering the Dayton Peace Accords to end or substantially reduce four years of fighting in Bosnia; his leadership of the NATO coalition in the Kosovo conflict; his support for NATO enlargement; Russian integration into the west; containing Saddam Hussein; and, above all, encouraging free trade and an open international economic and financial system by taking political risks in winning approval for important trade deals. Each of these areas has its pluses and minuses. Some of the proclaimed 'achievements', as in the Middle East, did not last long, while others were partial. The Clinton administration spent a lot of time worrying about the threat from terrorism and weapons of mass destruction – though this has naturally been overshadowed by everything that has happened since 11 September. Moreover, Republican critics argue that, for all the talk, President Clinton failed to act decisively against terrorists or what became known as 'rogue' states. On this view, the Clinton years were a transitional period, marked by *ad hoc* initiatives and the avoidance of American casualties. Even if the pattern is not clear – like a kaleidoscope in the words of Madeleine Albright, Clinton's second-term Secretary of State – there were recurrent doubts about when and how to use power and to intervene overseas.

These worries had been underlined by the Bosnian conflict, which the Clinton administration felt had been exacerbated by European weakness and only ended when the US intervened both militarily and diplomatically. The Europeans, and particularly the British, felt that Warren Christopher, the first-term Secretary of State, failed to appreciate conditions on the ground and that American opinion, particularly in Congress, took an over-simplified, good versus bad, view of a three-way conflict. The result was both a deterioration in Anglo–American relations (noted in the previous chapter) and a more sceptical view in Washington about Europe's ability to act together. These doubts were expressed with typical bluntness by Richard Holbrooke, America's chief Bosnian negotiator in the mid-1990s. Speaking at the annual Davos meeting in February 1996 of the World Economic Forum – a networking session for global super-egos – Holbrooke said, in relation to recent tensions between Greece and Turkey that nearly led to war: 'While President Clinton and our team were on the phone with Athens and Ankara, the Europeans were literally sleeping through the night. You have to wonder why Europe does not seem capable of taking decisive action in its own theater.' This was unfair to Sir Malcolm Rifkind, the then British Foreign Secretary, who later said that he had been up in the middle of the night working on the same problem. But no one disputed the general thrust of Holbrooke's remarks. He later wrote (1998, p. 331) about how his 'while Europe slept' remark was widely seen and reported as 'a metaphor for the confusion and drift that seemed to have settled over the European Union since the end of the Cold War.' Yet Blair largely ignored such tensions, and debates, in both his April 1996 visit to Washington and in his pre-election speeches on foreign policy.

The Labour election manifesto in 1997 included a lot of the 'new politics' language of the Clinton campaigns. But the foreign policy section of the manifesto contained not a single mention of the United States, or what the Clinton administration, in theory New Labour's closest ideological ally, was trying to achieve internationally. Instead, the primary emphasis was on Europe, together with references to 'strong defence within NATO', support for arms reduction talks, a tough attitude to arms sales, coupled with reforming the United Nations, attaching a much higher priority to international develop-ment and combating global poverty, and making 'the protection and promotion of human rights a central part of our foreign policy'. 'Leadership, not isolation' was the theme. But of Britain's close links with Washington, there was nothing. Various pre-election speeches had merely referred in passing to maintaining the Atlantic Alliance, with little evidence of any fresh thinking. In Bonn, May 1995, in his speech to the Friedrich Ebert Stiftung, Blair had said Britain should 'take steps towards building a stronger European foreign and defence policy in harmony with the Atlantic Alliance'.

On Europe, Blair was engaged in a careful balancing act – wanting to stress a positive and leading role, in contrast to the divisions and indecision of the Major Government, while not wanting to be out-flanked by the Conservatives. Blair has never been a European idealist, in the way that either Edward Heath has been or Roy Jenkins was, a believer in the vision of European unity to avoid any danger of repeating the horrors of 1939–45. Blair's commitment was less in some ways than that of the otherwise cautious John Smith, who had, after all, been one of the sixty-nine Labour rebels who voted for the principle of joining in October 1971. Blair was, and is, a pro-European in the sense that he feels at home around Europe, almost from his student days as a barman in Paris. He believes that Britain should naturally be a leading member of the European Union. In his first conference speech as party leader in October 1994, he said: 'I will never allow this country to be isolated or left behind in Europe', while the following spring he said that for Britain to remain at the edge of Europe would to 'deny our historical role in the world'. In his Bonn speech in 1995, quoted previously, Blair said, with selective amnesia about his 1982–83 election addresses: 'I grew up as part of a post-war generation. I voted for Britain to remain in the EEC. I fought to persuade my party to become a party of Europe, believing that to be in my country's interests.'

Labour's election manifesto in 1997 talked about a 'fresh start in Europe'. A new, united Government would be able to do things that the divided Tories could not. The objectives were rapid completion of the single market; a higher priority for enlargement; signing on to the social chapter of the Maastricht Treaty (from which Major had opted out), provided it did not involve forced harmonisation of social security or tax legislation; support for reform of the Common Agricultural Policy; and greater openness and democracy in EU institutions. But Blair emphasised retention of the national veto over 'key matters of national interest', including taxation, defence and security, immigration, decisions over the budget and treaty changes.

The euro was – and has remained – the most sensitive issue. Before the 1997 election, the euro was still a plan, not a working currency. The Major Government had an official 'wait and see' attitude, in part because of bitter divisions between supporters of entry like Kenneth Clarke and Michael Heseltine and strong opponents like Michael Howard, Michael Portillo and Peter Lilley, as well as a large number of vocal, sceptic backbenchers. Public opinion was hostile, as, more vehemently, were several prominent newspapers such as the *Sun*.

So Labour – eager to court the *Sun* and Rupert Murdoch, its proprietor – ducked and weaved about the euro. At its most demeaning, and dishonest, this involved letting an article appear under Blair's name in the *Sun* in April 1997 during the election campaign which proclaimed 'my love for the pound'. Abandoning sterling was not just about economics, Blair told *Sun* readers: 'It's about the sovereignty of Britain, and constitutional issues, too.' This was wholly different from the tone of his post-election comments when he said there were no constitutional obstacles to joining the euro, and he emphasised the economic aspects. The road to Wapping was apparently worth being economical with the truth. Or, as his advisers argued defensively in private, Blair had not formally conceded any ground which could not be later recovered. This turned out to be an over-optimistic gloss.

Labour's official policy was a more positive version of the Tories' 'wait and see'. The manifesto noted 'there are formidable obstacles in the way of Britain being in the first wave of membership, if economic and monetary union takes place on 1 January 1999.' So Labour promised to play a full part in the debate about the development of the euro and not to exclude membership forever. Reluctantly, Blair and Brown also agreed in November 1996 to promise a referendum on membership. This was largely to avoid being outflanked by the Tories who had already promised a referendum and to isolate the issue. The implicit, and often explicit, message was that people could vote Labour without being committed to the euro since they would have a separate vote on joining. This was also, it turned out, an ideal excuse for continuing indecision and inaction on the euro.

In office, in May 1997, Blair quickly affirmed both his pro-European credentials and his Atlanticist instincts – in the process revealing some of the tensions that were to become more apparent in later years. Within three weeks of taking office, Blair attended a summit of European leaders in the Netherlands to prepare for a full-blown inter-governmental conference to discuss changes to the EU constitution. But there were hints of triumphalism which did not go down well with his more experienced European colleagues. The Blair charm was balanced by talk of the dangers of a political elite getting out of touch and an evident dislike of euro-jargon. Other European leaders were reported as complaining that perhaps not that much had changed in the underlying 'we know best' British attitude. These worries were underlined two weeks later when Tony Blair flew to Malmo in Sweden for a conference of European socialists. While being personally acclaimed for his victory, Blair annoyed many tradi-tional socialists by warning of the need to abandon old-style ideas on spending and regulation. He was right, but his tone jarred, smacking of arrogance – particularly as a different approach also seemed to be successful electorally following the victory of Lionel Jospin's French Socialists in late May. Tensions between New Labour and the French Socialists over social and economic – as well as foreign – policy lasted until M. Jospin was trounced in the first round of the French presidential elections five years later.

In mid-June, Blair was more tactful at the Amsterdam summit to decide the new treaty. A new approach had been signalled when Blair announced that Britain would end its opt-out from the social chapter of the Maastricht Treaty. The message was clear: the new Labour Government wanted to be a good partner, though Blair bargained toughly before signing up to what became the Treaty of Amsterdam, whereas John Major would never have been allowed by his divided party to reach an agreement. This was the period when symbols were all. Television cameramen and photographers were given the gift of pictures of a youthful and energetic-looking Blair on a bicycle riding ahead of other European leaders: the cake-loving Helmut Kohl did not join them on two wheels.

Yet despite Blair's barrister-like skill in negotiations, and his personal charm, the net effect was not totally reassuring to other EU leaders. They welcomed the change of government but were not sure how much difference it would make to Britain's overall relations with the rest of the EU. These doubts were underlined later in October 1997, when a messy, semi-public negotiation between Blair and Brown led to a statement putting off indefinitely British entry into the euro. As significant, control over the issue was handed to the Chancellor by making the Treasury the guardian of the five economic tests of whether Britain had converged sufficiently with the eurozone.

While theoretically the option of holding a referendum later in the parliament was left open, the likelihood quickly disappeared, producing disillusionment among strong pro-Europeans.

During this honeymoon period, Tony Blair also cemented his personal alliance with Bill Clinton when the President visited Britain during a European tour. There was a 'laying on of hands', when the President addressed a Cabinet meeting, expressing envy at Blair's ability to act as a result of Labour's 179 Commons majority. The implicit message was, 'What could I have done with that?', especially as Clinton was still constrained by Republican majorities in both Houses of Congress after the 1996 elections. There was much mutual back-slapping, both at the Cabinet meeting and, later, at a press conference in the warm sunshine in the garden of 10 Downing Street. There was not much real news to discuss, so the two leaders talked about their political approaches. At one stage, as Blair was giving a particularly long answer, Sandy Berger, the US National Security Adviser, and his staff standing at the back noticed a visible sigh by Clinton. According to an American participant, 'the unmistakable message of the body language was I cannot keep up with him. I used to be like that.' Clinton, in his older brother mode, admired Blair's energy and command of the facts, 'what he [Clinton] used to be like'.

The President and the Prime Minister celebrated 'a new generation of politicians and a new generation of leadership'. This was a deliberate reference back to the Camelot days of JFK, Clinton's political hero, with whom, characteristically, he managed to get photographed. For Blair, there was a less happy parallel with Harold Wilson's bathetic posthumous invocation of Kennedy's youth and vigour during 1963–4. Blair and Clinton expressed a lot of self-admiring guff about the new approach being 'strong on ideals but indifferent to ideology, whose instinct is to judge government not on grand designs but by practical results'. They agreed about the need to promote employment through encouraging a more flexible job market. The self-congratulatory mood is caught by Blumenthal (2003, p. 299): 'When Tony Blair and Bill Clinton's parallel political lives finally intersected at the point of power, they had the chance to recast the alliance between the US and Britain.' But, even then, Blair's admiration of Clinton's political skills was qualified. Blair remarked to one of his advisers just after the Clinton visit that he thought there was a 'weird bit' to him – as became even more apparent the following year.

At the meeting, the two leaders also reaffirmed their belief in the importance of the transatlantic link. Blair said: 'A Britain that is leading Europe is a Britain capable of having close relations also with the USA.' Clinton replied that: 'It is good for the United States to have a Britain that is strong in Europe and strong in its relations with the US.' There was no sense of potential tensions between Blair's desire to play a leading role in Europe and to be close to Washington. Some euro-sceptic commentators were already pointing to the potential conflict between the European desire, backed by Britain, for a stronger European defence and security identity, and US worries, especially in the Pentagon, about whether this would undermine NATO. But these problems were mainly for the future.

The most lasting result of the affinity between the two leaders was the start that autumn of the first of a series of policy discussions between leading politicians and advisers in the Clinton and Blair camps. Hillary Clinton records in her memoirs (2003, p. 425) how after a discussion of 'shared ideas' about education and welfare over dinner at Le Pont de La Tour by the Thames – not the usual topics of conversation at one of London's most fashionable restaurants – the two leaders and their wives decided to initiate discussions among advisers to explore common ideas and strategies. That November, Mrs Clinton flew over with a strong White House team for a discussion at Chequers with the conscious aim of winning 'the battle of ideas' with the right, as well as to exchange thinking about specific policies. Sidney Blumenthal became the US organiser of these meetings. He gushingly records (2003, p. 308) how:

> *The Chequers meeting was the beginning of an international Third Way. The Anglo–American special relationship had never before been politically paralleled . . . Blair's success dramatically altered the international stage on which Clinton operated. The Prime Minister was an ally like no other through all sorts of difficulties and challenges, from foreign crises – the Balkans – to the domestic one over Clinton's possible impeachment. With Blair's election in 1997, Clinton felt that he himself was leading an international movement.*

The Chequers meeting was followed by a series of others, generally to coincide with normal bilateral or international meetings: Washington in February 1998, Chequers (again) in May 1998, New York University in September 1998, Washington (again) in April 1999, Florence in November 1999, and Berlin in June 2000 (from which Blair was absent following the birth of his fourth child Leo). The cast list broadened over time, to include centre-left leaders from Europe, Australasia and Brazil. It was never clear what was achieved, apart from boosting the egos of those participating. One British participant, who is both close to Blair and is still a public advocate of the Third Way approach, later complained that many of these 'grand policy seminars had been poorly prepared and ill-conceived. They were too diffuse and there was no follow up.' Perhaps the most important point was merely that the meetings happened, rather than that they had a lasting policy impact. Revealingly, Gordon Brown, for all his liking of the United States, and his interest in policy initiatives from across the Atlantic, was hardly involved in the meetings after the first one. He preferred to maintain his own separate, and parallel, transatlantic links. For both Clinton and Blair, what mattered was demonstrating that they were not alone, that others shared their ideas. Perhaps, also, they were keen to demonstrate that the Third Way was not only a slogan and an electoral strategy but also had an intellectual content: hence the welcome given to Anthony Giddens, director of the London School of Economics, as the ideologist of the Third Way.

The Anglo-American origins of the Third Way did not worry some on the left in Europe, but did concern the French Socialists. Blumenthal (2003, p. 668) notes that 'the most intensive co-operation existed with the British', while adding (p. 673) how Lionel Jospin sought to separate himself from the Anglo-American approach:

> *His presence at the Third Way meetings resulted in tensions*
> *because he was suspicious of Clinton's and Blair's inten-*

> *tions and clung to the other old socialist ways of speaking.*
> *Clinton wanted a broad, inclusive 'floating opera', with as*
> *many participants as possible. But Jospin did not want too*
> *many leaders of parties belonging to the Socialist*
> *International to become part of the Third Way, because he*
> *saw it as a co-option that would diminish the virtually*
> *irrelevant organisation, in which he believed he exercised*
> *influence.*

Blair himself believed, or perhaps hoped, that the Third Way approach discussed and reaffirmed at these meetings would be the model for the centre-left across Europe. He said, in an interview with the *Guardian* during his visit to Washington in February 1998, that his long-term plan was to put New Labour at the head of a 'worldwide movement of ideas . . . bringing together diverse programmes and parties of the centre-left in Western and Eastern Europe, and in North and South America.' But, as he had discovered at the Malmo conference of European socialists barely a month after coming to power, other centre-left parties disliked being lectured by him, and had their own national traditions and policies. Many within the Labour Party, on the left and in the unions, were deeply suspicious of all the talk about the Third Way, just as they had disliked 'Clintonisation' in early 1993. They were wary of the welfare reforms accepted by Clinton in 1996 and felt that both Clinton and Blair were not egalitarians. At that time, the Blairites found that they had most in common with the Dutch and Finnish social democrats, but least, at any rate publicly, with the French Socialists. The PS in France rejected the Blairite, and Clintonite, acceptance of globalisation, and the implicit assumption that there was no alternative to the neo-liberal orthodoxy. Many of the policies of the Blair and Jospin administrations were much closer in practice – notably in their attitudes to fiscal and monetary policy. Both believed in economic competition and the role of the state in assisting social cohesion. But their assumptions and language differed substantially. Writing at the end of Labour's first term, academic Ben Clift argued (in Ludlam and Smith 2001, p. 57) that: 'After several years of New Labour, the party is arguably now more influenced by Atlanticist links with Clinton. It is no longer so apparent that the trajectories of Labour and Continental social democracy run parallel.'

In personal terms, Blair had a non-ideological approach, working with whoever was in power. He got on well with centre-left leaders like Wim Kok in the Netherlands and Massimo D'Alema in Italy. But, over time, he became closest to José María Aznar of Spain, a centre-right leader until April 2004, and, until the Iraq war, with Jacques Chirac rather than Lionel Jospin. Blair had a good personal relationship with Gerhard Schröder, often having one-to-one dinners with him. But Blair was often frustrated by the German Chancellor manoeuvring to placate domestic opinion and party critics in the SPD, particularly in the run-up to his re-election campaign in September 2002. The attempt to form a close ideological bond was highlighted by the issue of a joint Third Way–Neue Mitte policy statement in early summer 1999. But this was soon played down by the Social Democrats, even though they continued, often inconsistently, to pursue a parallel policy agenda. By the middle of Blair's second term, Goran Persson of Sweden and, more erratically, Gerhard Schröder were his closest allies on the centre-left, all flexible reformers – who also managed to get re-elected for second terms.

European doubts increased when Blair flew to Washington in February 1998, when news of the Monica Lewinsky affair had just broken, and when tension was high over attempts to force Saddam Hussein to accept weapons inspectors (as discussed in the next chapter). Blair then held the six-monthly, rotating presidency of the European Council but – as widely remarked upon in Continental newspapers – he barely mentioned this role. He was visiting as British Prime Minister, supporting a friend and ally in trouble. His strong personal support for President Clinton was underpinned by a shared desire to present a united front over Iraq. The arguments over Iraq of early 1998, though largely forgotten now, revealed fault lines in the transatlantic relationship which developed into a wide chasm five years later. Tony Blair's attitudes and behaviour then – and the strained relations with France – were all apparent, even though on a minor scale compared with 2003.

Yet the February 1998 visit also marked the end of Blair's learning phase. His public support for Clinton reflected not only political calculation but also a shift in their relationship. Clinton said he was grateful for Blair's support 'when it would have been just as easy to walk away.' And, when the two leaders left the White House East Room, the President turned and said, in a quintessentially Clinton remark: 'I'm going to make sure you're proud of what you did in there.' James Steinberg, the Deputy National Security Adviser, turned to Sir Christopher Meyer, the British Ambassador in Washington, and said: 'We owe you big time.'

The British side debated – via a series of transatlantic exchanges – about how to call in the debt. The answer was Northern Ireland, where the US was an influential player and where there had been frequent clashes between London and Washington during the Major–Clinton period. One of Blair's closest advisers reckons that frequent exchanges between Downing Street and the White House over Northern Ireland were the basis of the warm working relationship which Blair and Clinton developed during 1997–8. Jonathan Powell, Blair's Chief of Staff, was increasingly involved in Northern Ireland; and, as noted earlier, he knew all the key figures in the Clinton administration dating back to 1992. So he was often the key link between Belfast, London and Washington. Clinton proved to be 'very helpful', in the words of one Downing Street adviser, at the most fraught point of the negotiations in Belfast leading up to the Good Friday Agreement two months after Blair's visit to Washington. The President followed the talks through the night and was available to call the participants. And he publicly backed 'Yes' votes in the later referendums.

However, privately, many on the British side – in Washington, 10 Downing Street and the Northern Ireland Office – argue that Clinton's role in Northern Ireland was 'hugely exaggerated'. The President's impact was more symbolic and presentational, than about substance, even in the Good Friday negotiations where the key roles were played by Blair and the direct participants. And there was disappointment over Clinton's lack of close involvement later. The British felt that the President could have done more. Sir Christopher Meyer argues that Clinton 'never quite gave the bite on Sinn Fein/IRA at crucial moments. I think we would have liked more pressure on decommissioning. I never thought we got the return we deserved.' That view was shared by some in the Northern Ireland Office who thought that the Clinton administration remained partial in its instincts, always being 'really close' to Sinn Fein and the nationalists, and leaning towards their views, despite giving access to the Unionists. Clinton's 'Green', rather than 'Orange', bias dated back to the 1992 election campaign and his courting of New York Democrats supportive of the nationalists, and even of the republicans. Clinton's willingness to defy London over the granting of a visa to Gerry Adams was seen as giving him some standing with the Irish republican community, which he failed to use. Apart from the continuing stalemate over decommissioning, the Clinton White House was also felt not to have put enough pressure on Sinn Fein over the Patten report on reform of policing in Northern Ireland. President Clinton 'never really put the boat out' in the view of one British Cabinet minister.

But the Blair team also began to think of life after Clinton. During his Washington visit, the Prime Minister spent a lot of time with Vice President Al Gore, who gave a typically wooden speech at a joint appearance at the State Department. The Vice President was invited to make a big speech in Britain. But in the hope of avoiding the mistakes of 1992, when the Tories became too closely identified with the Bush campaign, Mr Blair's advisers sought to keep open lines to possible Republican successors to Clinton, rather than just to Gore. A week after Blair's dramatic visit to Washington, Sir Christopher Meyer flew down to Texas to see George W. Bush, then campaigning for re-election as Governor, and already tipped as a stronger runner for the Republican nomination in 2000. These early contacts paid off in 2001.

4. Coming of Age

Strangely enough, it was reading the intelligence soon after I became Prime Minister.

Tony Blair explaining why and when he first became alerted to
the threat of weapons of mass destruction
(in comments to the author)

I have now seen some of the stuff on this. It really is pretty scary. He [Saddam] is very close to some appalling weapons of mass destruction.

Tony Blair, quoted in Paddy Ashdown's diaries,
November 1997

Just as I believe there was no alternative to military action, now it has started, I am convinced there is no alternative to continuing until we succeed . . . Success is the only exit strategy I am prepared to consider.

Tony Blair, speaking on the 'Doctrine of the
International Community', in Chicago,
22 April 1999, during the Kosovo war

Tony Blair was worried about Iraq and Saddam Hussein almost from the day he became Prime Minister. Few people noticed at the time. But most of the arguments over the threat posed by Saddam, and how to tackle it, were already present well before George W. Bush became President in January 2001. And Blair's response was virtually the same in 1997–8 as five years later. The Clinton years were a period of frequent tension and, often, disagreement: in the mid-1990s over Bosnia, and then, later, over Iraq and Kosovo. Differences emerged over the use of force, over the role of NATO and over the huge, and growing, imbalance in military capabilities between Europe and the United States. These events also shaped Tony Blair's attitudes, both towards military intervention and, specifically, about working with Washington.

The recurrent Iraqi crises of 1998 were dress rehearsals for the war of 2003. What Tony Blair said and did then explains most of what happened later. Far from being persuaded to take a tough line against Saddam Hussein in order to remain in favour with Washington – the widely held 'Bush's poodle' view – Blair had been arguing in favour of such an approach, including the threat of military action, since late 1997. Senior civil servants recall that very early on his premiership, he talked about the problems of weapons of mass destruction. This occurred at a time when, in the words of one close adviser, he was 'not yet particularly turned on by the intelligence agencies'. During the first comprehensive spending review in 1998, Blair had to be persuaded to take an interest in the budgets of the intelligence agencies – in marked contrast to his second term when he backed a big increase in their spending, particularly after 11 September. The main exception was Northern Ireland. Ahead of the Good Friday Agreement in spring 1998, Blair became closely interested in the assessments provided by the intelligence agencies. He was impressed by what he heard and read, especially when he could compare it with what happened later. But he did not become fully engaged with the intelligence world until the Kosovo conflict in 1999. After then, the leaders of the secret world became part of his inner circle of advisers during the frequent crises of his premiership.

Nonetheless, intelligence warnings about the threat of weapons of mass destruction, and particularly of Saddam Hussein, did make an early mark on him. When asked after the Iraq war, at the height of the row about the pre-war intelligence assessments, about what made him so interested in this issue, he replied: 'Strangely enough, it was reading the intelligence soon after I became Prime Minister.' He read about 'the threat from rogue states and about weapons of mass destruction getting into the hands of terrorist groups'. The main influence was the assessments by the Joint Intelligence Committee, based in the Cabinet Office. At this time, as before and later, the JIC was warning of the general threat from the proliferation of these weapons, particularly over the danger of a partial leakage of nuclear material from the old Soviet Union. Its warnings covered 'all the old culprits' and not just Iraq. In a sense there was nothing new in these assessments. What was new was the person reading them for the first time. For Blair, these warnings were both fresh and alarming. He picked up on them and they became an important part of his foreign policy viewpoint. One senior adviser in Downing Street says that when Blair saw the intelligence, he went to great trouble to find out more. The adviser sees this as an example of Blair's 'politician's instinct to see the coming issue'. This concern coincided with reports about the possible, illegal involvement of British firms in the arms supply chain to Iraq, contrary to UN resolutions. Blair was determined to stop these supplies and was 'quite worked up. He got religion about it', according to one American diplomat involved in exchanges over the issue. Paddy Ashdown notes in his diaries (2001, p. 127) a conversation with Blair in mid-November 1997:

> *We moved on to Iraq. He said that he had spoken to Clinton several times during the day. Clinton is trying to avoid military action, but doesn't quite know how to do it. Blair had said to him it was vital that we drew attention now to why the UN weapons inspectors were there. The world was being exposed to Saddam's viewpoint and had been allowed to forget the reasons for bringing them in the first place.*

Ashdown then quotes Blair directly:

> *I have now seen some of the stuff on this. It really is pretty scary. He [Saddam] is very close to some appalling weapons of mass destruction. I don't understand why the French and others don't understand this. We cannot let him get away with it. The world thinks this is just games-manship. But it's deadly serious.*

Blair said in his speech at the Lord Mayor's Banquet in the City on 10 November 1997:

> *Saddam Hussein is once more defying the clearly expressed will of the United Nations by refusing to allow UN inspec-tors to fulfil their task of ensuring that Iraq has no remaining weapons of mass destruction. It is vital for all*

of us that they be allowed to complete their work with no
suggestion of discrimination against our US allies. Only
then can the question of relaxing sanctions arise. The
Government's determination to stand firm against a still
dangerous dictator is unshakeable. We want to see a diplo-
matic solution and will work with others to achieve this in
the next few days. But Saddam should not take this as a
sign of weakness. He has made this fatal miscalculation
before.

Nine days later, Blair stressed publicly: 'It is absolutely essential that
he backs down on this or that he be made to back down. If he does
not, we will simply face this problem, perhaps in a different, and far
worse, form, in a few years' time.' Similarly, Robin Cook, who
resigned from the Cabinet over the decision to go to war in March
2003, then as Foreign Secretary took a very strong line against
Saddam. On 24 November 1997 he quoted reports showing that
Saddam continued to produce enough anthrax every week to fill two
missiles. Sanctions, he said, could only be lifted when he stopped
'trying to develop weapons of mass destruction'. In his resignation
statement to the Commons on 17 March 2003, the former Foreign
Secretary doubted whether Iraq now had the ability to deliver such
biological and chemical weapons. Cook argued that the circumstances were very different in March 2003 from 1997–8, not least
because the earlier operation was to reinforce containment, rather
than a full-scale invasion.

These lengthy quotations are revealing about the Blair
Government's attitude towards Saddam after only a few months in

office. Compare with what he said more than five years later in a statement to the House of Commons on 25 February 2003 about Saddam's options:

> *I detest his regime. But even now he can save it by complying with the UN's demand. Even now, we are prepared to go the extra step to achieve disarmament peacefully. I do not want war . . . But disarmament peacefully can only happen with Saddam's active co-operation. Twelve years of bitter experience teaches that. And if he refuses to co-operate – as he is refusing now – and we fail to act, what then? Saddam in charge of Iraq, his WMD intact, the will of the international community set at nothing, the UN tricked again, Saddam hugely strengthened and emboldened – does anyone truly believe that will mean peace? And when we turn to deal with other threats, where will our authority be?*

So as early as November 1997 all the strands of the debate over Iraq during the following five years were present: American and British determination to put pressure on Saddam over weapons of mass destruction, and differences with France. The main contrast is that Clinton was more reluctant than his successor to use military force on a large scale. Then, as in 2002–3, Blair used very strong language about Saddam. At the end of January 1998, Blair described the Iraqi leader as 'an evil dictator'. A few days later, a Foreign Office dossier was released about Iraq's build-up of chemical and biological weapons and its nuclear ambitions, prompting Blair to claim that Saddam was a 'threat to world peace'. During his visit to Washington in February 1998, Blair underlined Britain's support for America's tough approach when standing alongside President Clinton in the White House:

> *We have stood together before in the face of tyranny. It's important, not out of machismo or a test of international virility, but in the interest of long-term world peace that Saddam Hussein is made to back down. We've got to recognise, in the light of our experience with Saddam Hussein, that diplomacy simply won't work unless it's backed up by the threat of force or indeed the use of force.*

Just as in early 2003, public views were very different on either side of the Atlantic. Whereas a majority of the American public favoured strong action, and would support the use of force to overthrow Saddam, voters in Britain were much less bellicose. So Blair's tough language was intended not only to reinforce diplomatic efforts but also to educate and persuade the British public about the possible need for military action. The British Government then, as before the Iraq war of 2003, emphasised that the objective of any military action would be to secure compliance with successive United Nations resolutions about full inspection of Iraqi sites where weapons of mass destruction might be under development. So attacks would be concentrated on sites suspected of being involved in such programmes, as well as against Iraq's air force and missile capacity. Tony Blair and other ministers emphasised that military action would not be aimed at getting rid of Saddam, however welcome his departure might be as a by-product.

During the early 1998 confrontation, divisions also appeared with other European countries. America and Britain were highly sceptical about diplomatic initiatives being pursued by Russia and France, both of whom had close diplomatic and commercial ties with Iraq. In the end, the threat of immediate military action was removed after a visit to Baghdad by Kofi Annan, the UN Secretary General. This resulted in an agreement which averted air strikes. Some in the Pentagon and among Blair's advisers saw this as a fudge which allowed Saddam a way out without tying him down. In the event, it proved to be just a temporary respite, postponing military confrontation.

This episode highlighted the traditional British tendency to side with Washington when a security crisis develops. Even though Britain held the six-monthly presidency of the European Council for the first six months of 1998, achieving an agreed EU line was always a lower priority than maintaining a united front with the White House. Robin Cook sought to achieve common ground at regular meetings of EU foreign ministers, but this was never at the expense of the transatlantic link. Tony Blair spoke for Britain, not the whole EU. This was seen at the time as exposing the hollowness of talk of a common, let alone, a single EU foreign policy. Britain was not alone. On this occasion, Germany, Portugal and the Netherlands all favoured a tough line. But, as often, it was disagreement between Britain and France that undermined any hope of a joint EU position. Differences within Europe were further underlined in August 1998 when Tony Blair was largely on his own in backing President

Clinton's decision to order retaliatory attacks against Osama bin Laden's supposed operations in Afghanistan and Sudan, after the bombings of two American Embassies in east Africa. It turned out that the Sudanese factory produced pharmaceuticals, not chemical weapons. There were a lot of raised eyebrows in the Foreign Office, but Blair had no doubt of the need for transatlantic solidarity, just as Margaret Thatcher overcame doubts of her Cabinet colleagues in allowing the American use of British bases for the bombing of Libya in April 1986.

The ambiguities of the British position were further underlined by two sharply contrasting events later in the year. Tony Blair reached agreement with Jacques Chirac on a new European defence initiative in early December 1998 at an Anglo–French summit in St Malo. Having long resisted any separate European involvement in defence, for fear of undermining NATO, Blair cautiously put his toe in the water. The proposal was very limited: for EU countries to intervene in regional problems, either as peacemakers or peacekeepers, when the United States did not want to get involved. The St Malo declaration said that the EU 'needs to be in a position to play its full role on the international stage . . . To this end, the union must have the capacity for autonomous action, backed up by credible military forces, the means to decide to use them, and a readiness to do so, in order to respond to international crises.'

The declaration immediately added that this increased co-operation by EU states was intended to be 'in conformity with our respective obligations in NATO . . . we are contributing to the vitality of a modernised Atlantic Alliance, which is the foundation of the collective defence of its members.' Decisions would be taken by the various inter-governmental meetings of leaders and foreign and defence ministers. There was no suggestion of a single or binding security policy, and dissenting governments could stand aside. European troops sent to intervene in regional disputes would be taken from those committed to NATO, or from national forces outside NATO (the French), or from the minimal capacity of the Western European Union, the largely defunct European defence arm. The declaration also committed to further action to create joint European capacities for intelligence gathering, analysis and strategic planning.

This agreement was seen, and welcomed, by the French as a significant move by Britain in a European direction, away from its long-standing Atlanticist ties. The hope in Paris was that the St Malo declaration would mark the start of a coherent and effective European security and defence policy. Even years later, during the disputes over the Iraq war of 2003, French diplomats talked about the 'spirit of St Malo' and, by implication, its later betrayal by the British. The British hopes were more limited. Tony Blair and his advisers were partly in search of a fresh pro-European initiative after the decision to stand aside from the euro. They also believed that the Bosnian saga of the 1990s had exposed the inability of the Europeans to act effectively together if the United States was unwilling to become involved. Hence, Europe needed to build a credible joint defence capability. And, for the British, unlike the French, capability mattered more than organisation. Blair's belief that Anglo-French co-operation on defence need not conflict with co-operation with Washington had been expressed earlier in the year, on 24 March, when he addressed the National Assembly in Paris in French:

> *I know that some feel that being close with the United*
> *States is an inhibition on closer European co-operation.*
> *On the contrary, I believe it is essential that the isolationist*
> *voices in the United States are kept at bay and we*
> *encourage our American allies to be our partners in issues*
> *of world peace and security. Strong in Europe. Strong with*
> *the United States. That should be our goal.*

The declaration was, in practice, full of ambiguities, sufficient to alarm euro-sceptics in Britain, as well as many policymakers in Washington. While the Clinton administration, like its predecessors, favoured European integration and stronger European defence capabilities in theory, US officials were wary, in practice, of any change that might threaten America's leadership role and the primacy of NATO. Sir Christopher Meyer in Washington comments that 'it was a classic story of telling the Europeans to act together, then getting irked when we take a specific initiative'. In this case, there were complaints from Washington that the scope and language of the St Malo declaration had taken them by surprise – contrary to the spirit, and usual practice, of the close working relationships between senior officials in the two capitals.

The British had consulted the Americans beforehand on the rough text of what they were aiming for at the summit. And, according to British diplomats, senior American officials in the State Department and the White House were quite content with it. The British party then went to St Malo and negotiations began on the basis of a French text translated into English. But what came out at the end when translated from the French looked different from what the Americans had seen before. The tone – the reference to 'autonomous action' – was more French than Atlanticist. So, according to Meyer, Sandy Berger, the White House National Security Adviser, and Strobe Talbott, Deputy Secretary of State, were 'very upset indeed'. There was 'a significant element of disturbance'. Sir Kevin Tebbitt, the Atlanticist Permanent Secretary at the Ministry of Defence, flew over to Washington to reassure the Pentagon that Britain had not suddenly gone Gaullist and that the familiar arrangements through NATO would continue as before.

The American version of what happened is only slightly different. Administration officials complained about lack of consultation. They did not really understand why Blair had launched such an initiative with the French, raising fears of duplicating, and undermining, NATO's decision-making structure. There was an element of the Americans being forced to take their own medicine since their own initiatives were often launched without full consultation with allies. But this reversal was not appreciated in Washington. Talbott blamed Emyr Jones Parry, the Foreign Office's Political Director who was seen as strongly pro-European. Relations between the two were further soured during a sticky later visit to London in 1999. Talbott also made no secret in conversations with journalists about his unhappiness with the way St Malo had been handled, and with the failure of the declaration to take account of the worries of NATO allies not in the European Union, principally Turkey, about being excluded from European defence planning. Suspicions were aroused about the Blair Government's intentions over European defence which festered during the remaining two years of the Clinton administration.

Yet if St Malo underlined Blair's European aspirations, a very different message came from the other big event of the month: the four days of air attacks on Iraq by US and British forces after Saddam forced the United Nations weapons inspectors out of Iraq. Operation Desert Fox was the culmination of a year-long confrontation which had nearly led to military action earlier. The US and Britain halted air attacks at the very last minute on 14 November. The UN Security Council then commissioned Richard Butler, head of UNSCOM, the then weapons inspectors, to assess Iraq's compliance with UN resolutions on weapons of mass destruction. The Butler report concluded that Saddam Hussein was breaking his promises yet again. So President Clinton – then facing impeachment proceedings in the House of Representatives – felt he had to act this time.

Tony Blair was not a reluctant warrior. Just as in 2003, he faced charges of being the American President's 'poodle'. But he said on a BBC *Breakfast with Frost* interview on 20 December that: 'I was very, very insistent myself that this action was right. To those people who say, "Well, the timing of all this was geared to internal affairs," I find that grotesque and I find it offensive . . . I myself was insistent that we made sure the action was taken as quickly as possible after the Butler report.' Blair argued in the House of Commons on 17 December, as he had earlier in the year, that the operation had two objectives: 'To degrade the ability of Saddam Hussein to build and use such weapons of mass destruction, including command and control and delivery systems, and to diminish the threat he poses to his neighbours by weakening his military capability.' As often during the long Iraq saga, Blair insisted, in contrast to Washington, that the aim was not to remove Saddam – 'But no one would be better pleased if his evil regime disappeared as a direct or indirect result of our action.'

The operation was short, and sharp. But, immediately, there were doubts about its effectiveness. Saddam's air and missile defences were certainly damaged. But Iraq's weapons of mass destruction were probably not destroyed since the UNSCOM inspectors did not know where they were. The inspectors had been frustrated in finding them. The action was also highly unlikely to topple Saddam, and did not do so. Instead, there was talk of containment. But that strategy was shown to be flawed, both because the weapons inspectors were not allowed to return and because Iraq was able to evade existing sanctions.

There was little dispute, however, about the diplomatic costs, particularly for Britain. Not only were the raids widely criticised in the Arab world, but Tony Blair also stood alone with Bill Clinton. No other European countries participated in any way. Even though he knew about the likelihood of air strikes well before the action, Blair did not discuss the matter with fellow EU leaders at their mid-December summit in Vienna. His priorities seemed yet again to be Atlanticist rather than European. The French were doubly furious. First, Paris dissociated itself from the attacks. Within an hour of the first strikes, a statement from the French Foreign Ministry said: 'France deplores the escalation which led to the American military strikes against Iraq and the grave human consequences which they could have for the Iraqi people.' France was more outspoken than any other EU country.

Second, senior French officials complained about being let down by Britain, less than two weeks after the St Malo declaration. I heard senior French diplomats express exasperation, even anger, at what they saw as the inconsistency between the pro-European spirit of St Malo and the virtually immediate return to what they saw as the familiar British ways of following Washington's lead. It seemed to be yet another re-run of the familiar pattern, first seen when the Skybolt–Polaris agreement at Nassau between Kennedy and Macmillan was quickly followed in January 1963 by de Gaulle's veto of Britain's application to join the European Community. From the British point of view, there was no inconsistency. Tony Blair, as always, believed that his desire to strength European defence capabilities to deal with conflicts in places like the Balkans could, and should, be compatible with Britain's active involvement in action against Saddam Hussein. For Blair in December 1998, as in March 2003, there was no contradiction in the two approaches.

Tony Blair's 'bridge' strategy faced a much greater, and more unwelcome, test in the first six months of 1999 over Kosovo. This conflict saw the first and clearest expression of his moral vision. It is misleading to bracket this with the 'ethical' dimension to foreign policy which Robin Cook so controversially announced as part of his early mission statement at the Foreign Office. Blair certainly talked about human rights. But his outlook had less to do with a traditional socialist foreign policy as interpreted by Cook, than the Prime Minister's Christian outlook and personal sense of right and wrong. It owed more to Gladstone than to Lansbury.

The classic expression of the Blair view came at one of the most fraught moments of the conflict, in April 1999, during a visit to the United States for the NATO summit. On a brief visit to Chicago, before going to Washington for the summit, Blair delivered one of the most important speeches of his premiership, entitled 'Doctrine of the International Community.' This was no spur-of-the-moment address, quickly cobbled together on the way across the Atlantic, but reflected considerable thought in Whitehall, notably the views of Robert Cooper, an original and free-thinking senior Foreign Office official, whose views are discussed in more detail in Chapter 7. Much of the original draft was written by Professor Lawrence Freedman, a leading international relations academic who often participated in public debates on foreign policy (Kampfner, 2003, pp. 50–53). The Chicago speech offered a striking illustration of how, even at this early stage of his premiership, Blair had developed an interventionist view. He argued that 'the most pressing foreign policy problem we face is to identify the circumstances in which we should get actively involved in other people's conflicts.' He said the long-standing principle of non-interference in the affairs of individual countries 'must be qualified in important respects. Acts of genocide can never be a purely internal matter. When oppression produces massive flows of refugees which unsettle neighbouring countries, then they can properly be described as "threats to international peace and security".'

Blair set out five major considerations to determine whether or not to intervene:

> *First, are we sure of our case? War is an imperfect instru-*
> *ment for righting humanitarian distress; but armed force*
> *is sometimes the only means of dealing with dictators.*
> *Second, have we exhausted all diplomatic options? We*
> *should always give peace every chance, as we have in the*
> *case of Kosovo. Third, on the basis of a practical assessment*

of the situation, are there military operations we can sensibly and prudently undertake? Fourth, are we prepared for the long term? In the past we talked too much of exit strategies. But having made a commitment we cannot simply walk away once the fight is over; better to stay with moderate numbers of troops than return for a repeat performance with large numbers. And finally, do we have national interests involved? The mass expulsion of ethnic Albanians from Kosovo demanded the notice of the rest of the world. But it does make a difference that this is taking place in such a combustible part of Europe.

Blair acknowledged that these were not 'absolute tests'. But the implications were, and are, far-reaching – raising worries, particularly at the senior level of the armed forces, that he has been too willing to commit British troops. The five questions were posed directly in relation to Kosovo, but would also apply to Afghanistan and Iraq. For Blair, these questions were also a test of will. 'One of the reasons why it is now so important to win the conflict is to ensure that others do not make the same mistake in the future.' And, at a time when there were widespread doubts about the success of the campaign, Blair was typically single-minded: 'Just as I believe there was no alternative to military action, now it has started, I am convinced there is no alternative to continuing until we succeed.' In language reminiscent of Margaret Thatcher, he said: 'Success is the only exit strategy I am prepared to consider.'

The intensity of Blair's commitment led to tensions not only with European allies but also with President Clinton. Blair learnt about the limits both to his influence in Washington and to American willingness to risk the lives of its servicemen in European conflicts. As with Iraq, Blair was early on willing to consider the use of force against the Milosevic regime in Serbia to prevent/reverse the actions against ethnic Albanians in Kosovo. This is not the place to revisit all the twists and turns of the lengthy run-up to the start of air attacks in late March 1999. My concern, rather, is with Blair's views, and relations with both Washington and other European capitals. Ivo Daalder and Michael O'Hanlon of the Brookings Institution, both acute observers of the transatlantic scene, report in their aptly titled book *Winning Ugly* (2000, p. 35) that: 'Arguing most strongly in favour of the possible use of force was Great Britain, where as of early June [1998] the mood had hardened from "the top downwards". According to one British official, London now firmly believed that "the only thing that would change Milosevic's actions will be [military] actions in and over Kosovo itself".' They note (p. 54) that by early August

> *The British Government had concluded not only that any solution to the crisis in Kosovo would involve the threat of the likely use of military force, but also that ground forces would have to be deployed in Kosovo – if not to end the violence, then to enforce the terms of any agreement that was reached. The Cabinet also agreed that Britain would play a leading role in any military action and that London would therefore be prepared to deploy ground forces in large numbers.*

Blair held this view consistently in face of the doubts and outright opposition of many in Europe, as well as in Washington. Before the

conflict started, even Blair saw ground troops more in an enforcement role rather than invading Kosovo against Serbian opposition.
When the bombing campaign began in late March, there was an
allied consensus against the use of ground forces for anything other
than implementing a negotiated withdrawal by the Serbs. President
Clinton did not want the subject to be aired publicly.

But the air campaign failed to make any noticeable impact on
Milosevic's resolve – as television reports night after night showed
pictures of refugees being forced over the border into Albania and
Macedonia. In Clinton's view (as recorded by Blumenthal, p. 639),
'Great Britain was firm and would be staunch to the end. Clinton
said he'd told Blair that the bombing had to be kept up: there could
be no pause, not even for Easter. Blair had to keep the alliance
together and avoid being "nickle and dimed". Clinton was on the
phone every day with his counterpart, and he and Blair worked as a
tag team, dividing up the allies to speak to them.'

Yet it was a tag team with increasingly different views on what
should happen. Blair appreciated Clinton's engagement in an essentially European problem and his commitment to seeing the conflict
through to the end. But there were worries over the flood of refugees,
over bombs hitting civilians and over a muddled media message –
which led to the close involvement of Alastair Campbell and his team
from 10 Downing Street in improving the presentation by NATO. It
was then that Blair started seeking advice on the deployment of ground
troops. He began saying that 'the way to avoid war is to make serious
preparations for war'. This became a familiar mantra to his inner circle
during the Kosovo conflict and on many later occasions. Advisers
remember a bizarre meeting in Blair's small study in 10 Downing Street

next to the Cabinet room when Sir Charles Guthrie, Chief of the Defence Staff, tried to educate the Prime Minister in the military difficulties of invading Kosovo. There were no visual aids in the study so a map of Kosovo was suspended from the mantelpiece and held in place by heavy weights brought in by the military. However, the map kept slipping and had to be held in place by a senior civil servant as the suave Sir Charles pointed to the very few, often crumbling roads leading into Kosovo through the clouds from the outside.

Blair had become increasingly worried about the military situation by mid-April, especially after he visited Brussels and met General Wesley Clark, the NATO Supreme Commander, and later unsuccessful candidate for the Democratic presidential nomination in 2004. Clark (2001, p. xxxiv) gives a vivid account of their private conversation:

> *Immediately he came straight to the point. 'Are we going to win?' he wanted to know. 'Yes, Prime Minister, we are going to win,' I assured him.*

After a further exchange to test him, the General records:

> *We looked at each other for a long moment, and then he leaned further forward on the couch. 'Good,' he said, 'because the future of almost every government and leader in Europe depends on our success here.' It was said with finality. This was personal for both of us.*
>
> *Tony Blair was representing Europe. He was saying what Washington had not: that we must win. He must*

> *make certain that I understood that the outcome of this*
> *campaign was much more significant to the Europeans*
> *than to Washington. And he was driving home to me as*
> *Supreme Allied Commander Europe, that I was respon-*
> *sible for its success or failure.*
>
> *Then he continued, 'Now, are we going to win without*
> *ground troops?'*

Clark said he could not guarantee victory with air power alone to which Blair responded: 'Will you get ground troops if you need them?'

Clark knew that Blair and the British Government supported moving ahead with preparations for ground troops. And Clark, the senior US General in Europe, knew that he could not overcome Pentagon resistance to such preparations without British help and leadership.

This extraordinarily frank discussion between a British Prime Minister and an American General set the stage for bruising exchanges between Blair and Clinton at the NATO summit less than a week later. Blair flew over determined to press for decisions to commit ground troops in sufficient numbers for an invasion later in the summer. There was still an ambiguity in his advocacy about the circumstances in which troops would enter Kosovo. Nonetheless, Blair's resolve was clear. Daalder and O'Hanlon argue (2000, p. 132) that Blair's determination may have reflected his stronger political position compared with other alliance leaders:

> *Some also argue that Britain is generally more willing to*
> *accept combat losses than the United States at this point in*

> *history. Both countries ran risks in Desert Storm (the first Gulf War in 1991), but their experiences diverged in the early 1990s. In Bosnia, Britain lost eighteen soldiers as part of a feckless UNPROFOR operation, yet sustained its role in the operation. At roughly the same time, the United States ended its participation in the 1992–3 Somalia mission after suffering similar numbers of loses.*

But whatever the motives and the background, Blair was the bearer of an unwelcome message in Washington. On Wednesday 21 April, Blair arrived at the White House for a pre-summit discussion, two days before the formal NATO meeting. Blair argued both for deploying ground forces and for using the NATO meeting to persuade the main European allies to accept this approach. Clinton was unwilling to accept Blair's argument, and was not prepared to undertake even contingency planning about ground troops. This would, Sandy Berger, the National Security Adviser argued, be seen as a vote of no confidence in the air campaign, which the Pentagon still insisted would work. Moreover, the President did not want such a divisive issue raised at the summit which, he believed, should project a message of unity. Clinton's argument throughout was the need to preserve NATO unity in order to put pressure on Milosevic. Blair agreed not to raise the ground troops option at the summit. News of the disagreement soon reached Clark in Brussels. He records on 23 April (2001, p. 270): 'I learned about the stormy discussion on ground troops between President Clinton and Prime Minister Blair.' Clinton's irritation with Blair was further increased by Blair's vigorous stance in his Chicago speech justifying intervention, noted above, as well as in his numerous television appearances during the visit.

The most that Blair could claim from the visit was a 'very secret' agreement that bilateral conversations should open between the British and American sides about contingency planning for ground troops. But nothing really ever happened, such was the hostility in Washington. There were also ambiguities in Blair's position. He talked about deploying ground troops in a 'semi-permissive environment', meaning when they would not have to invade in the face of an entrenched enemy putting up strong resistance. It was unclear how such an environment could be achieved, especially since the British were more sceptical than the Americans – the Pentagon rather than General Clark – about the efficacy of air power. But Daalder and O'Hanlon (2000, p. 138) argue that 'these talks just before the summit may have planted a seed in President Clinton's mind. As Blair pointed out, failure was not an option for NATO and air power was hardly guaranteed to work.' So, they conclude, Clinton would need to do what was necessary to win the war, including a ground invasion of Kosovo, if necessary.

Nonetheless, Blair left empty-handed, and the British side was discontented. Andrew Rawnsley (2001, p. 270) reflects the Downing Street mood in reporting that 'Blair had found him [Clinton] frustratingly unfocussed, frequently confused, and fixated with American public opinion.' Blair is quoted as referring sarcastically to 'my buddy Bill'. This irritation was reciprocated in Washington where Clinton and his advisers disliked the praise which Blair received in the American press, particularly at the President's expense. Clinton's advisers felt that Blair failed to appreciate the problems that the President faced in Congress and did not give enough credit to his determination to stay the course against Milosevic – a point later acknowledged by Blair's advisers. Problems arose out of the time difference between London and Washington. Before Americans got up in the morning, Blair had often been on the airways, delivering a clear-cut message, which was seen on the US breakfast shows. This often irked Clinton's advisers, given the uncertainties of the President's approach. Rawnsley (2001, p. 274) writes:

> *Tony Blair returned from the NATO summit feeling bleak. 'Nothing has been resolved,' he despaired to one side. He was fearful that he had strutted too hawkishly in Washington. 'I've gone at it too hard,' he confided to a close friend back in London. By 'upstaging' Clinton, he had made the President look 'weak' and the situation 'worse'. Clinton would be 'even more reluctant' to make a commitment to troops because it would look as if he had been 'bounced' by me.*

In face of the continuing apparent stalemate on the ground, Blair feared that Clinton and European leaders might try and reach a compromise with Milosevic. Blair's close advisers in London were worried that Blair was getting into a very exposed political position which could destroy his premiership. His language was increasingly outspoken, and moralistic – talking of a 'battle of good against evil, between civilisation and barbarity, democracy against tyranny'. The high moral tone was reinforced when he visited refugee camps in mid-May and, in a speech in Sofia, he even compared himself to Gladstone, the ultimate Victorian moralist of international affairs.

Gladstone, he said, is 'one of my political heroes', Sir Richard Wilson, then Cabinet Secretary, noted the intensity of Blair's commitment in a conversation with him in the first half of May. Asked about his reaction if Clinton told him that there was no option but a diplomatic solution, the Prime Minister was passionate and insistent: 'I will not do it.' Blair believed it would not be right. Fortunately for him, his defiance was not tested.

Yet Blair's increasing frustration about the American unwillingness to consider ground troops, and some 'fairly aggressive briefing on his behalf by Alastair Campbell' (in the words of one senior adviser), kept surfacing in the US press. And a front page story in the *New York Times* on 18 May 1999 led to what Sir Christopher Meyer describes as a 'very angry' 90-minute telephone call from Clinton to Blair. There was a 'huge, monumental explosion' from the President about Downing Street briefing, which had to stop. Clinton blamed Campbell (though their subsequent relations were close and harmonious). Blair denied any briefing against Clinton. This may have been literally true, though continuing to talk about the ground troops option sounded the same in Washington. Downing Street advisers also noticed counter-briefing against Blair's stance in some American newspapers. But tempers cooled, and relations were harmonious for the rest of the war, although Blair's view of Clinton altered.

Blair's advocacy of ground troops also put him at odds with several European allies. Gerhard Schröder, the German Chancellor, who had already taken the unprecedented step of involving his country's armed forces in the NATO action, described Blair's call for ground troops as 'unthinkable' and called it 'British war theory'. Blair faced strong criticism in much of the Continent. The *Frankfurter*

Allgemeine Zeitung, reflecting the view of many in the German Government, dubbed Blair 'know-it-all' in late May. There was criticism also in Italy where the Government was anyway under strong public criticism for allowing its bases to be used for air attacks against Serbian forces and targets.

Blair was very, very lucky. Milosevic backed down and withdrew Serbian troops from Kosovo without a ground invasion. Blair's own role in this outcome was limited. He was helped out of an exposed political and diplomatic position by Milosevic, but he was only indirectly an architect of victory. The fair-minded Daalder and O'Hanlon conclude (2000, p. 141):

> *The story of the second, and victorious, part of the war is primarily a story of the evolution in American and Russian thinking. Prime Minister Blair's continued steadfast support of a more muscular strategy, and his patient and dogged lobbying of Clinton to join him in promoting and pursuing that strategy, were important. But by itself Britain could not win the war, and its position was clear from the conflict's early going. What changed in the war's second half, what tilted the balance from a strategy that was producing failure to one that became sufficiently muscular to produce success, took place primarily in Washington and Moscow.*

Kosovo provided several very important lessons for Blair. At a personal level, the conflict marked a change in his relationship with Clinton. He had come of age. He was no longer the younger brother over-awed by his glittering, if flawed, older brother. Rawnsley (2001, p. 280) again reflects the views of Blair's closest advisers in observing the relationship:

> *Blair's exasperation with Clinton was the more intense because it was accompanied by disillusionment. 'The scales fell from Blair's eyes about Clinton', according to a senior military officer.*

Relations remained warm and friendly at a personal level, both for the remainder of Clinton's term in the White House and afterwards when the former President made frequent trips to Britain. These included visits, usually unpublicised, both to 10 Downing Street and to the Prime Minister's country residence at Chequers, as well as regular phone calls, particularly ahead of the Iraq war. But, after Kosovo, Blair was now more aware of Clinton's limitations, and less willing to defer to him. In the eyes of Blair's advisers, Clinton had been demoralised, and weakened, by his year-long battle over impeachment and 'could never make up his mind whether Kosovo was an opportunity to rise above the battles with his critics or too risky to touch'. The other side of this coming-of-age was a greater personal self-confidence on Blair's part. He had been the leading European spokesman for the anti-Milosevic coalition, articulate, widely praised, though also widely criticised, particularly in the rest of Europe. The main personal consequence was that he became more sure of his views and more assertive internationally.

The outcome of the Kosovo conflict – NATO's first military operation in its fifty-year history – may have been successful, but few wanted a repeat of the arguments and tensions of those spring and early summer weeks. NATO reached decisions by discussion and consensus, but that also proved to be cumbersome. There were leaks and, many Americans suspected, treachery as information was, they believed, passed by some French staff to Belgrade. This created tensions between Washington and Paris long before the arrival of George W. Bush in the White House. The Americans who flew the overwhelming majority of air missions resented decision-making by committee, and, in particular, President Chirac's desire to approve specific targets and his reluctance to broaden the air campaign. The conflict also starkly highlighted the huge gap in military capabilities between the US and Europe, particularly in missile guidance and electronic warfare. The question was not just whether the Americans and the Europeans wanted to fight together, but could they?

A common reaction in the American military was 'never again'. Many in the Pentagon concluded not only that some European allies were untrustworthy but also that alliance decision-making imposed unacceptable political constraints – particularly when the US now obviously had the capacity to perform such military operations on its own. Even the internationally minded Strobe Talbott argued a few months after the Kosovo conflict that many Americans were saying 'never again should the US have to fly the lion's share of dangerous missions and foot by far the biggest bill'. He found Europeans 'determined never again to feel quite so dominated by the US as they were during Kosovo'. Talbott wanted the Europeans to ensure that their fledgling defence plans matched those of NATO. But others in Washington reached harsher conclusions about the pluses and minuses of involving the European allies.

So well before the Bush administration came to office, there was already a shift in thinking in Washington, particularly among the military, away from alliance operations based on NATO, to creating coalitions of the willing, led by the US – as happened in Afghanistan and Iraq. Insofar as there was a role for NATO, on this view, it was in clearing up afterwards, in peacekeeping. This produced considerable tensions on the ground since European, and particularly British, commanders felt that American troops were contributing little to peacekeeping operations since the priority was 'force protection' rather than getting out to help local communities. The conflict led to lengthy soul-searching in the British defence world. Britain flew 10 per cent of NATO's strike sorties during the campaign, but released less than 5 per cent of the total munitions used in the operation. On several occasions, British aircraft had to abort missions because they could not 'see' through clouds to bomb. The Defence Select Committee of the Commons concluded in its report on the 'Lessons of Kosovo' (Fourteenth Report, 1999–2000, p. xlviii):

> *The alarming deficit in European capabilities for suppressing and destroying even relatively unsophisticated air defences suggests that Europe must either accept that its scope for action independent of the US is very limited indeed, or face up to the requirements of improving its capabilities sufficiently for it to act independently.*

Blair reached four distinct, though, overlapping conclusions.

The first was to reinforce his belief in the priority of being on the inside with whoever was American President, trying to influence US decisions – the 'hug them close' approach. Blair now understood the risks of allowing private doubts to emerge publicly (as happened in April and May 1999). So he resolved to keep his worries and differences private in order to secure maximum influence on the White House. This was linked to a specific, and very Blairite, lesson about the need to improve the co-ordination of information in such conflicts. After the application of the Alastair Campbell approach to briefings by NATO headquarters in Brussels during the Kosovo conflict, a strengthened and formalised international communications strategy was developed, and used, during both the Afghanistan and Iraq wars. In parallel with the close ties between national security advisers, there were daily conference calls between London, Washington and the regional head-quarters to co-ordinate the presentation of information.

Second, Blair recognised America's overwhelming military superiority as the sole superpower. So, if Britain wanted to shape global events and affect the outcome of crises, it had to work with the United States. This was a double-edged point. Working closely with the United States was not only in Britain's interests, but also, he believed, in America's. Blair saw the dangers of the US acting alone – or more likely, he feared, not acting at all when intervention was desirable to prevent the spread of regional conflicts. These views were expressed repeatedly and forcefully during the run-up to the Iraq war during the winter of 2002–3.

Third, Blair saw the all-too-apparent political and military weaknesses of Europe as reinforcing the case for increased foreign and defence co-operation, building on the St Malo declaration. This would be to make the European Union more credible as a partner of the US, not as rival to it, as the French often saw in their Gaullist moments. As George Robertson, British Defence Secretary during Kosovo and, from October 1999, NATO Secretary General, argued a month later: 'The European Security and Defence Identity (ESDI) is no longer just an attractive idea, it has become an urgent necessity.' These hopes would mean increased defence spending and, as important, a shifting of existing budgets away from the largely defensive approaches of the Cold War era to more mobile and rapidly deployable forces. Only the British and, to some extent, the French possessed limited forces which could be deployed in this way.

Fourth, Blair saw a special role for Britain, and particularly for himself, as the 'bridge' between Europe and the United States. A year later, in April 2000, Blair repeatedly told Jim Hoagland, the *Washington Post* columnist, during a conversation in Downing Street about Britain's desire to 'help Europe understand where America is coming from, and to explain European concerns to America' on trade, missile defence and other matters. Hoagland stressed that the bridge was 'not simply a rhetorical device for Blair. It is a deep belief about Britain's role in world affairs.'

During the remaining eighteen months of the Clinton era, there were continuing tensions over the development of a specifically European security and defence policy. The NATO summit in Washington in late April 1999 – though inevitably dominated by Kosovo – agreed a formula acceptable to both Americans and Europeans. But this begged a lot of questions about when and how NATO assets could, and would, be used by the EU when the alliance as a whole (meaning the US) was not involved. A European spin was put on this approach at the Cologne summit of EU leaders in June 1999. American worries that the ESDI would duplicate, and ultimately rival, NATO kept re-surfacing, and were not really put to bed until the Helsinki summit at the end of the year. Strobe Talbott said in London in October 1999 that: 'We would not want to see an ESDI that comes into being first within NATO but then grows out of NATO and finally grows away from NATO but that could eventually compete with NATO.' The Americans wanted more European defence spending, but as part of a US-led, and -dominated, alliance.

In parallel, many European countries were alarmed about the American programme for National Missile Defence (NMD), often dubbed 'Son of Star Wars', after Ronald Reagan's initiative. They feared that NMD would destabilise the nuclear balance, particularly by requiring the abrogation of the 1972 Anti-Missile Defence Treaty, the cornerstone of arms control over the previous quarter-century. The British worry was that there would be a precipitate request by the Clinton administration to use the Fylingdales early warning station in Yorkshire for NMD. Fylingdales would be vital for the radar for interception. This programme would require new facilities on the site and be very controversial domestically in Britain. Consequently, the development of NMD aroused probably exaggerated fears in the Government about protests like the Greenham Common demonstrations of the early- to mid-1980s against the deployment of cruise missiles. Talbott recalls (2002, p. 390) how 'America's allies became, without exception, apprehensive about NMD.' Problems with tests of the system led to the announcement by President Clinton that decisions on development would be left for his successor. Nevertheless, Sir Christopher Meyer recalls how ESDI and NMD were 'niggling problems over the period. We worried about NMD and they worried about ESDI. We worried at each other. Neither side was totally satisfied by the explanation and answers of the other.'

These tensions were matched by recurrent differences about how to handle the Israel–Palestine conflict. Blair had more sympathy than some other European leaders with Israel's plight and determination to defend itself, in face of suicide bombers and other terrorist attacks which killed so many of its citizens. But like other EU leaders, Blair also felt that Washington failed sufficiently to understand the plight of the Palestinians and was not doing enough to put pressure on Israel to negotiate and to close down some of the settlements in the occupied territories. But Blair recognised that the United States was the only country with the authority and weight to make a difference, and that Europe, and Britain, had a subsidiary role. However, Blair's attempts to help push along the peace process at times irritated Washington. And one of Blair's close political allies recalls how in this period Clinton got 'very shirty' in a telephone conversation about a British initiative. Blair was told 'this is not for the Europeans. It is our show.' But Blair persisted and, as later with George W. Bush during 2001–2, the Middle East peace process was one of the very rare issues where Blair let his impatience with Washington surface, at least semi-publicly.

As the Clinton administration came to a close, Blair had become his own man with his own firm views on foreign policy. He was worried by weapons of mass destruction, believed that the threat of Saddam Hussein must be tackled, supported a strengthening of European defence, but, like so many of his predecessors, argued that Britain must, and should, work closely with Washington. Blair saw himself as having a central role between the United States and Europe. He believed he could, and should, be the leader of Europe and act as the bridge between Europe and America.

5. The Colgate Summit

He is strong, straightforward, with an underlying serious-
ness. You know where you are with him. I like him.

Tony Blair's description of George W. Bush after their
first meeting at Camp David in February 2001,
as reported by a close political ally

Nobody needs to tell me what to believe. But I do need
somebody to tell me where Kosovo is.

George W. Bush comments on the campaign trail,
August 1999

You're going to spend more time during your four years on
terrorism generally and al-Qa'eda specifically than on any
other issue.

Sandy Berger, Clinton's National Security Adviser, briefing
Condoleezza Rice, his successor on the
Bush team, January 2001

The first face-to-face meeting between new President George W. Bush and Tony Blair at Camp David in February 2001 was as carefully prepared, and orchestrated, as any arranged marriage. Inquiries were made about both families – their views and their backgrounds. A school contemporary of Blair's, in the same house at Fettes, turned out to be an old friend of the Bush family and put in a good word for the Prime Minister with the President-elect. Emissaries shuttled to and fro, generally in secret, to ensure that everything would go smoothly on the day. The apprehension was almost entirely on the British side. The junior partner – the once grand family – sought to remain on as close relations with the Bush White House – the now all powerful ruling family – as it had enjoyed during the Clinton years.

The new President was still largely unknown in Britain: and what impressions he had made had been generally unfavourable. The controversial method of his election, finally settled by the Supreme Court in mid-December, predisposed many on the left in Britain against him. Claims that Bush had somehow 'stolen' the election or that the result was 'fixed' persisted until the 11 September attacks. This cast doubt on the new President's legitimacy and made many Labour MPs and ministers suspicious of him. Moreover, New Labour had close links with the camp of Al Gore, the losing Democrat candidate. Gordon Brown kept in regular contact with Bob Shrum, one of Gore's campaign advisers, while Philip Gould, New Labour's opinion adviser, had formed a transatlantic partnership with Stan Greenberg, a leading Democrat pollster.

Tony Blair, however, took a more detached view. He has never found it hard to separate such personal and ideological ties from the need to work with whoever is in the White House, or as head of any other government. While, as we have seen, Blair has strong personal views, these do not fit easily into any neat party or ideological label. He has happily worked with leaders from a wide variety of political backgrounds. What has mattered to Blair – as to Bush – is whether he can work with other leaders, and trust them. Ideological and tribal ties have been far, far behind in importance. So he reacted to the election of George W. Bush in an ideology free manner, unlike many of his Labour colleagues and supporters.

Moreover, the Blair camp was well aware of the need to avoid repeating the alleged (though, in reality, exaggerated) mistakes of the Major Government 1992 in appearing to give excessive favour and help to one candidate. The Blair private office was, and is, very interested in American domestic politics since both Jonathan Powell, the Number 10 Chief of Staff, and John Sawers, then the main Foreign Policy Adviser, had served in the Washington Embassy (in Sawers' case as Minister, or number two, directly before going to Downing Street). Sir Christopher Meyer, Britain's Ambassador in Washington, remembers 'an insatiable demand for information from Downing Street'. Matthew Rycroft, in the same role as Powell eight years earlier, was sent out on the campaign trail – another useful link since Rycroft later returned to London to join the Downing Street foreign affairs team during the run up to the Iraq war. Meyer repeatedly warned during the summer and autumn of 2000 not to make Al Gore the only bet and to take Bush's chances seriously. The 'don't rule out Bush' message was conveyed to any visitor to the Embassy that autumn as well as directly back to London. Meyer says that some in 10 Downing Street thought that the British Embassy and he had become 'biased' towards Bush. It was more a question of a tilt to offset the pro-Gore bias of some of the New Labour political, though not policy, advisers in the Blair team.

Yet Meyer was closer to the Bush team than to Al Gore and, more important, felt that a Bush presidency might be as much in Britain's interests as a Gore one. This is not just a later rationalisation, though at the time it reflected one probably correct assessment and one partially mistaken one. The correct assessment was that a Gore presidency would not be just a Clinton third term. A Gore presidency would have been very different from what London had been used to under Clinton, with different people and different approaches – in just the same way as George Bush senior's presidency marked a distinct shift from Ronald Reagan's two terms, initially to the discomfort of Margaret Thatcher. The 'don't worry about Bush' message rested heavily on the links between candidate Bush's team and his father's: notably Condoleezza Rice, his closest foreign policy aide, who had been the Russian expert on the old Bush's national security staff; Colin Powell, a detached though important backer of Bush and likely Secretary of State, who had been chairman of the Joint Chiefs of Staff a decade earlier; Dick Cheney, the Vice Presidential candidate, who had been Defense Secretary during the first Gulf War; Robert Zoellick, James Baker's closest aide at the State Department and then the White House; as well as a host of other advisers, some of whose service went back to the Reagan and even Ford years. This familiarity was important, and Meyer knew many of them, particularly Rice and Powell, from his earlier period in the Washington Embassy. Meyer had kept up these contacts, both before and during the campaign. Any likely Bush foreign policy team would be very experienced, much more than many new presidential appointees.

Yet these links with the past were deceptive, and misled many on the British side to believe that there would a revival of the cautious internationalism of the Bush–Baker approach of the 1989–93 period. This was wrong. Many of the Bush team – particularly Cheney and Donald Rumsfeld, who returned to head the Pentagon after a 24-year gap, as well as their talented and vocal advisers – were consciously reacting against the elder Bush's approach, as well as against the Clinton years. Their agenda was very different. Meyer concedes now that 'we underrated Bush's conservatism'. But this is not, he insists, because 'we related him to his father, but because of the way in which he campaigned and ran as Texas Governor'. The British Embassy assessment applied the Texas model to how he might behave as President. In Texas, Bush had governed as a centrist. But this was a mistaken parallel since he had little choice as Governor. The Texas governorship is traditionally a weak position, often weaker than the Lieutenant Governor who was more powerful in the legislature. One experienced American official at the heart of the transatlantic relationship dismisses the remarks of Meyer and others. In his view, when Bush was finally elected, there was 'a huge intake of breath in the diplomatic world. No one knew what this meant. No one really understood, in the US, or anywhere else.'

There were clues, but they were mainly of a negative kind. Bush freely admitted his lack of knowledge as the campaign began, as the quotation at the start of this chapter underlines. His ignorance about foreign affairs was firmly set in the public mind when he was trapped by a grandstanding television interviewer and could not name certain foreign leaders. Al Gore, by contrast, merely confirmed his image as a cocky know-it-all when, subsequently, he went out of his way to name obscure heads of government. Bush's gaps of knowledge, as well as his frequent linguistic slips, led many – in Europe as well as in America – to depict the President as a crude, know-nothing Texan. This was a serious error, as all those who have had direct dealings with him confirm.

A related misconception was that he would be at the mercy of his advisers. Bush undoubtedly surrounded himself with a bright team, veterans of both the Reagan and earlier Bush administrations. Known as the Vulcans, they included Rice; Paul Wolfowitz, later the cerebral deputy to Rumsfeld at the Pentagon; Richard Armitage, the bull-like later deputy to Powell at the State Department; Stephen Hadley, later a key player on the national security team at the White House; Zoellick, who became the internationally respected and effective US Trade Representative; and Richard Perle, the ubiquitous and amiable 'prince of darkness', without whom no British television or radio programme on America would be complete. This was a formidable group with strong, and often divergent, views, but all believed in free trade and an assertive American foreign policy. This was in contrast to the more protectionist and isolationist strain powerful among Congressional Republicans.

Bush's ability to take advice from this group, and a similar one when he became President, led many outsiders to underestimate him. British doubts were reinforced by his tendency to mangle the language and talk in folksy American terms, which often jarred to European ears. However, unlike many of his predecessors, and his own father, Bush adopted a corporate approach to leadership. This reflected his time at the Harvard Business School, his own mixed period running a business and, above all, his experience of observing the drift in his father's White House. Then – with no official position – he had taken on the tough task of telling John Sununu, his father's tough Chief of Staff, that he was fired. That showed that he was no pushover. As Ivo Daalder and James Lindsay (2003, p. 33) argue in their authoritative summary of the Bush foreign policy, as a candidate during the campaign he had been blunt about how he viewed the presidency. He would be the Chief Executive Officer of the United States of America. This involved three things: outlining a clear vision and agenda; building a strong team; and sticking to his position and priorities. He was also stubborn and persistent, almost regardless of what others said, as European allies found to their chagrin after January 2001. This corporate style permitted vigorous internal debate between his powerful advisers and heads of department. The public, and often chaotic, nature of these inter-agency disputes – particularly between the Powell and Rumsfeld camps – frustrated and infuriated the Blair team when trying to reach agreement with Washington on a particular policy approach. But these arguments also obscured the fact that Mr Bush ultimately took the decisions and laid down the line.

During the 2000 campaign, the main theme of the foreign policy comments of Bush and his advisers was, in Daalder and Lindsay's words (2003, p. 37), 'Anything But Clinton'. The charge sheet was long: a lack of clarity in goals; vacillation in implementation; inconsistency – all adding up to what Bush described in November 1999 as 'action without vision, activity without priority, and missions without end – an approach that squanders American will and drains American energy.' The Bush team was critical of what it saw as vague internationalism in the name of human rights and attempts at 'nation building.' Instead, the focus was on power and the national interest. In his 1999 speech, delivered at the Ronald Reagan Presidential Library in California, Bush set out what he described as a 'distinctly American internationalism.' This reflected a shift of emphasis from the Clinton approach, in stressing that the American definition of its national interests, rather than international agreements, would set the terms of its relations with other countries: 'The United States needs its European allies, as well as friends in other regions, to help us with security challenges as they arise.' He would never put US troops under United Nations command, but 'the UN can help in weapons inspections, peacekeeping and humanitarian efforts'. In an article revealingly entitled 'Promoting the National Interest' in the January/February 2000 issue of *Foreign Affairs*, the journal of the foreign policy establishment, Rice develops this thinking. She says that, in the Clinton view, 'the national interest is replaced with humanitarian interests or the interests of the international community'. Consequently, while foreign policy in a Republican administration would be internationalist, it will proceed 'from the firm ground of the national interest, not from the interest of an illusory international community'.

The underlying approach was what Daalder and Lindsay (2003, pp. 40–45) describe as 'hegemonist'. What this meant was that, in the words of the immortal *1066 And All That*, the US was now indisputably 'top nation' and should use its power accordingly (contrary to Sellar and Yeatman's view that this was 'A Bad Thing' and the end of History). Or, in the words of foreign policymakers, the unipolar world in which the US was the sole superpower was beneficial – to both the US and the world. This reflects a long-standing belief in the inherent virtue of America's motives and behaviour because of its unique belief in freedom, democracy and peace. (This assertion of exceptionalism has been the most important single factor fuelling the widespread European hostility to what is seen as American self-righteousness and hypocrisy.)

A prime goal of US strategy should therefore be to prevent the emergence of any potential competitor or challenger, particularly in military terms. This is underpinned by a *realpolitik*, rather than an idealist, view of the world based on competing nation states which respect assertions of power, including the use of force. A blueprint was produced towards the end of the first Bush administration in 1992, appropriately within the Pentagon for Cheney and Wolfowitz. Entitled 'Prevent the Re-Emergence of a New Rival', the study expressed scepticism about the value of multilateral agreements or institutions. Contrary to the thrust of post-war US policy, the 1992 paper argued that 'we should expect future coalitions to be *ad hoc* assemblies, often not lasting beyond the crisis being confronted, and in many cases carrying only general agreements over the objectives to be accomplished'. So the US should be 'postured to act independently'. Moreover, the US should not be constrained by well-intentioned international agreements which limited US flexibility and favoured rogue states.

Bush was seldom so explicit. Yet there was a vigorous debate between various strands in the Republican Party and Washington think tanks. At one end were the isolationists and protectionists, arguing a very narrow definition of American national interest. They opposed American involvement in Bosnia and Kosovo. At the other end of the spectrum were the traditional internationalists, represented by Colin Powell and Brent Scowcroft, the elder Bush's National Security Adviser. They were cautious about the exercise of American power and stressed the value of working with allies in multi-national institutions and via international treaties. In between were two strands of hegemonists, or sovereigntists, often misleadingly lumped together as neo-conservatives, or neo-cons. One camp, later associated with Cheney and Rumsfeld, favoured a strong, if necessary military and unilateral, assertion of American national interests, but not a long-term commitment to re-making the world along US lines. Another group, associated with Wolfowitz, saw active involvement as a chance to change the nature of currently hostile and threatening regimes and to create more democratic, and pro-American, governments. The debate between the assertive nationalists and the democratic imperialists has rumbled along throughout the Bush administration, but really only emerged from 11 September, and particularly from early 2002 onwards.

Yet it is misleading to look back from a post-11 September perspective to this or that policy paper written before 2001 – however influential and important its author later became – and claim that all along there was a hidden agenda by a tightly knit neo-conservative group to conquer Iraq, or whatever. Such conspiracy theories are usually fatuous: the neo-conservatives are vocal but do not speak with one voice and are only among several groups competing for Bush's ear. Of course, plenty of ideas were in circulation. But candidate, or even newly elected President, George W. Bush had not endorsed them then, whatever he might do after 11 September. More interesting, and relevant, is what Bush and his team said at the time. Apart from claiming that his general approach would differ from Clinton's, candidate Bush was vague about details. On Iraq, he merely said that there would be 'consequences' of an unspecified nature if Saddam developed weapons of mass destruction. He never promised to use American troops to remove Saddam, even though regime change in Baghdad was by then the official, Congressionally approved, policy of the United States.

For the Blair team, there were apprehensions about what an assertion of the American national interest might involve, particularly after the October flap over Condoleezza Rice's remarks about a possible withdrawal of American troops from the Balkans. After a diplomatic flurry, she later 'clarified' these comments by saying that a reduction would only happen gradually after consultation with NATO allies. There appeared to be a clash between Blair's support for 'humanitarian intervention' (as advocated during the Kosovo war in his Chicago speech in April 1999, discussed in the previous chapter) and the Bush team's hostility to 'nation building'. The existing tensions with the Clinton administration over missile defence also threatened to get worse given the Bush team's desire to rid itself of the limitations imposed by the 1972 Antiballistic Missile Treaty. The incoming Bush team was being encouraged by the British Conservatives to oppose the European defence initiative because of its impact on NATO, despite attempted reassurance by the Europeans at their Nice summit in December 2000.

The British side was also worried about how a conservative Republican President and administration would treat Blair and New Labour in view of its close ties to Bill Clinton. During a visit to Washington near the end of the 2000 campaign I heard mutterings from senior members of the Bush team about Blair having 'to prove himself'. There would be no more of 'the woolly thinking of the Third Way'. (In practice, as noted in Chapter 3, the Third Way meetings carried on, slightly less often than before, under the Progressive Governance banner, with now ex-President Bill Clinton as the charismatic policy wonk-in-chief emeritus.) Karl Rove, Bush's political strategist, told one senior British official, in characteristically biblical terms, 'By your works you shall be known.' According to Meyer, who was acting as match-maker at the time, the signals from the Bush camp were reassuring: 'It's not a problem that you have had a good relationship with Bill Clinton. The President regards Britain as America's closest ally and will judge Tony Blair by how this develops.' The Bush team had seen how Blair was prepared to commit British troops to military action, both in the air strikes against Iraq in December 1998 and against Kosovo the following spring.

The relationship had got off on the right note in mid-December 2000 when Blair made the obligatory phone call congratulating Bush – in fact from Warwick University, where the Prime Minister was attending a lecture by outgoing President Bill Clinton. This was during Clinton's farewell tour at which he gave Blair the advice to 'get as close to George Bush as you have been to me', as noted at the beginning of Chapter 1. Bush's first words in the phone call were 'I believe you know my friend Bill Gammell.' Blair did, indeed, know Gammell, who was in the same house as him at Fettes, and later went on to become a Scottish rugby international and head of a successful oil and gas exploration company. In his teens, Gammell was also host to the young George W. since their fathers were friends and business associates in the oil industry. Bush made five subsequent trips to Scotland, one to attend Gammell's wedding. Gammell, who is publicly reticent about his two old friends, helped clear the way for their first discussions and meeting. In the words of one senior Downing Street adviser, Gammell 'softened things up by telling each side what a good guy the other was'. The first brief conversation went well, with Bush underlining how Blair's friendship with Clinton need not stand in the way of them having a good working relationship.

These signals were reinforced by diplomatic activity between mid-December 2000, when the election was resolved, and Blair's visit in mid-February 2001. Robin Cook quickly sought to establish close links with Colin Powell, as Colin replaced Madeleine (Albright) in the British Foreign Secretary's list of close contacts. In mid-January, a week before the inauguration, Jonathan Powell and John Sawers flew to Washington for an unpublicised series of meetings with everyone who mattered but the new President – Cheney, Powell, Rice and Rumsfeld. In American eyes, the British were behaving in their familiar fashion; Blair was 'doing what prime ministers have always done, not waiting for the grass grow, but jumping in there to get himself invited'.

Nevertheless, there was a good deal of nervousness in London before the first face-to-face meeting in February 2001. Meyer's advice was that Blair should 'play to his strengths, be informal, practical and direct, and it'll work'. Ahead of the trip, Blair stressed the importance of Europe and America working closely together since 'only bad people . . . the Saddam Husseins of the world' rejoice and benefit when 'we are apart'. Blair's objective, in the words of a Downing Street spokesman, was to underline how 'we are proud to be America's closest allies' and how 'we in Britain are uniquely placed to bring the United States and Europe together in a way that is to our mutual benefit'. The close relationship had been underlined just before the visit when US and British planes attacked Iraqi installations outside Baghdad.

Before going to Camp David, Blair had 'a rather stiff' interview with Vice President Dick Cheney, with whom the Blair team continued to have prickly relations. Unlike Bush, Cheney has always been more sceptical than enthusiastic about Blair. In the event, all went well with Bush. Meyer later recalled in an American television interview (2003): 'My hunch was that there was a kind of no-nonsense quality and informality to the two of them, which would enable them at least to start bonding very, very quickly, and that's what happened. We were there for twenty-four hours, and it warmed up rapidly over that very brief period.' The 'personal chemistry' was said to be fine in the two leaders' discussions, according to another participant. However, some on the British side later reported that Blair was irritated when John Sawers, his main foreign policy adviser, talked too much, and across him, in trying to catch the President's eye. On such occasions, Blair does not like interruptions and concentrates on his conversation with the other leader. This report partly appears to have arisen from an accident of seating at breakfast on the second day when Sawers was two away from Bush, with Blair on the other side of a longish table. After a sharp exchange over the extent of Chinese support for WMD proliferation, which the British felt that the Americans were exaggerating, Bush pressed Sawers directly with difficult questions about Iraq, Korea and related matters. Blair was half-listening and it was clear from his looks after a few minutes that he would rather himself be having that conversation with Bush. So Sawers then shut up and Blair began a direct exchange with Bush. Afterwards, Sawers was teased, particularly by Alastair Campbell, about talking too much, and, while Sawers immediately cleared the air with Blair, reports about the meeting got back to Downing Street. Sawers was seen by some of the Blair circle as too opinionated, in contrast to Sir David Manning, his more self-effacing successor.

(Sawers, however, maintained good relations with Blair and kept in touch with the Prime Minister after he left Downing Street. He hosted the Blair family on a holiday in Egypt where he became British Ambassador in autumn 2001. Sawers then took on the role of the Government's special emissary in Baghdad for three months after the end of the Iraq war, ahead of his appointment to the key job of Political Director in the Foreign Office.)

Both the President and the Prime Minister were keen to show how well they had got on – immediately moving on to Tony and George terms, as the press were told, in order to show that the arranged marriage would work. Bush remarked at their joint press conference at Camp David on 23 February: 'And as they [his advisers] told me, he's a pretty charming guy. He put the charm offensive on me.' Later, when asked whether they shared some personal interest in common, Bush replied, to Blair's evident embarrassment: 'Well, we both use Colgate toothpaste.' So the first of what has turned out to be many Bush–Blair meetings became known as 'The Colgate Summit'. Beneath the public relations claims, the two leaders did appear to strike up a good working relationship. One senior Blair adviser said there was 'no edge' in the meetings with Bush. Their talks were 'friendly, straightforward and open'. The relationship was much less complicated than the Blair–Clinton one, where there had always been the undercurrent of the older–younger brother or master–pupil tensions.

The two sides also reached understandings on sensitive policy areas. In a sense, there was a bargain: despite doubts about the feasibility of missile defence, the British recognised the dangers of weapons of mass destruction and proliferation, shared US concerns, and agreed to give backing in principle to the general aims of the American strategy, provided there was consultation with other countries, including Russia. Blair's tactic was to play the issue long, avoiding an early request to use the facilities at Fylingdales which, he knew, would ignite substantial opposition within the Labour Party. The left suspected, rightly, that Blair and Geoff Hoon, the Defence Secretary, would eventually agree to the use of Fylingdales – a US request could never have been refused without causing immense damage to the alliance. An admiring American diplomat says: 'the Brits played it very well. Lots and lots of notes were sent to Washington saying that before you go ahead and negotiate, consult us.' In return for this support over missile defence, the Americans accepted British assurances that European plans for a rapid reaction force were not intended to undermine NATO. At the press conference, Bush carefully referred to assurances given by Blair about the primacy of NATO, which would continue to be responsible for planning. Blair stressed that 'in circumstances where NATO as a whole chooses not to be engaged [that is the US], it is limited to peacekeeping and humanitarian tasks. It is not a standing army.' As both leaders knew, others took a different view, and their joint statement begged several questions about the co-ordination of EU capabilities with NATO and the position of non-EU NATO members such as Turkey. The Pentagon remained highly suspicious of any separate European operations, while the French wanted a planning and command structure clearly distinct from NATO. The discussions began with the Middle East and Iraq. The main focus then was on making the existing sanctions regime work better. The oil-for-food programme was proving to be cumbersome, while the sanctions were increasingly porous. But this talk was secondary to the main items of the meeting – Russia, the ABM treaty and the European defence initiative.

On returning to London, the Blair camp put out a reassuring message. Blair had told journalists on the way back about how Bush had been 'impressive', 'really on the ball', and 'extremely bright' (Webster, 2001). Implicit in such briefings was an element of surprise on the British side that Bush was different from what Blair had expected. Such warm words were, of course, the classic, and deliberate, British insider tactic, talking up close relations in order to gain influence. Blair seemed 'terribly pleased with his visit to Camp David', according to one Downing Street adviser who asked him how it had gone. Blair's relief was evident. In a private conversation with one of his closest political allies, Blair sounded relieved about his meeting with Bush: 'He is strong, straightforward, with an underlying seriousness. You know where you are with him. I like him.' Blair was impressed by the private Bush: 'a man with whom he could do business', in Margaret Thatcher's famous words about Mikhail Gorbachev.

However, the first few months of the Bush presidency created strains with Europe, partly because of the administration's desire to reject many of the Clinton era's international obligations. Other European leaders were less willing to accept the bargain which Blair struck at Camp David. Just before Blair went to the US, Donald Rumsfeld had repeated the US desire to design and develop a missile defence system when he had visited the annual conference of the defence world in Munich. Rumsfeld was more tactful than he subsequently was in his transatlantic contacts. But several European ministers expressed their worries that missile defence might trigger a new international arms race. Many Europeans remained openly critical of missile defence, particularly given Bush's intention to withdraw from the ABM treaty.

Bush rightly calculated that what mattered here was the attitude of Russia. He sought to establish a new relationship when he met Vladimir Putin for the first time in mid-June 2001 at a summit in Slovenia. Bush cloyingly said that, after looking into the eyes of the ex-KGB head, he had 'got a sense of his soul'. Yet these talks were the start of a gradual US–Russian process of reaching an understanding. The involvement of Russia, a real diplomatic success for Bush, is still largely under-appreciated in Europe. After all, so much had changed since 1972. So the abrogation of the 1972 ABM treaty did not cause an international crisis. Defusing the issue was underpinned by the later big cuts in the two countries' arsenals of strategic nuclear missiles, which Bush and Putin later discussed virtually on the back of an envelope.

The biggest cause of tension – indeed of denunciation – was the Bush administration's rejection in March 2001 of the 1997 Kyoto agreement on climate change because it would 'cause serious harm to the US economy'. This was partly bowing to political reality. President Clinton had known full well that the 1997 Kyoto Protocol would never have been approved by US Senate, but he paid lip service to its goals to gain the maximum goodwill. Bush was more direct. The administration looked at the treaty, confirmed that they did not like it, and decided that is what they would say, without apparently a second thought about the international response. The administration had a case that the Protocol was flawed but, at times, senior officials, notably Vice President Cheney, appeared to be rejecting all the scientific evidence over global warming – though, in the end, the President did recognise that global warming was a problem which needed to be addressed. The administration failed to offer any credible alternative methods of controlling emissions. The dismissive manner with which the decisions were made and announced reinforced European opposition. Bush, who hardly knew Europe, did not enjoy his first exposure to EU leaders together at summit meetings in June 2001. In general, he preferred Latin-American leaders, many of whom he already knew well from his time as Governor of Texas.

Overall, the fear in Europe was of blundering and insensitive American unilateralism. Apart from Kyoto and ballistic missile defence, concerns had arisen over American hostility to agreements on trade in small arms, new controls on biological weapons, the Comprehensive Test Ban Treaty and the proposed International Criminal Court. Again, there were legitimate US worries over the drafting of the ICC treaty – particularly over the terms of prosecutions which the Americans feared could produce a politically driven process. These fears had been highlighted since Kosovo, the Pinochet extradition case in Britain and the political activities of prosecutors in Spain and Belgium. Yet the Bush administration was, from the first, wholly hostile over the ICC, in what one close observer in the State Department sees as the 'first evidence of the Washington neo-conservatives using their political leverage.' So the message from the administration was that there was no way they could sign up to this. The EU was also critical of the US decision to end talks with North Korea over curbing their missile and nuclear programmes (angering many in South Korea in the process) and over cuts in spending on joint programmes with Russia to prevent proliferation of nuclear materials. The Bush administration also signalled that it did not want to be involved in the day-to-day details of the Middle East peace process and its officials were much less involved in Northern Ireland than the Clinton team.

Throughout this period, Blair characteristically sought to minimise differences with Washington, with the main exception of Kyoto. He decided to 'talk up' Bush in face of widespread criticisms in the rest of Europe and among the Labour Party in Britain. Blair's desire to play the traditional bridge between Europe and America was becoming harder and harder – and in Blair's eyes even more necessary. The 'bridge' metaphor was resented in the rest of Europe. Gerhard Schröder, in general a friend of Blair, was widely reported as saying that the traffic across Blair's bridge always seemed to be in one direction (Stephens, 2001). It is hard to be an even-handed inter-locutor: and during his visit to Washington in February 1998 when Britain held the European presidency, other European leaders saw him as more of a spokesman for the US view in Europe than the European view in Washington. Nonetheless, smaller European countries increasingly saw Blair as the only way to influence Washington's thinking. However, as a senior official in the Clinton administration put it (Baker, 2001): 'The ground on which Blair is standing is getting narrower and narrower by the day.'

Blair faced a tricky task since members of the Bush administration, though not Powell, seemed to take a delight in ignoring the views and interests of other countries, including close allies. As Daalder and Lindsay (2003, p. 73) argue, this reflected the belief that Clinton had sacrificed American national interests in his keenness to please allies over international agreements (not the European view at the time). Moreover, Bush, in his chief executive officer mode, wanted to show that he was not going to alter his plan simply because others disagreed. This applied both externally, in relations with allies, and internally, in taking decisions. The White House set the policy and only then delegated implementation. As one senior American diplomat noted at the time: 'there was a dawning realisation in London that this was not a Clinton-like administration. Europe would not get a free pass on issues. Where Clinton had dodged around, Bush addressed them directly.'

Yet, strangely given later events, the Bush administration did little on Iraq and terrorism during this period. Two days before the 11 September attacks, Bush had been in discussions with senior advisers about how to apply 'smart sanctions' against Saddam regime – a long way from seeking to overthrow it by force. If anything, Blair was more concerned with the threat of weapons of mass destruction at this time. Despite the remarks of Sandy Berger to Rice, quoted at the start of this chapter, and repeated warnings about the al-Qa'eda threat from George Tenet, director of the Central Intelligence Agency, not much happened, apart from discussions among officials. Terrorism was not treated as a top priority. The Bush administration was accused of largely ignoring the dangers of an al-Qa'eda attack by Richard Clarke, the head of counter-terrrorism at the White House during this period. Clarke's book (2004) and public testimony to the independent National Commission on Terrorist Attacks Upon the United States in March 2004 fuelled a fierce controversy about the administration's record on terrorism. Republicans accused Clarke of disloyalty and inconsistency, while Democrats used his charges to attack the Bush administration in an election year. Paul O'Neill, the Treasury Secretary, had even suspended American participation in international efforts to track and control terrorist money flows. Bush later told Bob Woodward (2002, p. 39) about his attitude to bin Laden before 11 September. He was prepared to look at a 'thoughtful plan that would bring him to justice' and had 'no hesitancy about going after him.' But, Bush acknowledged, 'I didn't feel that sense of urgency, and my blood was not nearly as boiling.'

That all changed on the morning of Tuesday 11 September, as Bush was listening to children read in an elementary school in Sarasota, Florida.

6. How is Bush Going to React?

*Every nation, in every region, now has a decision to make.
Either you are with us, or you are with the terrorists.*

President George W. Bush, address to Joint Session of
Congress, Thursday 20 September 2001

*The kaleidoscope has been shaken. The pieces are in flux.
Soon they will settle again. Before they do, let us re-order
the world around us.*

Tony Blair, speech to Labour Party conference, Brighton,
Tuesday 2 October 2001

*It has taken the foreign policy of the Prime Minister finally
to lay the ghost of Suez. I think what we have now done is
to establish a role for Britain in international affairs with
which we are entirely comfortable. It is Britain not as a
superpower but as a very powerful force for good*

Jack Straw in an interview with *The Times*,
Tuesday, 1 January 2002

Tony Blair understood almost instantly that the world had changed
on 11 September 2001. His public statements then, and in the
following few days, not only changed his relationship with George W.
Bush but also set Britain on a path which led to war with Iraq
eighteen months later. Blair's response to the attacks on the World

Trade Center and the Pentagon was dominated by questions about how Bush would react – and the need to ensure that America did not act recklessly, or alone.

Everyone remembers where they were when they first heard about the hijacked planes hitting the World Trade Center. It was morning on the East Coast of the United States: five hours later, just after lunchtime, in Britain. The horrible, at first unbelievable, images of that lovely late summer's day remain vivid. As a shattering global event etched in the memory, 11 September 2001 ranks alongside the assassination of John F. Kennedy on 22 November 1963. Yet unlike JFK's murder, or, for that matter, the death of Diana, Princess of Wales, the 11 September attacks were 'real time' television. Millions of viewers around the world saw the second, if not the first, plane hit the twin towers of the World Trade Center as it happened, then, just over an hour later, the collapse of, first, the south tower and, then, half an hour later, the north tower.

The live television pictures are what first brought home to Blair the immensity of the atrocity. He was in Brighton, due to make a very difficult speech to the annual conference of the Trades Union Congress about the involvement of the private sector in the provision of public services. The text of the speech had already been issued to the press. He was waiting to go on to the conference platform when news came through, just after 1.45 p.m. (8.45 a.m. East Coast time) about a plane crashing into the north tower of the World Trade Center. At first, no one knew whether this was just an accident, involving a light plane according to the immediate rumours. That had been the reaction of Bush's advisers in Florida when they heard about the crash of the first plane. Blair and his advisers waited, despite understandable pressure from TUC leaders to carry on with the speech. Alastair Campbell remembers it was a close-run thing about whether to go ahead. Then, twenty-one minutes later, at 2.06 p.m. British time (9.06 a.m. in New York), the second plane hit the south tower. It was then clear that the crashes were not just a tragic accident, but almost certainly involved terrorism – especially as reports came through of other planes going missing. This was when Bush was told about the second plane as he was listening to the children reading. That evening he wrote in his diary: 'The Pearl Harbor of the 21st century took place today.' The other two hijacked planes crashed into the Pentagon at 2.40 p.m. (9.40 a.m.) and into the Pennsylvania countryside at 3.37 p.m. (10.37 a.m.). Blair immediately decided to abandon his prepared speech. Instead, he made brief remarks from the platform about the attacks, before returning hurriedly to London.

But before setting off there was a conference call to his close advisers in London, Jonathan Powell and Sir Richard Wilson, the Cabinet Secretary. Wilson had quickly pulled out contingency plans in case of terrorist attacks in Britain, including banning commercial planes from flying over central London, and increasing surveillance at airports. Blair was briefed on what was going on: policing, protecting London and so on. At this stage, no one knew whether similar attacks might not be about to happen in Britain. One of Blair's closest advisers, who was involved in the afternoon discussions, recalls that the Prime Minister 'immediately spun into action, realising at once the importance of what had happened and what he should do.'

The rest of 11 September and the following day were hectic as emergency precautions were put in place and Blair rapidly sorted out his own thinking. Initially, several key people were out of London: not just Blair but also intelligence chiefs and some members of the Overseas and Defence Policy Secretariat in the Cabinet Office, while the newly reorganised Civil Contingencies Unit was away in Yorkshire for a 'bonding session'. Most important of all, Sir David Manning, who had just taken over from John Sawers as Blair's Foreign Affairs Adviser, was in the United States on a 'get-to-know you' visit. His meeting with Condoleezza Rice in Washington would later turn out to be very helpful in creating the key day-to-day link between 10 Downing Street and the White House. But on 11 September, he was on a plane flying up to New York. From his window seat, he had seen smoke coming from the north tower of the World Trade Center. On landing at JFK airport, like other passengers, he moved to and fro. But with mobile phones out of action and telecommunications networks inundated, he was unable to contact anyone, either in London or Washington. Eventually, after sharing a taxi with a young English couple who were also stranded, the Prime Minister's Foreign Policy Adviser ended up staying in a hotel in the New York suburb of Queens, which the dry and cerebral Manning later described as 'not normally used for purposes of sleeping'. It usually let out rooms by the hour. The next day he contacted the British Embassy in Washington, was rescued and returned to London later in the week.

Back in London later on the Tuesday afternoon, Blair had to decide what to do. Sir Richard Wilson was summoned out of a meeting of Cobra, the emergency/contingencies committee, to go to Blair's study next to the Cabinet room. Blair at once began to focus on the strategic implications, the likely US response, how Britain should handle the Americans and the need for a co-ordinated inter-national drive against terrorism. One adviser remembers Blair saying that afternoon: 'How is Bush going to react? What will he do?' This was his constant refrain over the next few days. Blair quickly approved and announced security precautions against any attack on London. There was no known threat, but jitteriness continued all day since it was not until very late that all civil airliners in the US were fully accounted for. The Whitehall machine responded rapidly under pressure, learning lessons from the bruising experiences of the fuel protests of September 2000 and the foot-and-mouth outbreak of spring 2001. These had exposed major weaknesses in central govern-ment's contingency preparations and in its handling of emergencies.

Blair was immediately briefed on what the intelligence agencies already thought was probably an attack by al-Qa'eda. (This opinion hardened into a certainty in the view of both the British and American intelligence agencies over the coming days. Some of the reasons were set out in a sixteen-page dossier published by Downing Street on 4 October, though much crucial information was held back for fear of revealing sources.) For all his long interest in weapons of mass destruction, Blair knew relatively little about al-Qa'eda. And while he had heard about Osama bin Laden, he knew next to nothing about Afghanistan, according to one official briefing him. He was not alone. Virtually no one in 10 Downing Street knew anything about al-Qa'eda. One senior adviser said, later: 'We thought al-Qa'eda was a bit of an American obsession.' That week Jonathan Powell, Blair's Chief of Staff, went out and bought a book on the Taliban by Ahmed Rashid, a leading Pakistani journalist who writes for the *Daily Telegraph* and the *Far Eastern Economic Review*. Published the previous year, Rashid's book offers an authoritative account of the complicated recent history of Afghanistan and was regarded in Downing Street as the best of a series of books on the subject. Over the coming weeks it was passed round the Blair inner circle.

Overnight, a huge briefing paper on al-Qa'eda, the Taliban and Afghanistan was prepared. But Blair was still unsure about all the implications and did not yet appear to be on top of the issues. So a meeting was arranged, involving the Foreign Office, the Secret Intelligence Service (MI6), and the Ministry of Defence, as well as John Scarlett, the new Chairman of the Joint Intelligence Committee. Sir Richard Dearlove, Director General of the SIS, and Scarlett, a former senior SIS officer, were the best informed of Blair's advisers about al-Qa'eda and the Taliban: and over the following weeks and months this gave them increasing influence with him. Originally scheduled for half an hour, the meeting lasted for two hours. Blair quickly absorbed what he had been told. As Wilson recalls: 'Tony Blair had an intuitive instinct for spotting issues important to him.'

Blair then decided to let Bush have a note about his initial views. As usual, he wrote it himself, and the typewritten note was immediately faxed to Bush, though the President did not read it until the following day. The five page memorandum was in Blair's own words and style, 'weaving in a lot of information and reflecting his instinctive grasp of a situation', according to one adviser. Blair writes in a rather jerky style, like his speeches, with lots of bullet points highlighting areas for action. This clipped approach – unlike the drafts of civil servants and the Foreign Office's diplomatic exchanges – also suits Bush. This was the first of a regular stream of such personal notes, like those Churchill sent to Roosevelt throughout the war. In this, possibly most important one, Blair argued that tackling al-Qa'eda and the Taliban was the immediate issue. He left Iraq out of the argument.

Some of Blair's advisers had been worried about how Bush would respond: whether America would strike out blindly and prematurely. These fears were triggered by Bush's strong and sometimes clumsy language. David Blunkett, the Home Secretary, said on the BBC's *On the Record* programme on 24 September that there had been fears in London for the first two or three days about an 'immediate, inappropriate and indiscriminate response'. The worry was that hasty military action would not only fail to deter future terrorism but would also undermine hopes of creating a broadly based international coalition. Blair himself was less worried, particularly after he spoke to Bush at lunchtime (London time) on Wednesday 12 September – the President's first talk with a foreign leader. Balz and Woodward (2003, part 2) record how: 'Blair did not share those fears about the United States acting prematurely, confiding to an adviser his belief that American public opinion would give Bush breathing space and adequate time to prepare.' The two leaders agreed that it was important to move quickly on the diplomatic front, to gain support from NATO and the UN, and to provide the legal and political framework for any military response.

> *Before hanging up, Bush and Blair returned to the question of a military response. Blair told Bush he had to make a choice between rapid action and effective action. And effective action would require preparation and*

> *planning. Bush agreed. He said he didn't want to fire*
> *missiles at targets that did not matter.*

But by expressing such strong support for Bush, Blair was tying Britain into a potentially large and limitless commitment. The scope of Bush's anti-terrorist policy became apparent in his broadcast on the evening of 11 September after the President finally returned to Washington: 'We will make no distinction between the terrorists who committed these acts and those who harbor them.' This implied not only retaliatory strikes but also a far-reaching, long war against terrorism, included in his speech without any discussion with his main foreign policy advisers.

Blair's crucial insight over these days was that the attacks would dramatically change America's sense of its own security. He appreciated the scale of the impact on American attitudes, and why Bush compared 9/11 to Pearl Harbour. The attacks both unified and energised America. As Blair later argued, this understanding about the enormous importance of the attacks for American attitudes was the root of the later division in European attitudes towards the United States, especially ahead of the Iraq war. Virtually everyone in Europe condemned the attacks, except for fringe Muslim extremists and some hardline anti-Americans on the intellectual left, such as the *New Statesman* in Britain, who took the morally bankrupt line that America somehow 'had it coming.' Even in anti-American France, the newspaper *Le Monde* proclaimed 'nous sommes tous Americains', while Gerhard Schröder, the German Chancellor, expressed 'unlimited solidarity', a very different tone from the anti-American language of the SPD's election campaign a year later.

But there were soon differences of interpretation. For many Europeans, and some policymakers in London, the 11 September attacks, while obviously horrific and barbarous, did not fundamentally change everything in global politics. The terrorists, and particularly al-Qa'eda, should be tackled, but not to the exclusion of other, equally pressing problems. On this view, to talk of a war against terrorism was itself a mistake, almost a victory for the terrorists. Sir Michael Howard, the eminent British military historian, received a lot of attention for a speech at the end of October warning that the Bush administration had made 'a terrible and irrevocable error' in declaring that America was 'at war'. He argued that the use of the term 'war' would arouse 'an immediate expectation, and demand, for spectacular military action against some easily identifiable adversary, preferably a hostile state; action leading to decisive results.' He compared the aerial bombardment of Afghanistan, which was then well under way, to 'trying to eradicate cancer cells with a blow-torch'. Sir Michael presciently warned about the prolongation of war:

> *Even more disastrous would be its extension, as American opinion seems increasingly to demand, in a 'Long March' through other 'rogue states' beginning with Iraq, in order to eradicate terrorism for good and all so that the world can live at peace. I can think of no policy more likely, not only indefinitely to prolong the war, but to ensure that we can never win it.*

These views – strongly represented in the Foreign Office and among the foreign policy think tanks – were certainly not anti-American.

Most strongly sympathised with America's plight after the 11 September attacks and praised President Bush's willingness to create a broad international coalition. However, they worried about his language and the expectations that he raised. Any campaign against terrorism would be indefinite, and would require intelligence and police operations as much as, if not more than, military action. It should also involve political initiatives to tackle the causes of terrorism, notably the Israel–Palestine dispute. Above all, what was needed was a sense of proportion and balance, a weighing of risks rather than a preoccupation with fighting terrorists and rogue states. To many Americans, within the administration and among their vocal allies, this European viewpoint amounted to weakness bordering on appeasement of the terrorists and, in some versions, smacked of ingrained hostility to Israel, if not anti-Semitism.

Blair believed that this view under-estimated the impact of 11 September on American attitudes. He favoured a measured, step-by-step response, but believed that it was vital to work with, rather than against, the grain of American opinion, and particularly the instincts of President Bush. Blair's view, honed as we have seen over the Clinton years, was that the right way to exercise private influence in Washington was to express total support in public. The price of private candour was public solidarity. This applied especially with George W. Bush, who, even more than his father, put a premium on personal loyalty and trust. If someone let him down, he remembered and did not trust him or her again. Similarly, trust and loyalty once earned, was repaid. This was the essence of the close personal bond between Bush and Blair after 11 September (or 9/11 as it universally became known using American terminology).

So Blair's post 11 September approach involved three strands.

First, he expressed solidarity and support for the American people, starting immediately on 11 September, both briefly on the platform in Brighton and then back in London. He returned to this message over the following days: in a Commons statement when MPs were called back for a special debate on 14 September, and particularly during his visit to New York and Washington a week later. His message was 'We stand side by side with the US – not least because 9/11 was the most serious terrorist attack on British citizens in modern times.' Even though early estimates of 200 to 300 British deaths were revised down substantially, the final toll of 67 was still larger than either Lockerbie or Omagh.

Second, Blair remained silent about any doubts he had over the American response. He was determined not to allow any hint of division with Washington. One revealing example was when he was asked in a CNN interview on 16 September about Bush's comments about a war between good and evil. Blair had discussed beforehand with Alastair Campbell how to respond if this was raised. He duly ducked and weaved. He emphatically rejected any suggestions of a war against the Islamic world, not least because many Muslims are victims of international terrorism. Instead, he talked of a war between 'the civilised world and fanaticism'. But, despite the doubts of many in London, he did not hesitate to use the word 'war'. Similarly, the Blair Government was silent when Bush talked the following day in the classic language of an American Western about wanting bin Laden 'dead or alive' and about a 'crusade against evil'. The President's tone and language infuriated many in the Muslim world and fuelled worries about American policy among many in the Labour Party.

Third, Blair was determined to persuade Bush to concentrate on al-Qa'eda and the Taliban and leave the problem of Iraq for a later date. As noted above, this was the main theme of his faxed note to Bush on the late afternoon of 12 September. This was followed up by further exchanges at all levels before his visit to the US a week later. In his CNN interview on 16 September, he talked of a two-stage approach: first, bringing those terrorists who committed the attacks to account; and, second, constructing an international agenda for 'dismantling the machinery of international terrorism', its financing and organisation. He talked of a 'broad-based coalition' and, significantly, he made no reference to Iraq.

However, during his statement to the Commons on 14 September, Blair argued that terrorist groups

> *would, if they could, go further and use chemical or biological or even nuclear weapons of mass destruction. We know, also, that there are groups of people, occasionally states, who trade the technology and capability for such weapons. It is time this trade was exposed, disrupted, and stamped out. We have been warned by the events of 11 September. We should act on the warning.*

Over the subsequent eighteen months, he repeatedly referred back to these words as evidence that his concern about weapons of mass destruction long pre-dated the decisions over Iraq.

But, as he quickly realised, Blair's calls to postpone action against Iraq were in line with how Bush was thinking. For the first few days after 11 September, there had been a vigorous debate among Bush's advisers. Several, especially from the Pentagon, had raised the possible links with Saddam Hussein, despite the absence of any evidence of a connection between the Iraqi regime and the attacks. During the rambling discussions on the following day, some of the later divisions emerged, according to Balz and Woodward's account (2003, part 2):

> *Rumsfeld then raised the question of Iraq, which he had mentioned in the morning meeting. Why shouldn't we go against Iraq, not just al-Qa'eda? he asked. Rumsfeld was not just speaking for himself when he raised the question. His deputy, Paul Wolfowitz, was even more committed to a policy that would make Iraq a principal target of the first round in the war on terrorism and would continue to press his case. Arrayed against the policy was the State Department, led by Powell, and among those who agreed with him was Shelton, chairman of the Joint Chiefs.*

Everyone agreed that Saddam Hussein was a menace and that any full-scale war on terrorism would have to make Iraq a target, eventually. Powell argued that the initial focus should be on al-Qa'eda because that is what the American people – as well as the international coalition – wanted. The Secretary of State concentrated on building up support in the region, notably from Pakistan which had previously had close links with the Taliban. Yet the debate continued. Wolfowitz talked in a daily briefing about 'ending states who sponsor terrorism', a potentially huge expansion of a then limited action to punish the Taliban if they did not break with bin Laden. At a Camp David conference of the Bush national security team on Saturday 15

September, the Pentagon again pressed the case for attacking Iraq. But Powell argued that the coalition partners who backed action against al-Qa'eda would go away if Iraq was attacked. Bush had strong doubts about going to Iraq then, largely because of the dangers of a lack of focus. In the afternoon discussion, Cheney intervened to argue that now might be a bad time to take on Saddam Hussein because of the danger of losing momentum. An attack on Iraq would be right at some point, just not now (Balz and Woodward, part 5). This issue was finally closed on Monday 17 September: 'Bush said he wanted them to keep working on developing plans for military action in Iraq but indicated there would be plenty of time to do that. Everything else, though, had to be done soon.' This was three days before Blair's visit. In the interim, Bush was mainly concerned with his speech to Congress and how he would tackle al-Qa'eda and the Taliban.

Blair's visit to the US involved a combination of public solidarity and private influence. Solidarity was expressed in a moving service for the victims at St Thomas's Church in Lower Manhattan when he said 'we stand side by side with you now'. Later, Blair attended the Joint Session of Congress addressed by Bush. The President pointed to Blair sitting in the guests' gallery and paid tribute to the support and friendship of the Prime Minister and the British people. This was the beginning of Blair's popularity in the United States. He was admired both for immediately standing by the American people on 11 September and for his eloquence. A banner was waved at a baseball game at Yankee Stadium saying 'God Bless George Bush and Tony Blair.' You cannot imagine that at Highbury or Old Trafford. After his earlier address at Washington Cathedral and his visit to New York,

Bush's speech to Congress erased most memories of his initial, uncertain response and defined the extent and scale of the campaign in stark terms.

Blair's influence was apparent in the earlier talks at the White House. As Sir Christopher Meyer recalled in a television interview (2003):

> *We finally got to the White House after this very emotional morning in New York. One of the issues was, were the Americans going to use 9/11, quite apart from hunting down al-Qa'eda, to go after Iraq as well? Tony Blair's view was, whatever you're going to do about Iraq, you should concentrate on the job at hand, and the job at hand was get al-Qa'eda. Give the Taliban an ultimatum, and everything else was secondary to that.*

After arriving at the White House, Bush 'immediately took Blair by the elbow and moved him off into the corner of the room, where we all congregated, and he said, I believe, to the Prime Minister, "I agree with you that the job in hand is al-Qa'eda and Taliban. Iraq we keep for another day."'

Blair's intervention was not crucial. He did not change US policy. Rather, the Prime Minister's repeated messages in this period about concentrating on al-Qa'eda and the Taliban reinforced the President's existing instincts and the view of both his Secretary of State and the Chairman of the Joint Chiefs of Staff. Yet there were revealing differences of emphasis. For the British, and particularly the Foreign Office, a decision on whether to take tough action against Iraq, including possibly a military operation, had been postponed until later. For the Americans, while action had been put off, there was already an implicit commitment to move against Saddam. It was a question of when, not if. Bob Woodward (2004, pp. 1–5) reveals how President Bush ordered Donald Rumsfeld to begin preparing plans for an Iraq war in November 2001. This work was in secret and denied publically by Bush. These ambiguities caused lots of problems for Blair the following year.

Then, over dinner at the White House with both teams of advisers, the main focus of the discussions was about how to deal with al-Qa'eda and the Taliban. Bush had already approved plans for a joint CIA–military operation in Afghanistan. The President outlined what he described as 'full force of the US military with bombers coming from all directions'.

Both sides broadly agreed about the strategy in Afghanistan: in Bush's words, they were 'on the same wavelength'. The British team was relieved by Bush's caution and realism; his reluctance just to send missiles and bombs into the sand for symbolic effect, as Clinton had done in his August 1998 attacks. Rather, Bush was concerned with an effective response.

It was at this time that Blair became in effect Bush's Ambassador at Large. In the eight weeks after 11 September, Blair had 54 meetings with other leaders, almost one a day; he had been on 31 flights and had covered more than 40,000 miles. This had benefits, in access to the White House, as well as risks, in fuelling the 'Bush's poodle' jibes. On an arduous two-day trip, he flew to Berlin to see Gerhard Schröder, before going to Paris for Wednesday night to meet Jacques Chirac, then flying on Thursday morning to New York, and down to Washington, before returning across the Atlantic that night for an emergency summit of EU leaders in Brussels on the Friday. And while flying from Paris to New York, Blair had spoken to Mohammad Khatami, the Iranian President. In many ways, Blair could talk to leaders that the Americans could not, and Jack Straw made parallel, controversial visits, notably to Tehran. In early October, Blair was off again to Russia and Pakistan. At the end of the month, Blair went on his most ambitious visit to Syria, Saudi Arabia, Israel and Gaza in the embryo Palestinian state. Each stop was difficult, particularly Damascus, where, against strong Foreign Office advice, he appeared at a news conference with President Assad. The young Syrian leader described Israel as a terrorist state and Palestinian suicide bombers as freedom fighters, like the French resistance under de Gaulle. There was nothing that Blair could say without creating even more stories about splits.

At first, many other leaders were reassured that the Bush administration had not acted unilaterally, but had gone to the United Nations and had consulted close allies. On 12 September, the Security Council approved a resolution condemning those responsible for 'aiding, supporting or harboring the perpetrators, organizers and sponsors of these acts' and authorising 'all necessary steps' to respond. In addition, Article 5 of the NATO Charter – setting out mutual obligations to come to the help of a fellow member under attack – was invoked for the first time in the alliance's history. This was largely thanks to fast footwork by George Robertson, NATO's Secretary General, on 12 September which put the onus on member countries to object – which none wanted to be seen doing in the post-11 September mood. So the initial emphasis was on creating a broad international coalition.

However, as Daalder and Lindsay argue (2003, pp. 79–81), 'the expectation that 11 September had fundamentally changed the Bush administration's approach to foreign policy was soon proved wrong. The decisions to go to the UN and accept NATO's invocation of Article 5 were tactical responses to the attack, not a strategic conversion to the multilateralist creed . . . In truth, September 11 did more to reaffirm Bush's view of the world than to transform it.' The Bush administration was grateful for international support, but it had to be on America's terms and under American leadership. Many European leaders became annoyed with Washington for spurning their offers of military help. The US did not use NATO's co-ordinated command structure, which only came into play much later in the summer of 2003 in running the multinational peacekeeping operation around Kabul. In the autumn of 2001, the US picked among the military resources made available through NATO by its members. This involved overflying rights, the provision of intelligence (probably the most important of all in the long-term campaign against terrorism), bases, and some ships and aircraft. The ships of some European NATO members were deployed to the eastern Mediterranean, freeing up American vessels to sail to the Gulf. In addition, some AWACS early warning aircraft flew over the eastern United States. But, with the partial exception of the British involvement in the campaign against Afghanistan, this help was secondary.

The Pentagon's insistence on the Afghanistan operation becoming not only US-led but also mainly involving US forces was partly because of the disillusionment of many American commanders with NATO's collective decision-making in the Kosovo conflict (as discussed in Chapter 4). They did not want to be constrained by other countries. Moreover, for many at the top of the Bush administration, the attacks had exposed the weakness and cosy illusions of American policy during the decade after the end of the Cold War. So 9/11 had confronted the American people with the brutal realities of a dangerous world, and the only response was to assert American power against the terrorists and those who backed them. And because America's sense of invulnerability had been destroyed, the response had to be primarily American. Other countries had obligations to fight terrorism, but 9/11 showed that America should lead the way. In his speech to the Joint Session of Congress on 20 September, the one attended by Blair, the President said: 'Every nation, in every region, has a decision to make. Either you are with us, or you are with the terrorists.' This meant strong US leadership.

In this period, the Bush administration began talking about assembling 'a coalition of the willing' rather than working through established alliances – a phrase which was repeated several times over the following eighteen months, particularly in the run-up to the Iraq war. That was linked to the view, expressed by both Rumsfeld and Cheney, that 'the mission determines the coalition and we will not allow coalitions to determine the mission.' This represented a not-so-subtle message to allies: 'We decide and you can join if you want to.' This phrase was also a counter to Secretary of State Powell's worries about unilateral actions that might undermine the international coalition of support created in the immediate aftermath of 11 September.

The course of the Afghanistan campaign was not smooth. As Bob Woodward vividly records in his book on the first year after 9/11 (2002), there were endless debates within the Bush inner circle about how to respond. This did not just reflect the usual inter-agency arguments – notably between Rumsfeld and the Pentagon, and between Powell and the State Department. Bush became frustrated at the absence of credible military operations given the elusive nature of al-Qa'eda. The Joint Chiefs of Staff were operating in unfamiliar territory and their options did not impress the politicians. Into this gap stepped George Tenet of the CIA who put forward what turned out to be the successful strategy of small CIA and Special Forces teams co-ordinating air strikes and working with the Northern Alliance forces and other warlords to defeat the Taliban. On 7 October the air and missile strike began, attacking the relatively few fixed and military targets in Afghanistan. This was linked to the clandestine work of the CIA and Special Forces, including some British forces, both providing money and supplies to the warlords and directing air strikes at the Taliban frontlines. After a period of frustration, this 'bribe and bomb' campaign produced a sudden breakthrough in the second week of November as the Taliban collapsed. Yet this limited type of campaign – partly intended to minimise American casualties – also had major flaws. It involved relying on unreliable allies, both in Afghanistan and among neighbouring countries, which may have allowed bin Laden and many al-Qa'eda/Taliban forces to escape in December 2001.

So the outcome was inconclusive since fighting against remnants of the Taliban and al-Qa'eda continued, especially in the mountainous areas bordering Pakistan. Moreover, the warlords were allies of convenience. They were happy to accept the CIA's money and saw who had the most military clout, but they were determined, above all, to preserve their dominance in their own areas. The Afghanistan

Government under Hamed Karzai really only controlled the area around Kabul, and the international peacekeeping force was specifically limited to the capital. This reflected only a half-hearted financial and military commitment by the United States and other countries to the rebuilding of Afghanistan. The Taliban might have been ousted, and the worst horrors of its regime removed. But Afghanistan was still a very precarious and unstable state and remained so in 2004. Moreover, bin Laden and many of his close advisers were still at large and al-Qa'eda remained a formidable international threat, as shown by terrorist attacks in Bali and elsewhere.

During the Afghanistan campaign, the first signs of divisions within Europe, and with America, began to appear – though in a very different way from the run-up to the Iraq war eighteen months later. During the Afghanistan war, Blair was largely in agreement with President Chirac and Chancellor Schröder, in marked contrast to their later, public disagreements. Indeed, the meeting of the three leaders in Ghent ahead of an EU summit in mid-October to discuss the battle against terrorism annoyed many other countries who had been excluded, as well as Romano Prodi, President of the European Commission. He said this separate meeting was a 'shame', while 'solo' diplomacy by some leaders (meaning Blair) undermined the EU's attempt to speak with one voice. The discussions of Blair, Chirac and Schröder were explained on the grounds that Britain, France and Germany were the only European countries then militarily involved in Afghanistan. But it was essentially a matter of *realpolitik*. These three countries mattered in these circumstances, the EU collectively did not.

These tensions were underlined when Blair arranged a Sunday evening dinner on 4 November, ahead of a brief visit to Washington that Wednesday. Originally, the dinner was to have been with Chirac and Schröder. But the guest list doubled over the preceding two days, reflecting Blair's genial unwillingness to offend his fellow EU leaders. First, Blair had seen Silvio Berlusconi during a brief stop-over in Genoa on the way back from Jerusalem, and made the mistake of mentioning his dinner. The prickly Italian Prime Minister was still annoyed at being excluded from the Ghent meeting and virtually invited himself. To avoid further embarrassment, Blair then included José María Aznar, his close ally. Then, in an almost farcical way, Guy Verhofstadt, the Prime Minister of Belgium, which held the EU presidency in the second half of 2001, was added to the list, along with Javier Solana, the European Council's foreign affairs representative. And if the Belgians were there, so too must the Dutch be. Such was the hurry that Wim Kok arrived late. The countries not invited complained about European unity and anti-terrorist coalition being undermined. The official Downing Street explanation was that those invited were the 'heavy players', a pretty elastic definition both of heavy and of players. The Prime Minister was said to think 'it important to establish that things can be done without all fifteen nations being present. The mechanism is not really there for all of Europe's nations to work in an operational way.' Quite so. But such gatherings had the reverse effect of reinforcing the division of greater and lesser powers.

The confusion of the guest list overshadowed the generally pessimistic tone of the discussions. The aim of the Sunday supper summit had been to co-ordinate policy on the campaign against terrorism and to stress the need to re-invigorate the Middle East peace process. But participants recall the gloomy intervention by President

Chirac, warning about the scale of civilian casualties and the dangers of a humanitarian catastrophe. The leaders also complained about feeling excluded by American military planners, despite agreements in early November on the involvement of German and Italian forces.

Blair himself faced a conflict of roles, as missionary round the world on behalf of President Bush and as messenger between Europe and America. Of course, he was not the only messenger since Bush still had close and regular contacts at that stage with both Chirac and Schröder. And Blair wanted to be seen to be working with the French and German leaders, hence the controversial Ghent and Sunday night meetings and his frequent phone calls to Paris and Berlin. The leaders also strongly backed new joint EU initiatives both to strengthen police powers against terrorists, to combat money laundering, and to increase humanitarian aid. But Blair already enjoyed a privileged status, reflecting both his staunch support immediately after 11 September and the scale of the British military contribution. But some European leaders even then worried that Blair was too much the missionary, the number one ally, and not enough the messenger of European worries. As Bush said when welcoming him to the White House on 7 November: there was 'no better person to talk to than Tony Blair. He brings a lot of wisdom and judgement.' But there were dangers of hubris. In an interview with *The Times* just before this visit, on 6 November, Jack Straw claimed that there had been a 'psychological shift' among EU partners so that Britain was now expected to take the lead in any discussion about the fight against terrorism. At the start of 2002, in a further interview with *The Times*, Jack Straw invoked the ghost of Suez in arguing that Tony Blair had now established a new role for Britain in international affairs – 'not as a superpower but as a very powerful force for good'.

However, Britain's relations with the Bush administration also had their bumpy periods during the Afghanistan campaign. British military commanders at times felt excluded by General Tommy Franks, despite the arrival of a sizeable British military mission at Centcom headquarters at Tampa in Florida. The British believed they could contribute more. At the end of the war, there was confusion about the scale and timing of the deployment of British paratroopers and marines to the stabilisation force in and around Kabul. London was keener than Washington to deploy a substantial peacekeeping force. The differences of approach were highlighted with typical candour by Admiral Sir Michael Boyce, Chief of Defence Staff.

Blair, as always, was keen to press for a revival of the Middle East peace process. On that, he was closer to fellow EU leaders. But unlike some of them, Blair recognised that any EU role was secondary and that Washington was crucial. Yet at their brief White House meeting on 7 November, Bush was reluctant to be rushed. There were also differences over relations with Yasser Arafat. The Americans increasingly did not want to have anything to do with him, while the British, though fully recognising his many faults, believed he could not be ignored as the elected head of the Palestinian Authority. The Prime Minister warned that the war on terrorism could not be won without an American drive to secure peace and stability in the Middle East. That was too much for many American conservatives, and many in the administration, who refused to make the link between the campaign against terrorism and the Israel–Palestine dispute. The President insisted that the coalition would defeat al-Qa'eda, 'peace or no peace in the Middle East'.

At this stage also, Tony Blair was expressing caution about action against Iraq in face of renewed rumblings from Washington hawks against Saddam. At a meeting with President Chirac on 29 November, the Prime Minister stressed that the focus was still on Afghanistan: 'We have not finished and it is essential that it is completed.' Chirac went further and said that action against Iraq or any other country was 'not a topical issue. I hope it will never become a topical issue because intervention would have serious consequences for the international coalition against terrorism.' Both leaders feared that an attack on Iraq would fracture the international coalition. Moreover, in an important difference with Washington, British ministers insisted that there was no evidence of Iraqi involvement in the 11 September attacks by the al-Qa'eda network on the United States. This reflected the consistent view of British intelligence.

Blair's vigorous response to the 11 September attacks was not a diversion from his natural foreign policy instincts, but rather a confirmation of them. His long-standing worries over terrorism and weapons of mass destruction had been highlighted. They reinforced his belief in humanitarian intervention, as set out in his Chicago speech of April 1999 at the height of the Kosovo war. He returned to the same themes in his speech to the Labour Party conference in Brighton nearly eighteen months later on Tuesday 2 October 2001. Blair is not a natural or classical orator. But this was one of his commanding performances, matched only by his speech to the House of Commons on Tuesday 18 March, at the start of the debate authorising British involvement in the Iraqi war. His theme was the same as in Chicago: global interdependence and the justification for intervention. In Brighton, on that afternoon, his rhetoric soared. In what was widely described – both with approval and alarm – as a messianic tone, Blair talked of a fight for freedom and justice: 'justice to bring those same values of democracy and freedom to people around the world . . . the starving, the wretched, the dispossessed, the ignorant, those living in wanton squalor, from the deserts of North Africa to the slums of Gaza, to the mountain ranges of Afghanistan: they are our cause.'

Blair's critics claimed that he almost seemed to be promising to solve all the world's problems. His moralistic tone worried many, particularly in the foreign policy and military worlds, who otherwise admired his qualities as an international leader. Blair did allow a touch of reality to intrude: 'We can't do it all. Neither can the Americans. But the power of the international community could, together, if it chose to.' Blair later admitted in his speech to the Lord Mayor's Banquet on 12 November that:

> *Some say it's Utopian: others that it is dangerous to think that we can resolve all these problems by ourselves. But the point I was making was simply that self-interest for a nation and the interests of the broader community are no longer in conflict. There are few problems from which we remain immune. In the war against terrorism the moralists and the realists are partners, not antagonists. The fact that we can't solve everything doesn't mean we try to solve nothing. What is clear is that 11 September has not just given impetus and urgency to such solutions, it has opened the world up.*

Blair also saw Afghanistan as reinforcing his twin track foreign policy approach, being both close to the American President and closely involved in Europe, and acting as the 'bridge' between the two:

> *We have buried the myth that Britain has to choose between being strong in Europe or strong with the United States. Afghanistan has shown vividly how the relationships reinforce each other; and that both the United States and our European partners value our role with the other. So let us play our full part in Europe, not retreat to the margins; and let us proclaim our closeness to the United States and use it to bring Europe closer to America.*

That view just about survived the Afghanistan conflict, despite the increasing strains noted above. But the 'bridge' was tested to near destruction over the following eighteen months.

Blair was in danger of over-reaching himself. His very skill as a missionary, an ambassador-at-large, and his eloquence unquestionably gave him access in the White House – a say in the President's decision-making. But, at times, Blair appeared to be taking responsibility for what he could neither deliver nor control. Blair in many ways had a more open, and more candid, relationship with Bush than with Clinton. The Prime Minister was no longer the pupil, or the younger brother, to the more experienced master, or older brother. But, as he well knew, any British leader was still very much the junior partner. This implied risks, as well as benefits, in attaching himself so closely to the American President. He could be tied publicly into the US policy, whatever his private reservations. Yet the nature of the close alliance was that these private discussions never became public. That did not matter in the weeks and months after 11 September since Blair largely agreed with Bush. But Blair's 'insider' approach caused him domestic political problems when the campaign against terrorism broadened during the course of 2002.

7. Axis of Evil

States likes these, and their terrorist allies, constitute an axis of evil, arming to threaten the peace of the world. By seeking weapons of mass destruction, these regimes pose a grave and growing danger. They could provide these arms to terrorists, giving them the means to match their hatred. They could attack our allies or attempt to blackmail the United States. In any of these cases, the price of indifference would be catastrophe.

President George W. Bush referring to North Korea, Iran and Iraq in his State of the Union address to Joint Session of US Congress, Tuesday 29 January 2002

The doctrine of international community is just enlightened national self-interest, so whatever the different rhetorical perspectives you come to the same point.

Tony Blair talking about differences between the British and American approaches in an interview in *Prospect*, August 2002

Today the international community has the best chance since the rising of the nation state in the seventeenth century to build a world where great powers compete in peace instead of continually prepare for war.

President George W. Bush, letter accompanying 'National Security Strategy of the United States', 20 September 2002

'Axis of evil' is the phrase that, above all others, has defined the Bush administration's foreign policy since 11 September. No matter that the three words were the creation of speech-writers looking for a catchy phrase. 'Axis of evil' has become the symbol of a more assertive American attitude to global problems – particularly the linked policies of pre-emptive action and regime change. As such, the words and the associated policies have been publicly criticised by many European politicians and on the left generally. However, Bush's 'conservative' approach has overlapped in several respects with Tony Blair's 'liberal' doctrine of 'international community'. The overlap turned out to be crucial during the discussions over Iraq in 2002–3.

In reality, 'axis of evil' was only the rhetorical gloss on the creation of what the administration's defenders have come to call 'the Bush doctrine'. (American presidents like to have a doctrine named after them, just as political commentators in Britain have sought to attach 'ism' to prime ministers since Margaret Thatcher, failing with John Major, though succeeding with Tony Blair.) The State of the Union address was the first of three major public statements in 2002 which defined the Bush doctrine – the others being the President's speech at West Point on 1 June, and the formal statement of the Bush National Security Strategy on 20 September.

The origins of the doctrine can be traced back to a number of positions taken by leading members of the administration during the 1990s – notably what became known as the neo-conservatives, such as Paul Wolfowitz and Doug Feith at the Pentagon; Lewis 'Scooter' Libby, Vice President Cheney's Chief of Staff; and John Bolton at the State Department. Outside the administration, the most active spokesmen for this viewpoint have been Richard Perle and Bill

Kristol, editor of the *Weekly Standard*. Several of the above were among the authors of 'Rebuilding America's Defences', a report published before the 2000 election.

This group criticises both what they call the narrow realism of Bush senior's team and the wishful liberalism of the Clinton administration. (Their case is clearly set out in Lawrence Kaplan and Bill Kristol's *The War over Iraq*.) As the title makes clear, Iraq has become the test case for the views. But the analysis is much broader. Bush senior's policies are criticised for being grounded only in vital interests, not ideals or abstract principles, too concerned with stability rather than the spread of democracy or freedom. The Clinton team is accused of being reluctant to use American power, of ignoring real security threats and of being ineffective. Yet, according to Kaplan and Kristol (2003, p. 63), the result of the liberal and realist approaches was the same: 'watching Saddam's arsenal grow ever more threatening'. Taking up George W. Bush's phrase, 'a distinctly American internationalism', the neo-conservatives maintain that American national self-interest, based on its values of freedom and democracy, is inherently compatible with the interests of humanity. What is right for America is right for the world. This justifies both pre-emptive action against security threats and regime change. Writing well before the start of the Iraq war, the authors argue: 'After Saddam Hussein has been defeated and Iraq occupied, installing a decent and democratic government in Baghdad should be a manageable task for the United States.' The neo-conservatives reject realist objections that democracy cannot be imposed from outside – pointing to Japan, Germany, Austria, Italy, Grenada, the Dominican Republic and Panama.

This approach involves a commitment to American pre-eminence, both economic and military, and a rejection of the constraints of international organisations and treaties. International co-operation might be desirable in certain circumstances, but only on American terms, hence the phrase 'coalitions of the willing'. That is what so worries many European leaders, in Paris and Berlin, as well as leaders in Moscow. What the neo-conservatives regard as beneficial is seen elsewhere as threatening. Take Kaplan and Kristol's grand assertion (2003, p. 119):

> *What upholds today's world order is America's benevolent influence – nurtured, to be sure, by American power, but also by emulation and the recognition around the world that American ideals are genuinely universal. As a consequence, when the world's sole superpower commits itself to norms of international conduct – for democracy, for human rights, against aggression, against weapons proliferation – it means that successful challenges to American power will invariably weaken those American created norms.*

America must 'not only be the world's policeman or its sheriff, it must be its beacon and guide'. They conclude that 'the mission begins in Baghdad, but it does not end there'.

These are breathtaking ambitions to re-make the world in the American image. Not only is the assumption of the universality of American values disputed by many in Europe, Asia and Africa, but the strategy implies that America can impose its view without the willing co-operation of others, as opposed to their acquiescence. You can agree that democracy, freedom and the rule of law are all highly desirable, while doubting that they can be created by one nation, however, powerful, according to a pre-set plan. Moreover, the experience of the Balkans, Afghanistan and, now, Iraq has shown that, while America can topple regimes largely on its own, it cannot create new ones without help from other countries. The US lacks the skills, the resources and the will to do nation-building on its own. That can only be done internationally and, preferably, via multilateral institutions. That is the neo-conservatives' dilemma.

The 11 September attacks gave this group the opportunity to press their existing views more forcefully. But while the neo-conservatives are unquestionably intelligent, influential and articulate, they are far from the only voice, even on the right, within the Bush administration. Some of the older generation, notably Donald Rumsfeld and, to some extent, Dick Cheney, have been wary of the interventionist and nation-building ambitions of the neo-conservatives, while the internationalists/realists headed by Colin Powell have been more hostile. Moreover, on particular issues, inter-agency and personality clashes have been as important as various shades of ideology.

In practice, Bush's gut instincts have often mattered most. The new Bush doctrine was initially articulated in his hastily written television broadcast on the night of 11 September, when he said, 'we will make no distinction between the terrorists who committed these acts and those who harbor them'. That implied a far-reaching change in US foreign policy objectives, particularly a much more aggressive attitude towards the state sponsors of terrorism. One of the central features of American thinking has been the stress on states – in contrast to the emphasis by European intelligence agencies, including the British, on looser terrorist networks operating independently of governments and often in failed or weak states such as Afghanistan or the Sudan. That explains the reference to the 'axis of evil' in the State of the Union address: 'to prevent regimes that sponsor terror from threatening America and our friends and allies with weapons of mass destruction.' He then listed the threats from North Korea, Iran, and particularly Iraq under Saddam Hussein: 'Iraq continues to flaunt its hostility toward America and to support terror. The Iraqi regime has plotted to develop anthrax, and nerve gas, and nuclear weapons for over a decade.' Moreover, the threat was urgent: 'We'll be deliberate, yet time is not on our side. I will not wait on events, while dangers gather.'

The phrase 'axis of evil' echoed round the world, creating alarm and provoking criticism. Herbert Vedrine, the French Foreign Minister, said US policy had become 'simplistic', while Chris Patten, the EU's External Affairs Commissioner, expressed the worries of transatlantic multilateralists in saying that the US was in danger of going into 'unilateralist overdrive'. Over the following months, Patten annoyed many members of the Bush administration by his criticisms of the US approach to the International Criminal Court as well as over its lack of consultation with European allies. On the left, the speech marked the end of the post-11 September phase of sympathy and solidarity. Instead, America, and particularly Bush, came to be seen as a threat to world peace. The critics were divided between those who regarded Bush as a knave, the tool of American corporate interests, or as a fool, an ignorant, blundering Texan.

The British Government's response was low-key – a world weary raising of an eyebrow. Sir Christopher Meyer later recalled in a

2003 television interview that his advice from Washington to London was:

> '*Cool it, no knee-jerk reactions, please. Understand why the phrase was used. Don't jump to conclusions. Start working immediately*' – as indeed we were in the embassy – '*with the administration about what the practical policy consequences were of putting Iran, North Korea and Iraq in the same box.*' Rhetorically, they were in the same box. But would it mean as a matter of policy being in the same box?

Meyer says the phrase 'didn't ring alarm bells' for him since he did not believe that the US was about to attack North Korea or Iran. The real issue was Iraq. As often, Colin Powell took a parallel view. He told Congress in early February that Iran and North Korea would be treated differently: 'There is no plan to start a war with these nations. We want to see a dialogue. We want to contain North Korea's activities with respect to proliferation, and we are going to keep the pressures on them.'

Yet language does matter. The phrase 'axis of evil' aroused fears in Europe about precipitate American actions that were not borne out by the reality of what happened. The words both exaggerated the extent of the contrast between the Clinton and Bush administrations and aggravated tensions within the international coalition. There were similarities with the alarmed response in Europe to Ronald Reagan's talk of the 'evil empire' of the Soviet Union in the early 1980s.

The full implications of the Bush doctrine were spelt out on 1 June in President Bush's speech at West Point:

> *For much of the last century, America's defense relied on the Cold War doctrines of deterrence and containment. In some cases, these strategies still apply. But new threats also require new thinking. Deterrence – the promise of massive retaliation against nations – means nothing against shadowy terrorist networks with no nation or citizens to defend. Containment is not possible when unbalanced dictators with weapons of mass destruction can deliver these weapons or missiles or secretly provide them to terrorist allies. We cannot defend America and our friends by hoping for the best. We cannot put our faith in the word of tyrants, who solemnly sign non-proliferation treaties, and then systematically break them. If we wait for threats to fully materialize, we will have waited too long.*

Consequently, the 'war on terror' required not only security measures like enhanced homeland defence and missile defence but also an offensive strategy. This would mean 'pre-emptive action when necessary to defend our liberty and to defend our lives.' Pre-emption challenged not only traditional doctrines about the nation state dating from the Treaty of Westphalia at the end of the Thirty Years War but also the stress in the United Nations Charter on self-defence as the only justification for military action. Under Article 51 of the Charter, this is only allowed 'if an armed attack occurs' – not if it might occur. Yet the Bush administration argued that the Charter's wording had to be updated to take account of newer threats from terrorist groups which could not be deterred or countered in the traditional way.

The expression of this doctrine of preventive intervention was seen within the administration to be as significant as the emergence of the doctrine of containing the Soviet bloc in the early Cold War days. Condoleezza Rice, the White House National Security Adviser, is quoted by Nicolas Lemann in a fascinating article on the shift in US policy in the *New Yorker* in April 2002: 'I really think this period is analogous to 1945 to 1947 in that the events so clearly demonstrated that there is a big global threat, and that it's a big global threat to a lot of countries that you would not normally think of as being in the coalition. That has started shifting the tectonic plates in international politics.'

The implications were spelt out by Richard Haass, Director of Policy Planning at the State Department, and seen by many Europeans as the acceptable internationalist face of the administration (before his departure in the summer of 2003 to run the Council on Foreign Relations in New York). In the Lemann article, Haass said that the new doctrine defined the limits of sovereignty:

> *Sovereignty entails obligations. One is not to massacre your own people. Another is not to support terrorism in any way. If a government fails to meet these obligations, then it forfeits some of the normal advantages of sovereignty, including the right to be left alone inside your own territory. Other governments, including the United States, gain the right to intervene. In the case of terrorism, this*

> *can even lead to a right of preventive, or peremptory, self-defense. You essentially can act in anticipation if you have grounds to think it's a question of when, and not if, you're going to be attacked.*

The new doctrine was translated into policy objectives and guidelines in the formal National Security Strategy of 20 September 2002. This explicitly stated that 'while the United States will constantly strive to enlist the support of the international community, we will not hesitate to act alone, if necessary, to exercise our right of self-defense by acting pre-emptively against such terrorists, to prevent them from doing harm against our own people and our country.' The strategy also underlined the President's desire to maintain the US as the sole superpower in military terms. 'Our forces will be strong enough to dissuade potential adversaries from pursuing a military build-up in hopes of surpassing or equalling the power of the United States.' There were references to working with allies and with NATO (which should develop 'highly mobile' forces available at short notice), but this would no longer be the only option. NATO was no longer the sole or pre-eminent security organisation as it had been for half a century. An equal preference was for 'mission-based coalitions' or 'coalitions of the willing', that is groups of countries assembled for a particular operation.

The lengthy statement also contained many references to a new relationship with Russia, pursuing 'common interests and challenges' rather than as 'adversaries' – a shift in thinking and attitudes by the Bush administration still widely under-appreciated in Europe. Similarly, the strategy aimed to integrate China into the west, in marked contrast to the administration's early approach when the Beijing regime was described as a 'strategic competitor'.

The overall goal was to expand 'the circle of development' through democratisation, free markets and free trade. As foreign policy analysts pointed out, there were continuities with the Clinton administration's approach: for instance, towards the enlargement of NATO to include former members of the Soviet bloc in central and eastern Europe as part of their transition to become part of the free market west. The Clinton administration had also talked about regime change, in respect of both Slobodan Milosevic and Saddam Hussein. The main difference between the Clinton and Bush strategies was the emphasis in the latter on a single overriding security threat from terrorists and their sponsoring states.

The strategy, like all such documents, begged a lot of questions. The promises to fight terrorism might not always be consistent with the goal of promoting 'free and open societies'. Many of the US's allies in the coalition against al-Qa'eda and the Taliban could not remotely be described as democratic or concerned with human rights. Moreover, critics argued that deterrence had worked with the three 'axis of evil' states, certainly in terms of their likely use of weapons of mass destruction against the US and its main allies. Nor did that strategy have clear guidelines about when pre-emptive attacks were justified, as opposed to the more traditional policy of deterrence or international negotiation. In practice, with the United Nations pushed to the sidelines, the answer was that the American President would decide.

While there was general agreement between the neo-conservatives and the assertive nationalists about pre-emptive action and regime change, they differed about what should happen next. Rumsfeld was very sceptical about committing American troops as part of a longer-term exercise in nation building. On his view, shared by Cheney, American power should be used to deter and defeat security threats and leave other countries to sort out their own governments. That approach was essentially seen in Afghanistan, where the Pentagon wanted a minimal US involvement in peacekeeping and reconstruction, and was content for the Europeans to take on these roles. The neo-conservatives are more interested in creating democratic societies in America's image, which will then, they believe, become allies of Washington. The choices have been more complicated in Iraq, and many of the post-war problems there have reflected the Pentagon's failure to think through and agree on what was needed after a military victory.

The main criticism outside America of the new strategy was that it set America up as a global policeman deciding when and where to intervene in what had been seen as the internal affairs of other countries. And, even if US interventions turned out to be well-justified (a strongly disputed point), a precedent might be created. Henry Kissinger argued in August 2002 that: 'It cannot be either the American national interest or the world's interest to develop principles that grant every nation an unfettered right of pre-emption against its own definition of threats to its security.' Moreover, the very breadth of America's ambitions is a worry for other countries. That was the root of the opposition of France, Germany and Russia to the Iraq war.

The Bush strategy partly overlaps with Blair's approach, at least in the analysis of particular dangers and threats. Blair's worries about weapons of mass destruction and their use by terrorist groups date back to 1997 – well before they went to the top of the Bush administration's priorities after 11 September. But their starting points are very different: on the one hand, an assertion of national power against global threats to security; and, on the other, a broadly liberal and moralistic concern with human rights. Consequently, the response in Britain to the Bush doctrine has not been straightforward. There have been supporters as well as critics in both main parties. Iain Duncan Smith, with his close links to the Bush administration and to the neo-conservatives, was a strong supporter during his two years as Conservative leader. Many Tory MPs wished his support had been more qualified, though, in March 2004, Michael Howard, his equally Atlanticist successor, maintained his firm backing for the Iraq war, which, he described, as not only justified, but also overdue. By contrast, many Labour MPs and activists, not just on the left, have been vocal critics of pre-emptive attacks, reverting to the anti-Americanism of the Vietnam era and the early Reagan years. Yet more interesting in many ways have been the Conservative critics of the Bush doctrine and its centre-left supporters, or, at least, sympathisers.

At the heart of these debates have been the similarities, and differences, between the Bush doctrine and Blair's defence of 'humanitarian intervention' in his Chicago speech of April 1999 and his Brighton speech of October 2001. Both accepted that longstanding ideas of national sovereignty could no longer be applied in all circumstances. Both justified external military intervention in the affairs of states because of wider security threats and dangers.

The main Conservative criticism was that the Bush doctrine was 'inherently destabilising of international relations', as Andrew Tyrie,

181

an independently-minded Tory backbench MP argued in a pamphlet produced shortly before the Iraq war (2003):

> *The notion that a pre-emptive strike may be undertaken without clear evidence of an imminent attack undermines the most basic principle of the relations between states – that military action can generally be justified only in self-defence. The doctrine of regime change is equally corrosive. For who should decide when a country's leadership must be changed?*

Tyrie recognised that the emphasis of the new doctrine varied, noting the contrast discussed above between the unilateralist and nationalist rhetoric of Donald Rumsfeld and the democratic missionary zeal of Paul Wolfowitz. Yet both accepted regime change and pre-emptive action against serious threats.

Tyrie distinguished this from the Blair view which he characterised as 'greater intervention around the world to impose our notion of freedom and justice. For him, globalisation means that anyone's internal conflict may affect everybody and, therefore, interference may be justified in the affairs of other states.' Tyrie saw this as 'dangerous talk', leading not towards a new international order, but towards a new international anarchy. He argued that the bedrock of order was the doctrine of non-interference and mutual respect of the integrity of states. Moreover, the British and American approaches are 'very different. The Prime Minister's new world order is internationalist, almost messianic, and draws on the rhetoric of human rights; America's is implicitly unilateralist and designed to facilitate the expression of US power.' These differences of approach have been reflected in the contrasting arguments used to justify specific interventions, as will be clear from the discussion of Iraq in the following chapters.

Moreover, Tyrie has reflected a profoundly Tory scepticism about the inherent moralism in both the Blair and Bush doctrines: 'the fundamental misconception that western values are inherently peaceful and that a fully democratic world would abjure war: that was the essence of the British and European objections to Woodrow Wilson's view of a new international order at the end of the First World War'.

By contrast, the traditional doctrine of non-intervention had been challenged by some of the more original foreign policy thinkers such as Robert Cooper and by centre-left commentators such as Michael Ignatieff and John Lloyd. Cooper was a senior, if unconventional, Foreign Office diplomat before becoming Director General for External and Politico-Military Affairs at the European council of ministers, working for Javier Solana, its foreign affairs representative. Well before the 11 September attacks, Cooper had highlighted the threat to stability from pre-modern states with pre-state, post-imperial chaos such as Somalia, Afghanistan and Liberia. They provided a breeding ground for international terrorists, cross-border crime and the drugs trade. Globalisation had eroded the distinction between the internal and the external. As Cooper argued on the first anniversary of the 9/11 attacks: 'This creates an environment in which the pressure for external intervention is greater than ever before. The characteristic post-Cold War conflict is a civil war; and the characteristic intervention is not, as in the past, intervention for conquest, but a peacekeeping operation designed to bring a civil war to an end or to solidify a shaky peace.'

Cooper went on to say that the 11 September attacks had exposed the vulnerabilities of the nation state – showing what damage could be done even without using any of the purpose-built technologies of mass destruction: 'Future attacks may be more devastating.' Consequently, 'the Bush administration's twin focus on terrorism and on weapons of mass destruction is precisely right.' Cooper expressed pessimism about threats to both internal and international order. He concluded that 'we have to adjust our legal concepts to take account of the new realities: pre-emptive force and covert operations may need legal recognition; and the UN Security Council may or may not be able to play a central role. At all events, we cannot continue as though nothing has happened, and assume that present conceptions of legal order must remain unchanged.'

Cooper's analysis was largely echoed by Michael Ignatieff. Based on several visits by him to failing states, and particularly the Balkans during the 1990s, Ignatieff – Director of the Carr Centre for Human Rights Policy at the Kennedy School of Government at Harvard – argues that only external intervention can prevent the horrors of ethnic cleansing and further instability. In a collection of essays, revealingly entitled *Empire Lite* (2003, p. 109), he describes the nation-building enterprise in Bosnia, Kosovo and Afghanistan as imperial because its 'purpose is to create order in border zones essential to the security of great powers – and because armed force, an instrument only great powers can use with impunity is critical to the task.' However, Ignatieff is worried that the 'imperial powers' are unwilling to make the necessary commitment. This theme has been argued from a Tory perspective by historian Niall Ferguson in his book *Empire* (2003), where he writes: 'The Americans have taken our old role without yet facing the fact that an empire comes with it.'

Ignatieff contends (2003, p. 126) that:

> *empire lite neither provides a stable long-term security guarantee, nor creates the conditions under which local leadership takes over. Everything is done on the cheap, from day to day, without the long-term security guarantees and short-term financial assistance that would genuinely create the conditions for true national independence.*

His approach is internationalist, not unilateralist. He criticises both some Americans for believing they can go it alone and the European left for failing to realise that they are being defended by the US, and that their core values of freedom are nearly identical in face of the terrorist threat. A year after the Iraq war, Ignatieff (2004) has admitted to second thoughts and doubts, not over the principle of intervention, but over its application in practice by the US:

> *An administration that cared more genuinely about human rights would have understood that you can't have human rights without order and that you can't have order once victory is won if planning for an invasion is divorced from planning for an occupation. The administration failed to grasp that from the first moment an American tank column took a town, there had to be military police*

> *and civilian administrators following behind to guard museums, hospitals, water-pumping stations and electricity generators and to stop looting, revenge, killings and crime. Securing order would have meant putting 250,000 troops into the invasion as opposed to 130,000. It would have meant immediately retaining and retraining the Iraqi Army and police, instead of disbanding them. The administration, which never tires of telling us that hope is not a plan, had only hope for a plan in Iraq.*

In Britain, John Lloyd, a leading centre-left journalist, has clashed sharply with his former allies on the left both by defending the war in Iraq and by arguing more broadly for multilateral intervention in the face of new cross-border security threats and all the problems of violence, poverty and starvation in failed states. He contests (2003) that the argument needed to be set out in terms of 'a positive agenda based on democracy, human rights and the rule of law'.

A further dimension to the debate – contrasting American and European attitudes to power – was opened by Robert Kagan, an American journalist living in Europe. His views, originally expressed in the journal *Policy Review* in summer 2002, were turned in the bestselling book *Paradise and Power*. His success was mainly based on his catchy phrase: 'Americans are from Mars and Europeans are from Venus.' But going beyond the trendy soundbite, Kagan argues (2003, p. 3):

> *It is time to stop pretending that Europeans and Americans share a common view of the world, or even that*

> *they occupy the same world. On the all-important*
> *questions of power – the efficacy of power, the morality of*
> *power, the desirability of power – American and European*
> *perspectives are differing.*

On Kagan's view, Europe is moving into 'a self-contained world of laws and rules and transnational negotiation and co-operation' – the realisation of Kant's perpetual peace. Meanwhile, 'the US remains mired in history, exercising power in an anarchic Hobbesian world where international laws and rules are unreliable, and where true security and the defense and promotion of a liberal order still depend on the possession and use of military might.' Kagan argues that European attitudes reflect their relative weakness, particularly in military power, compared with America. However, he does not just condemn, but recognises differences within Europe. Moreover, he is not a unilateralist: 'Winning the material and moral support of friends and allies, especially in Europe, is unquestionably preferable to acting alone in the face of European anxiety and hostility.'

Yet Kagan's book, for all its simplicities, highlights many of the transatlantic differences. But critics, such as Chris Patten, have argued that, while Europe does need to strengthen its military capabilities, it can never rival the US, nor should it. Instead, Europe, with its different history and dreadful experience of killing before 1945, has much to contribute through what Joseph Nye (2002) has called 'soft power'. That means peacekeeping, assistance with nation-building, persuasion and diplomacy. Patten points to what the EU has been doing in the Balkans. Patten is no Gaullist or cultural anti-

American; rather the opposite. He is an instinctive Atlanticist, entitling a speech in October 2002, 'America and Europe: an essential partnership'. Yet he criticises American unilateralism. In a BBC interview, also in October 2002, he said America could not

> *define its national interest entirely in terms of rules which other people have to play by, but America doesn't. If you're the biggest kid on the block, if you're the only superpower around, you have to lean over backwards to demonstrate that you're trying to consult and trying to bring people along with you, rather than simply laying down the law.*

Instead, he has urged a system of 'co-operative global governance', involving, for example, strengthening the global rule-book and more preventive diplomacy. In an interview with *The Times* in November 2002, he said:

> *The main argument against the sovereigntists/unilateralists is that the US should not contract out of leading the international community or institutions which it did more than anyone else to create. Leading those institutions of global governance is part of the job description of any American President. Europe's role is to help America in that task. Many of the things that Europe wants to achieve are incomparably more difficult if America is not on the same side.*

The real danger for the United States is that its natural allies in Europe and elsewhere will not accept its view of the world – even if they have to live with its overwhelming military power. As Daalder and Lindsay argue (2003, p. 196):

> *America's friends and allies might not be able to stop Washington from doing as it wished, but neither would they necessarily be willing to come to its aid when their help was most needed. Indeed, the more others questioned America's power, purpose, and priorities, the less influence America would have.*

8. Our Guy Tony

Maybe I should be a little less direct and be a little more nuanced, and say we support regime change.

George W. Bush explaining his Iraq policy at a joint press conference with Tony Blair, Crawford, Texas, 6 April 2002

The world works better when the US and the EU stand together. There will be issues that divide – issues of trade, most recently over steel, for example. But on the big security issues, the common interests dwarf the divide. Forget the talk of anti-Americanism in Europe. Yes, if you call a demonstration, you will get the slogans and the insults. But people know Europe needs America, and I believe America needs Europe too.

Tony Blair, speech at the George Bush Senior Presidential Library, College Station, Texas, 7 April 2002

There were concerns first over Afghanistan, and, secondly, over the issue of Iraq that America would take precipitous or unthought-through action. Now, as I keep saying to people here, they haven't done that, they have acted perfectly sensibly, responsibly and in consultation with international partners.

Tony Blair in an interview with *The Times*, 21 May 2002

Iraq was always going to be next after Afghanistan. But the course to war was not clear-cut. From spring 2002 onwards, military action to get rid of Saddam Hussein was probable at some stage. But that did not mean that George W. Bush and Tony Blair had irrevocably decided on military action. This chapter discusses the first part of this process – from early 2002 up to the unanimous agreement by the UN Security Council on resolution 1441 on 8 November. The central question is the one posed by Robin Cook after his resignation on the eve of the Iraq war: had Tony Blair, in effect, entered a Faustian bargain with George W. Bush? In return for access, and the hope of influence over US policy, did the Prime Minister tacitly, or explicitly, promise the President that Britain would support, and join in, eventual military action against Iraq?

Blair and his advisers challenge the determinist interpretation. On the Blair view, war was not inevitable and could have been avoided even as late as early 2003. In theory, perhaps, but in practice not. The real story is less straightforward, and cloudier, than either the press reports at the time or the retrospective assessments after the war. The movement towards war occurred in several stages during the course of nearly a year. Washington and London faced different domestic pressures. Legal and political constraints prevented Blair from making regime change an explicit objective. So their justifications differed. Blair believed – and may have convinced himself – that he had not irrevocably agreed to decisions to which the Bush administration thought he was committed. The Bush team believed that Blair was with them over Iraq, at least in principle, from the Crawford summit in April 2002, and more firmly from the Camp David meeting in September 2002. If Crawford was the engagement, then Camp David was the not-so-secret marriage. Blair became steadily more tied in to the Bush strategy during the course of 2002.

However, he believed at each stage that his support was conditional and that war was not inevitable. Blair hoped that the return of the UN inspectors in late 2002 would uncover Saddam's arsenal of WMD, and would lead to its disposal, thus making war unnecessary. On the other hand, if Saddam obstructed the inspectors, then there would be an unarguable case for military intervention which virtually all major countries would accept. The hawks in Washington were suspicious of a renewal of UN inspections precisely because they thought it might make it harder to take early action to remove Saddam. There were, therefore, significant underlying differences in the Bush and Blair strategies, and hopes. While the Bush approach was itself evolving during the year, there was at times an element of self-delusion about Blair's claims that all options were open. No formal decisions may have been taken, but Blair's options were narrowing fast. These contradictions came to the surface with a vengeance in February and March 2003.

Barely had the fighting stopped in Afghanistan in late 2001 than Iraq was on the agenda. Indeed, it had really always been there, as the accounts in Chapter 6 of the post-9/11 discussions in the Bush team show. For the Pentagon, and the President, it was only a matter of time. War planning had begun in late 2001. The hopes of some in the Foreign Office in London that there would be a fresh debate about Iraq were wishful thinking. Sir Christopher Meyer was at this time telling London that the issue was 'coming up. There was no way we could be head in the sand. Bush was serious about getting rid of Saddam. The only question was how do we handle America.'

Concern about Iraq and weapons of mass destruction came together in 'Blair's mind taking account of the realities of Bush', according to a senior adviser in London. But this was not the same as the British official mind since there was still considerable scepticism in the Foreign Office over support for the emerging American line towards Iraq. The Foreign Office as an institution did not play a central role in the development of Iraq policy during 2002–3. Jack Straw, his close advisers, and the ambassadors in Washington and the United Nations, were personally very involved in all the hectic diplomacy. But the two Ambassadors spent more time dealing with 10 Downing Street directly, and with Straw's office, over Iraq than with the relevant Foreign Office departments. No one had any doubt that the key decisions were made in 10 Downing Street. In formal, bureaucratic terms, control over Iraq policy was officially under Sir David Manning in Number 10 rather than in the Foreign Office. Robin Cook, who left the Foreign Office in only June 2001, told the Foreign Affairs Committee after the Iraq War that many career diplomats shared his concern about 'the consequences of us being involved in unilateral action with the Americans'. In her evidence to the MPs, Clare Short, admittedly a critic with attitude and several axes to grind, complained that 'decision-making was sucked out of the Foreign Office which, I think, is a great pity because there is enormous experience about the Middle East in the Foreign Office.' Yet, as the following chapter will discuss, it was not just a matter of the centralisation of decision making in 10 Downing Street. There were also major criticisms of the Foreign Office's assessments of French and German policy over the winter of 2002–3.

The Blair team regarded many in the Foreign Office as privately critical of their Iraq policy. During the summer one senior Blair ally described the Foreign Office as 'all at sea'. In the view of one senior official with experience of both periods, the distance between 10 Downing Street and the Foreign Office over Iraq during 2002 was as great as during the Thatcher years – with the significant difference that Blair and Straw got on well, and became closer, in contrast to the increasing personal friction between Margaret Thatcher and Geoffrey Howe, particularly in his last three years as Foreign Secretary.

From his vantage point in the British Embassy in Washington, Sir Christopher Meyer recalled in a television interview (2003):

> *There are a variety of tributaries that flow into this river*
> *that leads to regime change and disarmament. But it was*
> *becoming an active subject of discussion in the first quarter*
> *of 2002. I think Blair and Bush have come to the view*
> *that you have to deal with Saddam Hussein through very*
> *different paths. Blair was Prime Minister in 1997 and*
> *1998 when Saddam provoked the first crisis with the*
> *inspectors. So Blair has had experience from that time,*
> *and formed a view which said the international*
> *community, one way or another, has got to deal with*
> *Saddam. President Bush comes into government in*
> *January 2001 and was not immediately focused on Iraq*
> *from a war-fighting point of view, to put it crudely. For*
> *Bush, the transforming moment as far as Iraq is concerned*
> *was 9/11. They had an earlier priority, which is the*
> *Taliban and al-Qa'eda. But once they're out of the way,*
> *more or less, then Iraq comes up front. And, as it comes up*
> *front, the nexus, the two lines cross between the way in*
> *which Blair has first seized the issue and the way Bush*

> *subsequently has. They're not coming from identical*
> *positions; they come from positions which intersect.*

At this stage in the spring of 2002, the common assumption among politicians and commentators on both sides of the Atlantic was that Iraq was now the top priority. It was treated as a fact beyond debate, even though both North Korea and Iran had more advanced nuclear programmes. Iraq was the priority partly because it had always been top of the enemies list for many of the Bush team, and in part because of all kinds of retrospective judgements and regrets about the failure to get rid of Saddam in 1991. Moreover, many in the administration believed that Saddam was somehow involved in the 11 September attacks, even though there was no intelligence backing for this claim. British intelligence always denied any link between Saddam and 9/11. However, Iraq was also seen as a straightforward target compared with Iran or North Korea. Paradoxically, Iraq's military weakness since 1991 made it easier to attack. And, as Ivo Daalder and James Lindsay (2003, pp. 116–128)) argue: 'Regime change in Iraq would give the President what he and several of his advisers most wanted: the opportunity for a grand strategic play, the type that establishes presidential reputations.' So it became the 'inevitable war'.

The British tactic during the early months of 2002 was the familiar one: to ask questions. How should Saddam be tackled? How should the United Nations be involved? How should weapons of mass destruction be linked to regime change? Should America do this on its own? Or should Washington try to build a wide-ranging coalition?

The meeting between Blair and Bush at the President's Texas ranch in Crawford in April 2002 was when the British side fully realised the strength of Bush's resolve to oust Saddam, probably by military means. This was the first important step towards war, the second being at Camp David five months later. One close adviser to Blair remembers being taken aback at Bush's bluntness at the joint news conference on 6 April when the President said: 'I explained to the Prime Minister that the policy of my government is the removal of Saddam and that all options are on the table.' Regime change was not officially Britain's policy, so Blair approached the question obliquely: 'It has always been our policy that Iraq would be a better place without Saddam Hussein. I don't think anyone can be in any doubt about that.' Blair's emphasis was on weapons of mass destruction: 'You cannot have a situation in which he carries on being in breach of UN resolutions, and refusing to allow us to assess whether and how he is developing these weapons of mass destruction. Now, how we then proceed from there, that is a matter that is open for us.' But the President then left absolutely no doubt about how he intended to proceed: 'Maybe I should be a little less direct and be a little more nuanced, and say we support regime change.'

There, then, was a difference of emphasis in public statements that bedevilled the debate over Iraq during the following year. Blair could not be frank about his objectives. Sir Christopher Meyer (2003) noted that, while the British Government had never subscribed to the notion of regime change, 'as a matter of practical politics, or *realpolitik*, if you are asked a question, "Can you disarm Iraq without changing the regime?" your answer would have to be, "No, of course you can't", because if Saddam Hussein had actually come into compliance 100 per cent, as laid down by all these resolutions, he would have had to have a personality transplant, a soul transplant; he would not have been Saddam Hussein'. Blair and 'the realists in the British Government realised pretty early on that this was the way it would be.'

Tony Blair had three aims at Crawford: first, as we have seen, to emphasise weapons of mass destruction rather than regime change; second, to stress that all options were open; and, third, to persuade the Americans of the benefits of working with allies. The British desire to avoid talking explicitly about regime change opened up differences with more candid, and less constrained, American officials throughout the year. The emphasis on all options being open was partly to secure a step-by-step approach to decision-making, and partly to reassure opinion at home. Blair ended the press conference by saying that 'after 11 September, this President showed that he proceeds in a calm and a measured and a sensible, but a firm, way. Now, that is precisely what we need in this situation, too.' That was not just a compliment to his host, but also a message to Labour MPs: 'Don't worry, we're not going to rush into an invasion of Iraq.'

That was reinforced by his attempt to persuade the Bush team to seek international support. In a speech the following day, 7 April, at the Bush Presidential Library, Blair said: 'The international coalition matters. Where it operates, the unintended consequences of action are limited, the diplomatic parameters better fixed. The US and EU together is a precondition of such alliances. But it needs hard work, dialogue and some mutual understanding.' Yet, as often over the following year, Blair and the British took an over-optimistic view of Europe and America coming to a common approach on Iraq. Blair sometimes talked as if merely making the assertion, self-evident to him, that Europe and America needed each other would somehow ensure that both sides of the Atlantic worked smoothly together. Sir

Christopher Meyer later recalled (2003) that Crawford was the start of a process which went on for a few months:

> *We, the British, said to the Americans, 'If you are going to bring Saddam Hussein into compliance with all those resolutions of which he remains in violation, you could do this on your own. You have the military strength to go into Iraq and do it. But our advice to you is, even a great super-power like the United States needs to do this with partners and allies. And the best way of trying to get a good coalition together is to exhaust the processes which the UN offers.'*

The Crawford meeting sowed the seeds for all the differences of emphasis that caused so much trouble for Tony Blair in the run-up to, and after, the Iraq war a year later. Blair publicly talked about weapons of mass destruction when he, and his advisers, knew that the Bush team's real concern was removing Saddam Hussein – a goal with which he sympathised, but which he could not publicly make his primary objective. Bush was obviously determined to press ahead. The only questions were how and when. Blair elevated these questions into 'all options are open'. This was true in the formal and legal sense, but no one present at Crawford had much doubt about what was likely to happen. Moreover, the American side had concluded that Blair would be with them at the end of the day. This was hardly surprising since the two leaders had discussed the various phases of action against Saddam, starting with building up diplomatic support before taking military action, and then ensuring that a successor regime could run the country. As Blair said in his speech at the Bush Presidential Library: 'Leaving Iraq to develop WMD, in flagrant breach of no less than nine separate UN Security Council resolutions, refusing still to allow weapons inspectors back to do their work properly, is not an option. The regime of Saddam is detestable.' Moreover, in relation to terrorism and weapons of mass destruction generally, Blair argued: 'If necessary the action should be military and again, if necessary and justified, it should involve regime change.' So it was easy for the Americans to assume Blair's support. At the news conference, Bush went out of his way to praise Blair as someone 'who does not need a focus group to convince him of the difference between right and wrong'. At this stage, the Bush team had little idea of the political constraints which Blair faced at home.

Blair faced two critical audiences in Britain. First, and most obvious, were those in the Labour Party who were increasingly worried about Bush's general policies – particularly following the 'axis of evil' speech – and who were strongly opposed to military action against Iraq. Serious trade disputes, over steel and farm subsidies, increased criticism of the Bush administration. At minimum, these MPs insisted upon specific approval by the UN for any new measures against Iraq. Blair faced a mixed reception from Labour MPs on his first appearance back in the Commons after his visit to Texas. They were concerned about the possibility of military action, and were less impressed by his assurances that nothing precipitate would be done.

Second, and less widely appreciated at the time, was the scepticism of many in the foreign policy and intelligence worlds. This group included two recent Conservative Foreign Secretaries, Lord Hurd of Westwell and Sir Malcolm Rifkind, and Sir Michael Quinlan, a former Permanent Secretary at the Ministry of Defence, as well as many serving officials. They accepted that Saddam's regime was evil and nasty, especially to the Iraqi people. But they believed that the containment policy since the Gulf War in 1991 had worked reasonably well in isolating Saddam. So he was not an urgent threat either to his neighbours, or to peace generally. Writing in August 2002, Sir Michael invoked the doctrine of just war: 'Attacking Iraq would be deeply questionable against several of its tests, such as just cause, proportionality and right authority.' He warned that an assault 'looks like an unnecessary and precarious gamble, unless there emerges new evidence against Mr Hussein altogether more compelling than any yet disclosed.'

Moreover, despite recurrent assertions on the American right, British intelligence insisted that there was no evidence linking Saddam's regime to the 11 September attacks. Indeed, in the British view, there were only 'rough linkages' between Baghdad and al-Qa'eda. Other states, such as Iran and Syria, had a worse record as sponsors of terrorism, while, in terms of weapons of mass destruction, North Korea's nuclear programme has a far greater, and more immediate, threat to global security. The strongly Arabist group in both the Foreign Office and the Secret Intelligence Service was also very worried about the destabilising impact on the region of an invasion of Iraq. On their view, action against Saddam was a lesser priority than an American shift towards greater involvement in the Israel–Palestine dispute.

The Prime Minister shared these concerns about the Israel–Palestine dispute, and, as noted earlier, had sometimes faced frosty receptions from both Washington and the Israeli Government for repeatedly raising the question. This was the only issue where Blair did not hide his frustrations with Washington. He said privately that he would have tackled it differently, but acknowledged that America was in the lead. So it was self-defeating to stake out a separate European position which both antagonised Israel and was ignored by the US. Yet Blair took every opportunity to argue the importance of addressing the Palestinian problem, as well as satisfying Israel's desire for security. This was desirable not only in itself but also to secure the acquiescence, if not support, of many Arab states for action against Saddam. Hence Blair was effusive in his praise for Bush's speech on 4 April, just before his Crawford visit, which pointed to more active US involvement after an outbreak of suicide bombings and bloody retaliatory raids. Blair offered British help in sending in observers to monitor any ceasefire. Britain and the US differed, however, in their attitude to Yasser Arafat. Both regarded Arafat as weak and slippery, and criticised his failure to deal with the terrorist groups behind the suicide bombings against Israel. But Blair argued that Arafat, as the elected leader, could not be ignored, and that the priority was to find, and work with, those in the Palestinian Authority who were prepared to search for ways forward. In the short-term, this Bush initiative, and Colin Powell's subsequent trip to the region, achieved little, not least because the administration was not fully committed in the face of strong criticism from American conservatives and supporters of Israel. Blair later refused to back Bush's demands for Arafat to be replaced by a new leadership 'not compromised by terror'.

Blair followed a twin-track approach over the summer of 2002. First, he sought to convince the Bush administration of the need to work through the UN. Sir David Manning, Blair's foreign affairs adviser, went on an unannounced trip to Washington in July and told Condoleezza Rice, and others in the administration, that the Prime Minister had to have a UN resolution if he was to retain political support at home. This point was reinforced in another series of personal messages by Blair to Bush. A senior American diplomat talks, admiringly, about how 'Blair knew how far he could go in pursuing policy. It was less Blair calling up Bush with a specific agenda than an iterative process.' By his strong support for Bush, particularly after 9/11, Blair also won some freedom of manoeuvre. So during the course of a strongly anti-Saddam speech, Blair might sometimes include a declaratory policy, ahead of Washington's thinking, about, say, the Middle East peace process or the importance of the United Nations. According to this American observer, 'There were sometimes protests and teeth grinding at the medium-level. But since the big message was fine for Washington, the reaction of Bush, Rice and Powell was to talk warmly of "Our guy Tony". That mattered more than x or y point on page 5 of a speech.'

The Blair–Bush exchanges were matched by frequent conversations which Jack Straw had with Colin Powell and in the constant activity of the British Embassy in Washington. The British side found the inter-agency arguments that summer and autumn very frustrating. Cheney, Powell and Rumsfeld, and their main advisers, were all strong personalities and Condoleezza Rice, while close to Bush, was often unable to impose herself on their arguments. Manning and Meyer sometimes found that when they thought a point had been agreed and confirmed by Rice, nothing happened. It turned out that the matter had not been resolved and the argument continued between the Pentagon, the State Department and the Vice President's Office. Bush tended to float above these debates until a decision had to be made. And Powell's influence waxed and waned over this period.

Blair was well aware of the potential political risks of backing Bush but, characteristically, believed he could find a way through them if a UN resolution could be agreed. King Abdullah of Jordan embarrassed Blair at the beginning of August by saying the Prime Minister had 'tremendous concerns about how this would unravel'.

Second, Blair emphasised again and again the threat from Iraq's weapons of mass destruction, which, he said, must be addressed. In one of the many paradoxes of this story, Blair's concern had been shared for as long, and in some respects even longer, by Iain Duncan Smith, the leader of the Conservative Party. The latter's support was very important at Westminster during the following autumn and winter when Blair was struggling to cope with a deeply divided Labour Party.

At this time, there was talk of producing a dossier of intelligence about the threat, as had been done the previous autumn over bin Laden and al-Qa'eda's involvement in the 11 September attacks. But Blair told senior MPs (chairmen of Commons select committees on the Liaison Committee) on Tuesday 16 July that: 'The only reason we have not published some of this documentation [on weapons of mass destruction] is that you have got to choose your time for doing this, otherwise you send something rocketing up the agenda when it is not necessarily there.' At this session, Blair broadly endorsed the new doctrine on pre-emptive action: 'The one thing we have learnt post-11 September is that to take action in respect of a threat that is coming may be more sensible than to wait for the threat to materialise and then to take action.' But that only underlined the importance of making a convincing public case about the seriousness of the threat.

The decisions over both the UN and the British intelligence dossier reached their climax in early September. But, first, there was an unusually open argument, even by Washington standards, in the holiday month of August about the next steps. Even though Bush was thought by the British to be leaning towards going to the UN, no one was sure, and the battle to influence the President was waged fiercely. Policy drifted during the summer months. On one side were the State Department and some veteran officials from earlier administrations, and, on the other, the Vice President, the Pentagon and their allies. The first salvo came from the 'old and the bold', notably from Brent Scowcroft, National Security Adviser in Bush senior's administration. Scowcroft, who remained close to Bush senior, warned on 4 August that an attack on Iraq could turn the Middle East into a 'cauldron and thus destroy the war on terrorism.' Later in the month, both Henry Kissinger and James Baker, Secretary of State to Bush senior, intervened in the debate. While generally supporting tough action against Iraq, Kissinger warned about the broader implications of the doctrine of pre-emption. Baker said the US should go to the UN Security Council. He warned that the cost of occupying Iraq, 'politically, economically and in terms of casualties, could be great' and 'will be lessened if the President brings together an international coalition behind the effort'.

On 5 August, Colin Powell met Bush at the White House to make the case that action against Iraq should be via an international, rather than unilateral coalition. Powell raised British concerns since Straw had talked to him just before the White House meeting. On 14 August, with Bush on vacation in Texas, his key advisers met in Washington. Bob Woodward (2002, p. 335) says Powell talked about getting a coalition for action against Iraq to provide 'international cover at least. The Brits were with us, he noted, but their support was fragile in the absence of some international coalition or cover. They needed something.' The Blair and Straw messages had got through. The first opportunity that the President would have to raise the issue formally was his annual speech to the UN General Assembly in New York on 12 September. Cheney and Rumsfeld did not dissent from raising Iraq then, but argued that the speech ought to challenge the UN for not enforcing a decade of resolutions ordering Saddam to destroy his weapons of mass destruction.

Cheney raised the temperature in a speech on 26 August when he said, 'a return of the inspectors would provide no assurance whatsoever of his compliance with UN resolutions. On the contrary, there is a great danger that it would provide false comfort that Saddam was somehow "back in the box".' The next day, Rumsfeld seemed to cast doubt on the value of a broad coalition when he said: 'I don't know how many countries will participate in the event the President does decide the risks of not acting are greater than the risks of acting.' These speeches alarmed the Europeans and contributed to Gerhard Schröder's decision to take a strongly anti-war line in his party's campaign for re-election the next month. Powell was also worried. The American papers were full of stories of feuding at the top, especially as the Secretary of State had given the BBC an interview saying it was worth sending the inspectors back to see what they would find.

After Bush returned to Washington, he clarified the policy. He would seek UN support on Iraq and agreed that the weapons inspectors should return, despite his doubts about whether this would work.

Blair also returned from holiday towards the end of August. The conflicting reports from Washington had fuelled domestic opposition and the Government message had been confused. Blair quickly sought to get a grip, notably at a news conference, ahead of his visit to Washington. The British impact on President Bush's decision to go to the UN is, as always, not precisely measurable. Blair's own advisers believe that, on this issue above all others during the Bush presidency, the Prime Minister was 'very influential'. The best evidence, from both sides of the Atlantic, is that the Prime Minister's desire, and political need, for a UN resolution helped reinforce the President's tilt in that direction – especially when it coincided with what Colin Powell was saying. The 'deal', insofar as there was a formal deal, was reached during three and a half hours of talks at Camp David on 7 September when Blair made a day trip to the US. The two leaders' public comments highlighted the threat from Saddam not just, in Bush's words, to 'the neighbourhood in which he lives, or the region, but also the United States and Britain'. After the talks, Blair said they had 'a shared strategy on how we believe this should go forward. People should have confidence that we will approach this issue in a sensible and measured way. We will do it on the basis of the broadest possible international support.'

The 'deal' was essentially that the President would go to the UN Security Council to seek a further resolution to give Saddam one last chance to comply. In return, the Prime Minister would not allow America to go it alone and would back US-led military action if

Saddam Hussein failed to co-operate with the UN weapons inspectors. This implied that if Saddam surprised everyone, and did comply, then the Americans would not go in and bring about regime change. There were potential political difficulties for both sides: for Blair, with many Labour MPs opposed to war if Saddam did not co-operate; and, for Bush with the Washington hawks eager for regime change if Saddam did surprise everyone by dismantling Iraq's weapons of mass destruction. But the main risks were all on Blair's side. Bush thought Saddam would never do the right thing and there would be war. Moreover, the British feared that America might also still go ahead with ousting Saddam regardless. For the Americans, Camp David was a clear commitment of support. As Sir Christopher Meyer comments: 'Afterwards, Bush had little doubt that Tony Blair would be with him, however the cards fell.' For Blair, it was not yet a decision to go to war. Military action was still not certain. He still believed that the UN inspectors might find, and dismantle, Saddam's WMD programme. A few days later, Blair set out the terms of the 'deal' in telling sceptical and often hostile delegates at the annual conference of the TUC on 10 September: 'Let it be clear that he must be disarmed. Let it be clear that there can be no more conditions, no more games, no more prevaricating, no more undermining of the UN's authority. And let it also be clear that, should the will of the UN be ignored, action will follow.' As Meyer later noted in a television interview (2003), Blair was

> *pretty determined to go all the way with President Bush;*
> *not because he's sort of hanging on to this relationship for*
> *dear life, but because he truly believed, as he does today,*
> *that Iraq and Saddam Hussein were an offense to the*

> *integrity of the UN and the Security Council on which so*
> *much else depends. It was in that framework that he made*
> *that commitment to the President.*

Even after Camp David, no one was sure that President Bush would definitely commit to the UN route in the face of strong counter-arguments from Cheney and Rumsfeld. It was still unclear whether Bush would formally request a new UN resolution, as opposed merely to making a declaration about Iraq's breach of existing UN resolutions. Cheney feared becoming embroiled in the UN process. But the Pentagon was a long way off being ready for any military action against Iraq. The US did not have enough cruise missiles (a large number had been fired in the Afghanistan campaign) and there were not nearly enough troops on the ground. So for all their scepticism about the UN, Cheney and Rumsfeld accepted that military action could not be taken for several months. By chance, the key sentence was left out of the draft on the autocue when Bush addressed the UN General Assembly in New York on September. But the President ad-libbed and said: 'We will work with the UN Security Council for the necessary resolutions.' This sentence was greeted with relief around western capitals. The British Government was able to say to its critics 'I told you so, look Bush is no unilateralist.' The emphasis on the UN helped to limit the scale of a Labour backbench rebellion to fifty-six MPs at the end of an emergency Commons debate on Tuesday 24 September. This was large by historic standards but was dwarfed by the revolts of February and March 2003. Many Labour MPs then said they were only going along with the Government as long as it worked within the UN.

Going down the UN route also tied Blair – though not Bush – to stressing the threat from weapons of mass destruction. It was what a senior British official described as a 'scare them and prepare them' approach. Blair used every opportunity to stress that Iraq's possession of these weapons was a threat to Britain. To reinforce that argument, a dossier was prepared by the intelligence agencies through the Joint Intelligence Committee mechanism. This was published on the eve of the special Commons debate on 24 September. At the time, the main response was that no startlingly new evidence had been found, or, any rate, presented. There was no 'smoking gun'. The main firm evidence was about the past: about Saddam's appalling record in developing weapons of mass destruction, and about what had been found by the inspectors before they were forced out in 1998, notably the large unaccounted for stocks of chemicals. But the dossier was much vaguer in its Chapter 3 about developments since 1998. There were suspicions, suppositions and only partially substantiated assertions, reflecting reports about Saddam's attempts to acquire components and supplies which might be useful in weapons of mass destruction. The underlying theme was that Saddam's record has been very bad in this area and we know no reason to believe he has changed. These were reasonable conclusions, but they did not prove that Saddam was an urgent threat. However, after reviewing the Government's dossier, an assessment by the International Institute of Strategic Studies at the same time, and a report by the American Central Intelligence Agency the following month, the Foreign Affairs Committee of the Commons concluded in mid-December (Second Report, 2002–3, p. 29) that there was 'compelling evidence of Iraq's programmes to develop chemical, biological and nuclear capabilities, and the means to deliver them'. There was no dispute at this stage among the MPs on the committee about this definite conclusion.

The Government's 'September' dossier later became the subject of intense political controversy after the war when no weapons of mass destruction were found. Allegations were made in late May 2003 by Andrew Gilligan, a BBC journalist, that the Government, and in particular Alastair Campbell, the Downing Street Head of Strategy and Communications, had transformed the September dossier to make it 'sexier' by including a claim that Iraq could deploy weapons of mass destruction within forty-five minutes. Gilligan's claim was strongly denied by Campbell, producing a bitter confrontation between 10 Downing Street and the BBC, and a high-profile inquiry by the Foreign Affairs Committee of the Commons in June and July 2003. Jack Straw told the MPs: 'Let me make clear, nobody "sexed up" or exaggerated the September dossier, no one at all, and that includes Alastair Campbell.'

But the whole affair turned from brute politics into tragedy after the suicide on the night of 17–18 July 2003 of Dr David Kelly, a highly respected Government specialist in biological weapons. After the initial Gilligan–Campbell row, Dr Kelly came forward to tell his superiors in the Ministry of Defence that he had met Gilligan shortly before the latter's first BBC report. Kelly's name then became public, partly through the activities of Government press officers. He was questioned, at times toughly, by the Foreign Affairs Committee just over two days before his disappearance and death. The BBC then confirmed that Dr Kelly had been Gilligan's main source for his story. Questions were raised about the conduct of the Ministry of Defence and 10 Downing Street in helping to confirm

Dr Kelly's name to the press, as well as about meetings between Dr Kelly and BBC reporters.

Dr Kelly's death led to the establishment of an inquiry under Lord Hutton, a Law Lord. The hearings in August and September 2003 produced a mass of evidence about the inner workings of the Ministry of Defence, 10 Downing Street and the BBC. Frank e-mails between the participants were disclosed and the veil of secrecy was lifted on the heart of the Whitehall, and the BBC, during the public sessions when witnesses were questioned. Tony Blair himself appeared, as did Geoff Hoon and a long list of senior and middle-ranking civil servants, including Jonathan Powell and Alastair Campbell from 10 Downing Street. For the first time, the public heard, though only by an indirect audio link, from 'C', Sir Richard Dearlove, Director General of the Secret Intelligence Service. The inquiry questioned a whole heirarchy of BBC officials from the chairman of the Governor downwards; as well as journalists and the Kelly family itself. It was a compelling spectacle, from which no one at the time appeared to emerge much credit.

There was much speculation as 2004 started about whose heads would roll in Whitehall. In the event, after the publication of the report on Wednesday, 28 January, 2004, the only heads to roll were at the BBC, as Gavyn Davies, its Chairman, and Greg Dyke, its Director General, after Lord Hutton strongly criticised failings in its editorial procedures and over the role of the governors. By contrast, virtually all the charges against the Government were described as 'unfounded', apart from some mild criticisms of the Ministry of Defence for failing to inform Dr Kelly immediately his name was confirmed to the press. In particular, Lord Hutton concluded that the dossier was prepared in a proper way, and the controversial forty-five minute claim was included in good faith, despite ambiguities in statements at the time about the range of any missiles (the intelligence, in fact, applied to battlefield weapons). Tony Blair immediately claimed to have been vindicated by Lord Hutton's conclusions, and, in his statement to the Commons immediately after the publication of the Hutton report, he focussed on the attacks on the integrity of himself and the Government. 'The allegation that I or anyone else lied or deliberately misled the country by falsifying intelligence on WMD is itself the real lie'. However, the general media and political response was more critical. Lord Hutton was widely accused of being politically naive, particularly over the behaviour of Alastair Campbell in wanting the September dossier strengthened and in pursuing a relentless campaign against the BBC over its coverage of the Iraq war during the summer of 2003.

Yet much of the controversy over Hutton missed the point. The real question was not about the good faith of Mr Blair and his political advisers, or whether they overrode the doubts of the intelligence agencies. The reservations expressed by Dr Brian Jones of the Defence Intelligence Staff about the forty-five minute claim were largely about emphasis and the Joint Intelligence Committee was content with the final wording, as John Scarlett, its chairman, made clear in its evidence to the Hutton inquiry. The media focus on rumblings of dissent in the intelligence world obscured the much more significant factor: the extent of agreement among not only the British secret agencies but also among those in the USA, France, Germany and Israel about the dangers of Saddam's WMD programme. All these agencies believed in summer 2002 that Saddam did have WMD. Disagreement came later about the imminence of the threat, and about how to respond. The Intelligence and Security Committee, consisting mainly of senior MPs (though not a normal parliamentary committee), had access to all the intelligence assessments and concluded in its September 2003 report (p. 21):

> *Based on the intelligence and the Joint Intelligence Committee assessments that we have seen, we accept that there was convincing intelligence that Iraq had active chemical, biological and nuclear programmes and the capability to produce chemical and biological weapons. Iraq was also continuing to develop ballistic missiles. All these activities were prohibited under United Nations Security Council Resolutions.*

So the real puzzle, in the light of the failure to find WMD, was: were all the west's intelligence agencies wrong? Did a 'house' view develop within the intelligence agencies which ignored uncertainties about the strength of the evidence. That became the subject of official investigations in both the USA and in Britain (a broad-ranging inquiry into intelligence about WMD conducted by Lord Butler of Brockwell, the former Cabinet Secretary).

The debate over Hutton also largely ignored why the September intelligence dossier was published. The Government needed evidence about WMD to prove its case that Saddam was an urgent threat. The debate within the intelligence world during August and September 2002 about the publication of the dossier was less about presentation ('sexing up' the dossier) than about the dangers of revealing and compromising sources. Their unease was not so much about the content of the final dossier than about the unprecedented way it was prepared, which involved working closely with the Downing Street political and communications staff. The disclosures in the public hearings about the close, even 'matey', relations between John Scarlett and Alastair Campbell raised eyebrows amongst those used to more arms length relations between those preparing intelligence assessments and the political decision makers. But this was, of course, a unique exercise.

At the heart of the problem was a culture clash: between the worlds of John Le Carré's George Smiley and *The West Wing*, between the cautious words, caveats and nuances of the Joint Intelligence Committee and the megaphone communications of 'spin doctors' and the twenty-four-hour news cycle. The more public intelligence assessments are, the more that any qualifications and uncertainties disappear. In his conclusions, Lord Hutton considers: 'that the possibility cannot be completely ruled out that the desire of the Prime Minister to have a dossier which, whilst consistent with the available intelligence, was a strong as possible in relation to the threat posed by Saddam Hussein's WMD, may have subconsciously influenced Mr Scarlett and the other members of the JIC to make the wording of the dossier somewhat stronger than it would have been if it had been contained in a normal JIC assessment.' After saying that 'this possibility cannot be completely ruled out', Lord Hutton says he is satisfied that Mr Scarlett and the other members of JIC were 'concerned to ensure that the contents of the dossier were consistent with the intelligence available.' Even amongst those at the top of the intelligence world who claim that Mr Scarlett behaved properly in retaining control over the dossier, there was an acknowledgement of the term 'subconscious' and a sense of 'never again', a belief that intelligence assessment and the political world must be kept more visibly separate in future.

Tony Blair and the Government were at fault in not highlighting the uncertainties in any intelligence report. For instance, the Prime Minister's foreword to the 24 September assessment states that 'the documents disclose that his [Saddam's] military planning allows for some of the WMD to be ready within forty-five minutes of an order to use them.' There was no hint of qualification or doubt about the source. As the Foreign Affairs Committee said in its report (Ninth Report, 2002–3, p. 27), the forty-five-minutes claim 'did not warrant the prominence given to it in the dossier, because it was based on intelligence from a single, uncorroborated source'. The Intelligence and Security Committee criticised the Government in its September 2003 report (p. 31) for failing to clarify the nature of the forty-five-minutes claim. 'The omission of the context and assessment allowed speculation as to its exact meaning. This was unhelpful to an understanding of this issue'.

In the post-war debate in the US about the use of intelligence, the *Washington Post* revealed (Milbank, 2003) that the repetition of the forty-five-minutes claim by President Bush twice in the days immediately after the publication of the British dossier was made without consulting the Central Intelligence Agency. There was a similar controversy on both sides of the Atlantic over claims in the September dossier that Iraq had sought to buy uranium from Niger in Africa for enrichment, in order to develop nuclear weapons. It subsequently became clear that some documents appearing to back up this claim had been forged, though British ministers and officials continued to claim that there was good and unforged evidence that Iraq sought materials from Niger (Ninth Report, 2002–3, p. 23). There was also criticism in the US about the reliability of the claims of some of the Iraqi exile sources – for instance, about mobile laboratories involved in producing banned weapons – which had been trumpeted before the war by the Pentagon and its media allies, though had always been doubted by the CIA and British intelligence.

But the British Government was right to publish the overall intelligence assessment. If British troops were going to be sent to war in a pre-emptive action against a possible threat by Saddam, rather than in reaction to an aggressive action by him, then the case had to be strong and the reasons had to be set out as fully as possible. The central question is, rather, did the intelligence show such a threat? As discussed above in relation to the September dossier, the British Government's argument relied on Saddam's indisputably bad past record in developing chemical and biological weapons (and using chemical weapons against Iran and the Kurds) and on the danger of such weapons falling into the hands of terrorist groups.

The weaknesses in the dossier were recognised by Jonathan Powell, the Downing Street Chief of Staff, in an e-mail he sent to John Scarlett on 17 September 2002, a week before its publication. After saying that the 'dossier is good and convincing for those who are prepared to be convinced', Powell added:

> *The document does nothing to demonstrate a threat, let alone an imminent threat from Saddam. In other words it shows he has the means but does not demonstrate he has the motive to attack his neighbours, let alone the west. We*

will need to make it clear in launching the document that we do not claim that we have evidence that he is an imminent threat. The case we are making is that he has continued to develop WMD since 1998, and is in breach of UN resolutions. The international community has to enforce those restrictions if the UN is to be taken seriously.

The Blair case was always: here is an evil man with an evil record and we must prevent him and others with weapons of mass destruction from arming terrorists. As the Prime Minister argued on 15 October in the Commons after the Bali bombing had shown the continuing threat from al-Qa'eda: 'If, in times to come we allow these states to develop weapons of mass destruction – highly unstable, dictatorial, repressive regimes – and, if, at the same time, we have these terrorist groups operating, can we really be confident that at some point these two threats aren't actually going to be separate but will rather come together?' But that possibility was not the same as proving that Saddam was an imminent threat that justified pre-emptive military action. The damning charge was later made by Robin Cook in evidence to the Foreign Affairs Committee in June 2003 that 'there was a selection of evidence to support the conclusion, rather than a conclusion that arose from a full consideration of the evidence'. Yet such claims were politically necessary in Britain since, unlike the US, regime change was not a formal policy objective, even if, in practice, it was an informal one for Blair.

Going to the UN in order to secure the return of the inspectors was one way of establishing the existence, or otherwise, of such a threat. Cheney and Rumsfeld were sceptical about the UN route precisely because they thought the inspectors would be hoodwinked by Saddam and the whole process would be drawn out for a long time. At one stage that autumn, Lewis 'Scooter' Libby, Cheney's chief of staff, asked a senior British official why Blair was so worked up about the UN since he 'is going to be with us anyway'. In response, the British diplomat explained the domestic political pressures on Blair. Opposition to the possibility of a war built up throughout the autumn. After Blair's cool reception at the TUC conference in mid-September, there was strong criticism of – and a big grass-roots vote against – the Blair–Bush line at the Labour Party conference at the end of the month. However, delegates were charmed by a characteristically eloquent performance from Bill Clinton urging support for tough action against Iraq. In a series of Commons exchanges after the end of the party conference season, Blair and Straw were reminded of the strength of feeling among Labour MPs against Bush personally, whom they accused of being both ignorant and dangerously impulsive. In vain did Blair and Straw try to convince MPs to ignore some of the bellicose language coming out of parts of Washington and to assure them that Bush's actions had been both measured and fully discussed with Britain. A UN resolution was vital for Blair.

The Prime Minister favoured going to the UN, not only for domestic and international reasons, but also because he thought that the inspectors would confirm the existence of Saddam's biological, chemical and nuclear programme. At best, the inspectors would force full disclosure and the dismantling of these programmes, thus avoiding war. At worst, the inspectors would be so obviously obstructed, as in 1997–8, as to provide a cast-iron justification for military action. Life was, as often, much less straightforward.

The negotiations over what turned out to be Resolution 1441 took much longer than expected, six weeks rather than two weeks. This was partly because of the conflicting objectives of members of the Security Council. Initially, there were intensive negotiations over drafting the resolution between Washington and London: between Bush and Blair, between Straw and Powell, and between Sir Jeremy Greenstock, the British Ambassador to the UN, and John Negroponte, his American opposite number. The Americans wanted a brief, blunt resolution saying that if Saddam failed to make a full declaration of his weapons of mass destruction, then that should be enough to go to war. The US proposed that the UN inspectors should be accompanied by representatives of any of the Permanent Five members of the Security Council, as well as by armed security forces. This proposal for 'coercive inspections' made Hans Blix's 'few hairs stand up' (2004, p. 76–77). Britain dissented, both because such a resolution would never be approved and because the wording had to allow for what the inspectors might find in Baghdad. Awkwardly for Blair and Straw, a very tough American draft surfaced in the *New York Times* in the middle of the Labour Party conference. As Patrick Wintour and Martin Kettle report in their account of the negotiations (2003): 'Mr Blair and Mr Straw found themselves forced to spend far too much time in a small overheated secure room in the Imperial Hotel in Blackpool, discussing the wording with the British team at the UN, the Foreign Office and Washington.'

That pattern of intensive telephone diplomacy by conference calls between the US, Britain, France, Russia and China – the five permanent members of the Security Council with veto powers – continued for more than a month. Straw – working closely with Sir

Jeremy Greenstock at the UN – was at his best in such detailed, painstaking negotiations. He happily dealt with the subtleties of fine textual points in clauses and sub-clauses. This did not just involve negotiating between the five. At each stage, there were lengthy discussions within the Bush administration, notably between Powell and Cheney and Rumsfeld, before a fresh US line appeared. For Blair and Straw, what mattered was having an agreed resolution. Russia and France did not want to give the US and Britain a blank cheque. Even before Bush's UN speech, in an interview with the *New York Times* on 8 September, President Chirac had called for two resolutions: a first one to authorise the return of the weapons inspectors and to demand full compliance from the Iraqi government; and, if necessary, a second one specifically to authorise military action. In marked contrast to its co-operative stance over Afghanistan a year earlier, Russia was also initially cool even to a first UN resolution. During a visit to Moscow by Tony Blair in mid-October, President Putin dismissed the British intelligence dossier as 'propagandist'. He added: 'Russia does not have any trustworthy data which would support the existence of nuclear weapons or any other weapons of mass destruction in Iraq.'

The lengthy negotiations revolved around issues of what actions, or failures to act, by Iraq would trigger drastic responses – the so-called automaticity question. Dominique de Villepin, the new French Foreign Minister, was very active in negotiations. Jack Straw set out the issues in evidence to the Foreign Affairs Committee on 28 October 2002:

> *On the one hand, there are those, France and Russia particularly, who are concerned with the Security Council having*

> *in one resolution laid down the terms of the weapons inspec-*
> *tions and what would amount to a failure by Iraq. They are*
> *concerned that the resolution might be used to justify*
> *military action in circumstances where military action,*
> *although in practice justified, is taken. On the other side,*
> *there are the US and the UK with, if you like, the opposite*
> *concern, which is that we could end up with a situation*
> *where the future integrity of the whole of the international*
> *system of law is at stake: military action is necessary and*
> *palpably obvious and yet one or other members of the*
> *Security Council decides to veto it. It is how you square this*
> *circle which has been the matter in discussion.*

Both concerns turned out to be justified. As often in the past, Saddam attempted to divide the Security Council by reversing his previous policy and saying that UN inspectors could return to Iraq after all. This tactic did not affect the momentum towards agreement. In the end, no one wanted to be seen to block a further resolution. Russia and France accepted that it was better to have a resolution in view of the all-too-credible threat by Cheney and Rumsfeld to go ahead with military action against Iraq on a unilateral basis.

However, the celebrations by foreign ministers over the unanimous vote on 8 November by all fifteen members of the Security Council to back Resolution 1441 turned out to be premature. The resolution sounded strong, in calling for tough inspections and full Iraqi compliance and co-operation. There were deadlines for Iraq to supply full details of its weapons of mass destruction programme and to account for earlier stocks of chemicals and the like identified by the inspectors before they were forced out in 1998. Iraq was threatened with 'serious consequences' if it failed to comply, but only after further Security Council consultations.

The wording was ambiguous, intentionally so, since that was the only way that agreement could be reached. France, Russia and other countries did not believe that the resolution implied an automatic trigger for war. They argued that there would not only have to be further Security Council discussions on the inspectors' reports but also a further vote before going to war. The Americans accepted only that the Security Council would be consulted, but there did not have to be another vote before military action. The British sought refuge in the ambiguity: a further resolution would be desirable, but not essential, in these circumstances. The unanimous vote masked disagreement about what the resolution meant. Jack Straw praised President Bush for having worked through the UN: 'They have the military power to have gone down the unilateralist route and there is nothing the international community could have done about that. They made a choice to stick with the multilateralist UN route and we should applaud them for that.' But this did not mean that the US would continue to stick to the multilateralist route.

Even on 8 November, Jack Straw emphasised that the US and Britain reserved the right to use force even if a further UN resolution could not be agreed, as happened over Kosovo in 1999, in the face of the threat of a Russian veto. However, faced with pressure from Labour MPs, on 25 November, Straw hardened his preference for a second resolution which, he hoped, Britain might propose. This was linked to a promise of specific Commons endorsement of any military action, except when the security of British forces required an element of surprise. The Foreign Secretary – who was always particularly sensitive to the views of MPs – also distanced Britain from the zero tolerance view of some American hawks who wanted to treat any breach of Resolution 1441 as enough to justify war. A 'material breach' of the resolution must mean 'something significant: some behaviour or pattern of behaviour that is serious'.

The Security Council vote on 8 November was the deceptive high point of international unity. The relief of the British side at a successful exercise in diplomacy created over-optimistic hopes that perhaps, just perhaps, war could be avoided. In retrospect, Sir Jeremy Greenstock commented later (quoted in the BBC book on the war, 2003, p. 57): 'We sat on our laurels longer than we should have. With hindsight, we should have started negotiating straight after the first resolution in November. Instead, we sat back and thought how clever we'd been.' The fault lines soon emerged.

9   Old Europe and New Europe

I don't want him in the White House . . .

Condoleezza Rice, Bush's National Security Adviser, referring
to Joschka Fischer, the German Foreign Minister, during his
visit to Washington, late October 2002

*You're thinking of Europe as Germany and France. I don't.
That's old Europe. If you look at the entire NATO Europe
today, the centre of gravity is shifting to the east. Germany has
been a problem, and France has been a problem. But you look
at vast numbers of other countries in Europe. They're not with
France and Germany on this, they're with the United States.*

Donald Rumsfeld speaking at the Pentagon,
Wednesday 22 January 2003

*Now that I've lived through February and March 2003,
I understand how Europe slid to war in August 1914.
Events resembled a Greek tragedy, in which leaders follow
their passions and beliefs, rather than their interests, to the
point of self-destruction.*

French official involved in decision-making on Iraq, April
2003, quoted in Charles Grant's *Transatlantic Rift*, 2003

Tony Blair's transatlantic bridge collapsed in early 2003. The strains
had been growing steadily over the previous few years, and worsened

after President Bush's 'axis of evil' speech of January 2002. But a period of extraordinarily inept diplomacy by all the main countries fuelled a series of rows, confrontations and misunderstandings during the first eleven weeks of 2003 that created open fissures. As one international diplomat later commented: 'Everyone without exception did badly. Everybody under-performed.' There were disagreements not only between Europe and America but also within Europe, notably between Britain, on the one side, and France and Germany, on the other.

The British view, especially in 10 Downing Street and, to some extent in the Foreign Office, was, and remains, that the split could have been avoided, even as late as the end of February, *if*. . . and there is a long list of *if*s which made both sides more inflexible. Several incidents hardened attitudes: de Villepin's 'ambush' at the Security Council on 20 January; Rumsfeld's 'old Europe' remarks two days later; Fischer's confrontation with Rumsfeld at the Munich Wehrkunde defence conference in mid-February; the long running dispute over NATO support for Turkey, and Chirac's 'whatever the circumstances' veto threat on 10 March. However, war was probable from well before the start of 2003. The diplomatic errors on all sides just increased the mutual animosities when the fighting started. Nonetheless, Downing Street misread the attitudes and likely behaviour of President Chirac and Chancellor Schröder, and largely ignored the signs of a revival of the Franco–German alliance. This left Blair out on a limb in mid-March.

Afterwards, contingent explanations often look less plausible than a determinist one. It is much easier to put the messy events of history into a neat pattern. With hindsight, the train crash was always going to happen. Yet the divisions of spring 2003 cannot be explained just by a series of accidents, diplomatic errors or personal quirks. The causes can be traced to a deeper change in attitudes on both sides of the Atlantic, dating back to the end of the Cold War. These tensions were aggravated by the rows over the Balkans in the 1990s and, then, worsened further after the arrival of George W. Bush in January 2001. His administration's unilateralist/nationalist actions and rhetoric both puzzled and angered many Europeans. In retrospect, the international solidarity after 9/11 was deceptive, despite continuing co-operation between intelligence and police forces in fighting al-Qa'eda and other terrorist groups. As discussed in Chapter 7, Europe (or, rather, most of Europe) and America had increasingly distinct strategic outlooks and security concerns. These differences were highlighted, rather than blurred, by 9/11.

For many Americans, and particularly President Bush and his advisers, the attacks were a wake-up call. The terrorists were no longer at the gates. They were inside the previously safe walled garden and must now be hunted down not only inside but also outside the walls – wherever they and their supporters were. This was a life or death struggle. The European response was more world-weary. For many European politicians, the attacks were obviously an appalling tragedy but that did not mean 'everything has changed'. Britain, France, Spain, Italy and Germany have all experienced terrorism. They have lived with threats from terrorists and know there are no instant solutions. Tony Blair, as we have seen, was caught in the middle. He appreciated that American attitudes had changed. The challenge for the Europeans was to work with the US. Differences about how to handle Washington were at the root of the arguments within Europe. France and Russia were worried about American unilateralism and the enormous economic and military power of the US.

The end of the Cold War not only removed a common threat that bound Europeans and Americans together, but, less noticed, it weakened the previously close personal links between key policy-makers on either side of the Atlantic. Transatlantic co-operation had a lower priority. For instance, the 'quad' – involving key foreign policy officials from the United States, Britain, France and Germany – had allowed very secret discussions to be held around the main issues, thus anticipating and defusing arguments before they became serious. But during the Bush presidency, the Americans devoted less effort to working with the Europeans, while France and Germany never made a bilateral attempt to get alongside the White House and the US. The exception, of course, has been Britain, which has continued to make a priority of maintaining close relations with Washington. One Foreign Office diplomat recalls a rare meeting between the foreign policy advisers to the leaders of the 'quad' countries in the first half of 2002. While Condoleezza Rice, Bush's National Security Adviser, greeted Sir David Manning from Downing Street warmly as an old friend, her relations with her French and German opposite numbers appeared 'cold and formal'. After late autumn 2002, and particularly January 2003, contacts at any level between Washington, and Paris and Berlin were very limited.

Tony Blair talks to other European leaders frequently. However, throughout this period, Blair was always more concerned with his relations with Washington, than with either Paris or Berlin. This was reinforced by a change of organisation within 10 Downing Street.

After 2001, the Foreign Affairs Adviser's post was split because of the heavy workload. Sir Stephen Wall, in charge of the European Secretariat of the Cabinet Office, was also brought into 10 Downing Street to become the Prime Minister's European Adviser: in effect, his high-level personal representative around the EU. The Foreign Affairs Private Secretary, Sir David Manning from September 2001, in effect became a national security adviser on the American model. His main concern was non-European security issues, for which Sir David was well-qualified as a former Ambassador to both Israel and NATO. Yet, even though the two advisers got on well, this division of roles meant that European concerns were not always taken into account as much as they previously had been when the Prime Minister and Sir David were considering policy towards Iraq during 2002–3. During the critical period over the winter of 2002–3, Sir David never once spoke to Chancellor Schröder's chief foreign policy adviser.

Personal factors also unquestionably played a part. Even before the public differences of early 2003, President Bush was unimpressed by President Chirac, whom, he felt, did not have a clear view of what he wanted to do after the French elections. There was no rapport. The French elections made Chirac more self-confident. In the past, he had been inhibited, both as Prime Minister and as President by 'co-habitation'. But the squashing of Lionel Jospin in the first round of the French presidential elections and of the Socialists in the subsequent parliamentary elections freed him. The centre-right controlled both the Élysée and the National Assembly. Chirac was unchallenged, and determined to assert himself on the world stage. Dominique de Villepin, Foreign Minister after the elections, was on Chirac's wavelength, having previously been his chief of staff in the Élysée Palace.

Moreover, Bush was infuriated by the crude anti-American language and the attacks on him personally during the German election campaign of September 2002. This was a tactic of desperation by Gerhard Schröder as his SPD was well behind in the polls as the holidays ended. Moreover, the German Government had become increasingly worried by the belligerent language of Dick Cheney and Donald Rumsfeld. The best way to rally the SPD's core supporters was to play to the strongly anti-American (in part, anti-Bush) and anti-war sentiments in the German public. Schröder talked of action against Iraq as a 'military adventure'. This put Blair on the spot since he had promised to back Schröder in the election. After SPD attacks on the US, senior party officials spoke anxiously to Blair's advisers, hoping that a promised visit to an election rally would not be cancelled. It was not. Blair honoured his commitment. His hope was that the anti-American line was merely a regrettable election tactic; and that, afterwards, Schröder would distance himself from his earlier statements. As often during this story, British hopes of harmony were disappointed. Blair agreed not to take the disagreements over Iraq to a special meeting of EU leaders since this would only emphasise differences with Schröder. France was still sitting on the fence at this stage, arguing for two UN resolutions rather than one, but not opposed outright to military action. So Schröder's electoral needs undermined any chance of getting an agreed European position on Iraq in autumn 2002. After narrowly winning a second term on Sunday 22 September, Schröder felt he could not abandon his pre-election hostility to a strong line against Iraq.

Bush believed he had reached an understanding with Schröder over Iraq after talks in Berlin in May. Bush now felt let down, as well as insulted. Bush puts a strong emphasis on personal relations and loyalty – hence, his close personal relationship with Blair. Like Barbara Bush, his mother, the President is unforgiving about personal slights. After the German elections, Bush was in no mood to forgive or to forget. Schröder's post-election attempts to mend fences with Washington – for instance, by getting rid of the minister who compared Bush with Hitler – were brushed aside. Hence, also, the dismissive attitude of Rice at a senior staff meeting to any suggestion of a visit to the White House by Joschka Fischer (Riddell, 2002): 'I don't want him in the White House.' Instead, the German Foreign Minister was allowed a brief meeting with Colin Powell at the State Department, well away from the President. Other senior members of the administration – notably, and typically, Rumsfeld – also took a cool, and at times, hostile attitude to members of the Schröder Government in the weeks after the German election. There was virtually no direct contact between Bush and Schröder over the following critical months.

By contrast, Blair had dinner with Schröder in 10 Downing Street on the night after the German elections in an effort both to maintain cordial personal relations and in a largely unsuccessful attempt to repair the transatlantic bridge. What happened instead was something as worrying for British foreign policy: a revival of Franco–German co-operation. This had been largely in abeyance over the previous few years because of the coolness between Chirac and Schröder. Blair's long-term aim had been to form a close alliance between Britain and Germany and to detach Schröder from Chirac. These hopes were dashed. The reverse happened. France and Germany surprised Britain by producing joint proposals for the future financing of the Common Agricultural Policy at an EU summit in Brussels in late October. Blair had been out-manoeuvred by Chirac and Schröder. Chirac and Blair clashed angrily, and publicly, after the British had challenged French comments over reform of the CAP, and argued that the matter had not been settled. Chirac complained that he had never been spoken to in this way before. This led to the postponement of a regular Anglo–French summit until the New Year, and reinforced Chirac's natural Gaullist antipathy to the Anglo-Americans. The new Franco–German amity was underpinned by a grand celebration at Versailles on 22 January when members of the Bundestag and the National Assembly met to commemorate the fortieth anniversary of the Élysée treaty signed by de Gaulle and Adenaeur. This had immediately followed the French President's veto of Macmillan's application to join the European Community, largely because of Britain's continuing close ties to America, as discussed in Chapter 2. Little seems to have changed since 1963.

The cool relations between Bush and Chirac and the open hostility in Washington towards Schröder after the German election campaign reflected a more general disillusionment with Europe at senior levels of the administration. The exceptions were Blair and José María Aznar of Spain. These doubts were expressed not just by Pentagon neo-conservatives but by mainstream officials, many with long experience of Europe. During a visit to Washington in October 2002 (Riddell, 2002), an internationally minded member of the Bush Cabinet told me that he was annoyed by European 'smugness', 'intellectual arrogance', 'snobbishness', 'weak leadership' and 'vacillation' – as well as irritation at being patronised as ignorant and blinkered.

These tensions and differences of personality and attitude provided a fractious background to the start of 2003. The passage of UN Resolution 1441 on 8 November 2002 had been followed by the return of the inspectors under Dr Hans Blix on 27 November and the production of a lengthy declaration by Iraq on 8 December about its weapons of mass destruction. The ambiguities in Resolution 1441 immediately became apparent. The Americans and the British declared that the Iraqi Government's 12,000-page statement was full of gaps and evasions, so Iraq could already be said to be in 'material breach' of the resolution. This reinforced the case for early military action in the eyes of Washington. The Bush team concluded that Saddam was not interested in co-operation and a diplomatic solution, so war was now virtually certain. Blair also recognised then that military action would be very hard to avoid. By contrast, France and Russia saw the declaration as justifying the return of the inspectors. But, reflecting the 8 November compromise, there was no timetable for the inspectors or for the Security Council to take a decision on Iraqi compliance. Dr Blix himself talked of setting 'tasks' for Iraq to carry out by late March. This was far too late for Washington and Dr Blix agreed to make an interim report on 27 January.

Jack Straw said at the beginning of January that the odds were now 60–40 against war, compared with 60–40 in favour before Christmas. This reflected the British political need to show that all options were open, even though many in Blair's inner circle now thought that war was inevitable. Straw himself, like Powell in Washington, was still trying to avoid war. The British still wanted to play for time, to see what the UN inspectors produced, not least to ensure that any war was seen as a last resort caused by Saddam's intransigence. Straw got on well with the suave de Villepin after their lengthy negotiations over Resolution 1441, and tried to persuade the French that Britain was not irrevocably committed to go to war if Saddam complied. Yet British military preparations were stepped up during these early weeks of January when more forces and equipment were deployed to the region.

But the French soon undermined Blair's strategy. The key period for France was mid-January. But the signals were not picked up in London in part, the Foreign Office claims, because of contradictory statements by French officials as late as early February that Paris would not oppose military action. But President Chirac's views changed earlier. It is true that at the end of 2002 French officers had even talked to the American military about a possible contribution to an invasion force. However, in the second week of January, Maurice Gourdault-Montagne, Chirac's personal diplomatic adviser, went to Washington to find out the Bush administration's thinking. As reported in the *Financial Times* account of this period (2003), the Frenchman's cautionary words were brushed aside at a lunch with Condoleezza Rice:

> *His concerns were bluntly dismissed, 'They got the reply: boom, boom, boom,' a senior French diplomat recalls, 'Everything was impossible. The preparations for war must proceed. The message from Condi Rice was absolutely clear. The US had decided that military action was necessary to resolve the Iraq crisis and the only thing that could stop it was the fall, or departure of Saddam Hussein.*

Chirac and de Villepin then decided to oppose military action and to take the international lead in challenging the American and British approach, which they believed would lead to war within weeks. A weakened Schröder nestled up to Chirac. This not only reflected strong views in Germany but also the Chancellor's neglect by Bush. Germany had just taken over the rotating chairmanship of the Security Council (though without a veto), while any French threat to use its veto would be watched closely by Russia and China. The French tactics immediately became clear at a specially arranged session of foreign ministers at the Security Council on 20 January to discuss global terrorism. The Americans and the British had been reluctant to attend. Powell wanted to fulfil other engagements on Martin Luther King Day, a special day for black Americans. But he was persuaded by de Villepin to come. So both Colin Powell and Jack Straw were startled when de Villepin described military action as a 'dead end' and argued that the return of the UN inspectors meant that Baghdad's weapons programmes were 'largely blocked or even frozen. Since we can disarm Iraq through peaceful means, we should not take the risk to endanger the lives of innocent civilians or soldiers, to jeopardise the stability of the region. We should not take the risk to fuel terrorism.' Today, he said, 'nothing justifies considering military action', and, talking of an American 'adventure', he hinted that France would use its veto to block a further resolution authorising military action: 'France is a permanent member of the Security Council. It will shoulder all of its responsibilities faithful to all the principles it has.'

If de Villepin was trying to restrain America, he failed spectacularly. His words infuriated Powell, the main voice of caution in the Bush administration. This was the moment when divisions between America and France became open and, it turned out, irreconcilable.

Sir Christopher Meyer (2003) later recalls seeing 'Colin Powell pretty soon after the meeting on 20 January with his deputy, Rich Armitage. Their remarks were bordering on the unprintable. They felt they had been ambushed. They felt that they'd been called to New York on false pretenses, and had been put in an extremely difficult and invidious position.' Powell had an additional problem: 'There were always those in the administration who were questioning the usefulness of continuing this process of negotiation inside the Security Council. As the arch-apostle of trying to take the process as far as possible, he had the ground cut from under him.' Afterwards, Powell became a strong supporter of tough, early action against Saddam.

France and Germany reinforced their anti-war message on 22 January at the joint celebrations of the fortieth anniversary of the Élysée Treaty. At that stage, Chirac did not go as far as Schröder in refusing to approve any type of military action against Iraq. The French President then stressed that any use of force must be approved by the UN Security Council.

The Pentagon hawks seized their chance. When asked about European opposition on 22 January, Donald Rumsfeld sought to divide Europe. Like many famous phrases, his exact words were not the same as the headlines, or as entered folk and media memory. He did not talk about 'old versus new Europe.' But that was the thrust of his remarks:

> *You're thinking of Europe as Germany and France. I don't.*
> *That's old Europe. If you look to the east, Germany has*
> *been a problem, and France has been a problem. But you*
> *look at the vast numbers of other countries in Europe.*

> *They're not with France and Germany on this, they're with
> the United States.*

Of course, Europe was divided. If you did a head count of those
current, and new, members of the EU, a majority of the twenty-five
were with Washington in principle, even if few were vocal supporters,
and only Britain and Poland supplied forces. To dismiss France and
Germany in this way was inflammatory. Europe, and especially the
EU, was no longer a French – and to a lesser extent German –
dominated club as it had been for most of the post-1945 era. The
range of interests and views was more diverse. But any definition of
Europe had to have France and Germany at its core. These eastern
and central European countries, as well as Britain, Italy and Spain
wanted to have cordial relations with France and Germany.

But this was not just insensitive or opportunistic rhetoric by
Rumsfeld, compounded a few days later when he linked Germany
with Cuba and Libya as countries which 'won't help in any
respect'. His comments reflected a deliberate shift of policy in
Washington, which began after Kosovo and first became apparent
when the Pentagon largely spurned the offers of military help by
NATO and several European countries after 9/11. Rumsfeld and
his allies preferred to work not through formal alliances such as the
EU, and even NATO, which might restrict America's freedom of
manoeuvre, but through 'coalitions of the willing'. This meant
American dominated and led coalitions, as in both Afghanistan
and Iraq. A divided Europe was not to be regretted, as in the past,
but was seen as an advantage to Washington in recruiting
supportive allies.

Rumsfeld's remarks infuriated European leaders just as much as de Villepin's 'ambush' had angered the Bush administration. Criticism came from the right as well as the left. Bernd Posselt, European spokesman of the Christian Social Union, the Bavarian partners of the CDU, accused Rumsfeld of 'neo-colonialism' and said: 'The US has to learn that the EU is a partner and not a protectorate.' The dispute was fuelled by an argument within NATO over an American request to provide Turkey with AWACS early-warning aircraft and missiles to defend it in case of war. But this was blocked for several weeks by France, Germany, Belgium and Luxembourg on the grounds that agreement would be seen as an endorsement of preparation for war. Eventually, in mid-February, a deal was worked out on the Defence Planning Committee of NATO, of which France was not a member. This argument further soured relations within Europe, and increased the American preference for working on an *ad hoc* basis with coalitions of the willing, rather than through NATO.

Back in London, the UN strategy appeared to be unravelling. Not only was Europe divided, but the verdict from Dr Blix was inconclusive. His report to the Security Council did not give the Americans and the British the clear-cut verdict they wanted; and, consequently, was mainly of help to the opponents of military action. Dr Blix's report on 27 January merely deferred decisions. Iraq had not produced an adequate explanation of what had happened to its previous stocks of chemical and biological weapons, but that did not necessarily mean that they still existed. But the political pressures were increasing on Blair at home, as opinion polls showed the importance of securing a further UN resolution if he was to retain public and political support. This led to ever stronger warnings by Blair about the threat from Saddam.

So Blair was very much a supplicant when he travelled to Washington on 31 January. Shifted from Camp David to the White House because of bad weather, the meeting was not easy, and its public impact was unnecessarily worsened by an impression of disagreement at the concluding news conference. Blair wanted a commitment both to a further UN resolution and to a further push on the Middle East peace process (underlined by the British decision to go ahead by phone with a conference on the future of the Palestinian Authority in mid-January even though Israeli forces prevented Palestinian representatives from coming to London). Bush gradually became more willing than some of the British side expected to promise action on the Israel–Palestine dispute. But he continued to delay publishing the 'road map' on steps towards a settlement, which, he insisted, come only could after the Iraq war. The UN was the real problem. Sir Christopher Meyer says the Americans were getting impatient. He describes attitudes before the Camp David meeting:

> *The Americans wanted to attack in the second half of February. Blair wanted the end of March. Bush was not ready to compromise. Blair wanted Bush's backing for the second resolution and to find more time before an attack. But I warned that Bush was convinced of neither. The Prime Minister would have to argue for a second resolution, and for time.*

As so often, there was a vigorous debate for and against a further resolution within the administration and Bush had not made up his mind at this stage. Meyer said in a later television interview (2003): 'Blair made it perfectly clear that for all those who wished to be with the US in disarming Saddam Hussein – Britain, Turkey, Australia, Spain, Italy – there were others that were all saying that, more for political than for any legal reason, they needed to make a best effort attempt to get a second resolution.' But the Bush team was reluctant, and only agreed to help Blair because of his domestic political problems. Moreover, the American timetable was anyway slipping because the troops would not be ready to attack for at least another month. Then came the misunderstanding which gave the impression of more disagreement than there had been. As the two leaders and their advisers were standing around after the meeting, Bush referred to his notes for the press conference about seeking a second UN resolution. Karl Rove, his political strategist, intervened, 'You've already said that'; to which Ari Fleischer, his spokesman replied, 'No, you have never said it.' Blair and the British team said nothing. The result was an edgy press conference. Bush spoke in equivocal terms: 'Should the UN decide to a pass a second resolution, it would be welcome if it is yet another signal that we're intent upon disarming Saddam Hussein.' This did not exactly sound like a ringing endorsement.

Meyer took up the story in a later interview (2003):

> *It all looks terrific, in they go. And frankly, they make a bog of it; it just doesn't come out right. The President gets irritated with the first question he takes, because it's a double question or a triple question, which he doesn't like. The Prime Minister, I think, was over-anxious to make the case against Saddam from first principle. So the*

> *question took too long to answer. They didn't look particularly comfortable behind the lecterns, and I thought, 'Oh, God, this is not good.' Then we went up to supper in the private quarters. We were sitting around the table and, as prime ministers and presidents do, they look to their courtiers and say, 'Well, how did we do?' . . . There was a deathly hush around the table. Then I think it was, as you might imagine, Alastair Campbell who said, 'Well, I'm afraid that the journalists will go away from that press conference thinking the two of you have had a row.' And they both looked stunned, because they hadn't had a row.*

That episode was symptomatic of a deteriorating situation for Blair. But he still sought to paper over the cracks: at the postponed Anglo-French summit in Le Touquet on 4 February, the British and French leaders agreed proposals to strengthen defence co-operation in Europe, while avoiding mention of Iraq. A Foreign Office minister insists that senior French officials were still assuring him at Le Touquet that they would not oppose the war. This may have partly reflected divisions between Chirac and more cautious foreign affairs advisers. However, Charles Grant records (2003, p. 117) making a trip to Paris at the end of January and being told by senior figures in the French administration that 'Chirac was determined not to allow the passage of any UN resolution that gave diplomatic cover for war in Iraq.' But on his return to London, Whitehall officials still told him of their hopes that France – and Russia also – would not veto any resolution. 'The Government as a whole continued to believe for at least another month that the French would become more flexible. Several Foreign

Office diplomats blame 10 Downing Street for the excessive optimism, yet some overseas embassies shared that rosy view.'

Blair was also under increasing domestic pressure. A Populus poll for *The Times*, undertaken over the weekend of 7–9 February, showed that, while a majority of people regarded Saddam as a threat to Britain, nearly four-fifths believed that America had been determined to go to war all along regardless of the UN. Three-fifths said Britain should join military action against Iraq only if such action was backed by the UN.

These political pressures also led to serious errors. In its eagerness to prove the case against Saddam, Downing Street issued at the beginning of February what became known as the 'dodgy dossier'. This began as a proposal of the Iraq Communications Group – one of the attempts to improve domestic, as well as international, co-ordination of information during conflicts following the shortcomings in NATO's propaganda campaign in the Kosovo war of spring 1999. This group, chaired by Alastair Campbell, sought in his words to the Foreign Affairs Committee (Ninth Report, 2002–3, p. 35), 'to get our media to cover this issue of the extent to which Saddam Hussein was developing his programme of concealment and intimidation of the UN inspectors'. The paper relied on Foreign Office, Ministry of Defence and intelligence material. But, unfortunately, the procedures were sloppy and some other information was included, unattributably, from an article in the *Middle East Review of International Affairs*, by Ibrahim al-Marashi, an American citizen of Iraqi origin, who examined captured Iraqi state documents. His article appeared in the published British dossier, with neither attribution nor his consent, along with material from British intelligence agencies. The material was not cleared for use by the Joint Intelligence Committee but, apart from a confusion in presentation, there is no dispute about its accuracy. The Prime Minister, unwittingly, misrepresented the document's status to MPs by saying it was 'further intelligence'. The revelation of the error a few days later meant, in the words of the Foreign Affairs Committee (p. 42), that the dossier was 'almost wholly counter-productive. By producing such a document the Government undermined the credibility of its case for war'. Jack Straw did not disguise his anger, either in February or, later, during the Foreign Affairs Committee inquiry, at what he called 'a complete Horlicks'. This episode highlighted the importance of presentation for the Blair Government, and the power at the time of Alastair Campbell, as the Iraq Communications Group had a degree of autonomy and lack of proper accountability.

At the UN, Colin Powell engaged in a parallel exercise to persuade world opinion about Saddam's programme of weapons of mass destruction. Powell's presentation to the Security Council of the intelligence case against Saddam was professionally done with photos and tapes of bugged phone calls between Iraqi commanders. But there was a lot of surmise and inference. It was convincing for those willing to be convinced, but failed to include any decisive new evidence to win over the unconvinced.

Transatlantic divisions worsened dramatically in this period. On 30 January, eight heads of government – of Britain, Denmark, Italy, Portugal and Spain among existing EU members, and of the Czech Republic, Hungary and Poland among new entrants – signed a widely published newspaper article backing the enforcement of Resolution 1441. This was reinforced a few days later when the leaders of ten other eastern European countries signed a similar pro-US letter. This initiative appeared to reinforce Rumsfeld's 'old and new' Europe charge and hardened opinion in France, thus making agreement on a further resolution even less likely.

These tensions produced a memorable public confrontation at the annual meeting of defence ministers and policymakers in Munich in mid-February. Joschka Fischer, the German Foreign Minister and former street demonstrator from the 1968 protest generation, clashed directly and publicly over the case for war with Rumsfeld, the epitome of the assertive American nationalist. Abandoning his speaking notes, Fischer shouted in English: 'My generation learned you must make a case, and excuse me, I am not convinced. That is my problem. I cannot go to the public and say, "these are the reasons" because I don't believe in them.' He looked directly at Rumsfeld, who was unrepentant in his speech by warning that those countries, such as France and Germany, which refused to back the US were guilty of undermining the UN. Not surprisingly, participants at the conference worried about the threat to the future of NATO, let alone the slim chances of healing the rift between the US and Germany.

Chirac then went over the top at a summit of EU leaders in Brussels on 17 February and attacked the central and eastern European countries who had signed the letters (most were among the ten new entrants to the EU in 2004) as having 'missed a good chance to remain silent'. These countries 'have been not very well brought up and are rather unaware of the dangers of lining up too quickly on the American position'. He also accused Bulgaria and Romania, both still on the waiting list for EU membership, of 'damaging their chances of joining'. This attack was counter-productive since it alienated these countries who had originally been expressing general solidarity for the US rather than (apart from Poland) offering specific or active support in any war. These eastern and central European countries became wary of linking themselves to France or Germany, and they were actively courted by Washington.

Some French and other policymakers concluded – in a mirror image of Rumsfeld's attempt to divide Europe – that an inner core of EU countries would have to form their own foreign policy as an offset to the US. Charles Grant (2003, p. 21) quotes Francois Heisbourg, a leading French foreign and defence analyst, as saying that the letters were 'proof that we can't have a European foreign and security policy in a wider Europe on any issue that the US disagrees with'. At the same time, a new alliance was formed between Chirac, Schröder and Putin. After the Russian leader visited Berlin and Paris, a joint position was announced. On 10 February, they all made clear their opposition to war. Over the following few weeks, the French, German and Russian foreign ministers co-ordinated their anti-war statements.

Hopes of finding a solution at the UN were also disappearing. Dr Blix's eagerly-awaited further report to the Security Council on 14 February was inconclusive, disappointing British ministers watching on television who had hoped that, at last, firm evidence would be produced. The Iraqi Government had not yet been completely open in its declaration. The inspections were progressing steadily, but they needed more time. That was the French and German case. The suspicion in London and Washington was that Dr Blix did not want to be blamed for causing a war. As Robin Cook noted in his diary

(2003, pp. 293–4) this was Blair's 'nightmare come true . . . The ghastly dilemma he now faces is that without Hans Blix denouncing Saddam there is little chance of getting a majority in the Security Council for military conflict, and therefore even less chance of getting a majority among the British public'.

The Blix report came on the eve of a series of massive anti-war demonstrations around the world. In Britain, a march through London to Hyde Park attracted well over a million people, including many who were not politically aligned and had never been on a demonstration before. This was despite the fact that the Stop the War Coalition was dominated by the far-left and some militant Islamic groups whose posters were violently anti-Israel. These links were ignored in what became liberal England's equivalent of the pro-hunting countryside marches. Britain's liberal conscience was stirring. Charles Kennedy spoke at the rally, as the Liberal Democrats became the only major national party to oppose a war on Iraq. At the same time as the marchers were assembling, Blair was appealing for support from Labour members in Glasgow. His tone was both increasingly moralistic and, at times, desperate, prompting Michael Portillo, the Tories' 'nearly man' to comment on the BBC *Today* programme that Blair had changed from the focus-group-driven, risk-averse phase of the 1990s. He was now self-consciously bolder and moralistic. These traits had been apparent before: for instance, during Kosovo but were now much clearer. Blair was also concerned about the outbreak of anti-Americanism. America, he told reporters at his monthly news conference on 18 February, was 'not some alien power acting against our interests'. His main argument was: 'Don't look at the parody of what George Bush has done. Look at the reality.' Mr Bush had 'waited and acted deliberately' after 11 September. But this case cut little ice with many Labour MPs and activists who strongly disliked the President.

Much of establishment opinion was still cool about, if not openly hostile to, the likelihood of war (Riddell, 2003). This included such mainstream figures as Field Marshall Lord Bramall, Lord Hurd of Westwell and Sir Michael Quinlan, whose criticisms of the doctrine of pre-emption are noted in Chapter 7. Their main worry was that military action would aggravate, rather than alleviate, problems in the region, particularly the Israel–Palestine dispute, and would encourage terrorism. Lord Hurd warned in a speech to the Royal United Services Institute on 27 January that 'the reaction against what would appear as imperialism rather than liberation could be destructive. We might win the war in six days, and then lose it in six months.'

The Blair Government's political problems were underlined on 26 February when the House of Commons debated a motion broadly endorsing the Government's approach, but not backing military action. Nearly a third of MPs – including 121 Labour members defying their party's whip, 13 Conservatives and 52 Liberal Democrats – voted for an amendment arguing that 'the case for military action is as yet unproven.' This amendment – backed by former Conservative Cabinet ministers such as Kenneth Clarke and Douglas Hogg and Labour ministers such as Chris Smith and Frank Dobson – was defeated by 393 votes to 199, thanks to the support of most Tory MPs. The scale of the revolt – the largest against any governing party for more than a century – shook Blair. It would have been larger but for assurances by Blair and Straw that this was not the decisive debate and that MPs would have a later opportunity to discuss and vote on military action. Before the debate, Blair had assured MPs that he was working 'flat out' to secure approval of a UN resolution, saying that Saddam had failed to take his 'final opportunity'. A large number of Labour MPs privately warned that they remained loyal only on condition that such a resolution was obtained. The Government's critics argued that more time should be given to diplomatic efforts to disarm Saddam.

The Government was publicly resolved to carry on with its existing strategy. But Blair decided to confront his critics directly in a series of often-bruising television programmes with groups of people opposed to the war: what Alastair Campbell described as the 'masochism strategy'. It was certainly painful: at the end of one programme, Blair was slow handclapped. But these confrontations probably helped to convince many doubters about Blair's sincerity. As he often said at the time, he was not backing the US and taking a tough line to win popularity.

Moreover, in an interview with *The Times* on the day after the Commons vote, Jack Straw was still hopeful of getting a further UN resolution, but added significant caveats about an 'unreasonable veto' and how military action was already covered by Resolutions 687 and 1441. Like Blair, he put the point starkly: 'Do you seek to encourage and influence America to put its faith in the multilateral system, or work in a way that they can make a choice and go unilaterally if they wish?' A few days later, the Foreign Secretary told MPs: 'We will reap a whirlwind if we push the Americans into a unilateral position in which they are at the centre of a unipolar world.' That was the essence of the Government's case. The Americans were determined to get rid of Saddam, and must not be left alone. Yet, both for domestic political and legal reasons, it is vital to do this under the cover of a further UN resolution.

But over the following two and a half weeks there was an element of unreality, even of self-delusion, about ministerial claims that a further UN resolution could still be agreed. The belief in London was still that, despite all the anti-war language coming from Paris, the French Government would, in the end, not want to be seen exercising its veto against the US. This represented a serious misreading of French attitudes and policy. There is still a dispute about whether different parts of the French Government were sending out conflicting messages or whether the British were failing to spot the by now clear signals of French opposition.

Blair's perennial optimism at times bordered on self-delusion. He repeatedly told MPs and public alike that he was sure that a resolution would be agreed. But his words became more and more unconvincing. Bush and Blair, and Powell and Straw, worked desperately to try and secure support on the Security Council. This was in the hope that if America, Britain and Spain could secure the backing of a majority of the Council, then France – along with Russia and China – might abstain. But only Bulgaria was committed to joining the US side. Sir David Manning flew to Santiago for the day in an attempt to win over the Chilean Government, and Blair talked frequently to Ricardo Lagos, the Chilean President.

However, the Bush administration paid the price for an often high-handed approach to its neighbours since not even Mexico or Chile would commit to the US side. Much effort was devoted to courting smaller countries such as Angola, Cameroon and Guinea.

But while Bush and Powell were prepared to make one last effort at the UN, US officials made clear that a further resolution was not seen as in any way essential, and implicitly was largely being sought to help Blair. There was also increasing impatience in Washington. A lengthy attempt to persuade Turkey to allows its territory to be used by American troops in order to enter northern Iraq failed, partly because Colin Powell did not devote sufficient time and personal commitment to winning over the new government in Ankara. The Turkish refusal seriously disrupted American planning but, by early March 2003, US commanders were virtually ready.

After another ambiguous report from Dr Blix on 7 March, Straw tabled a resolution setting a deadline of Monday, 17 March. It was time, the Americans and British argued, for a decision and for the Security Council to stand up and be counted, the last thing many of its smaller members wanted. Their leaders knew that war was very unpopular in their countries. They wanted to ensure that responsibility for the fate of the resolution lay with the veto-wielding members of the Security Council. While the Americans were, in part, going through the motions at this time, the British were in an increasingly awkward position. During late February and early March, British ministers did look for a compromise – to which Hans Blix was sympathetic – involving specific benchmarks for Iraqi compliance. The problem was timing. The US firmly resisted any deadline lasting into the late spring or early summer. So Tony Blair could have been in an awkward position if such a proposal, with a deadline of, say, a few weeks, had gained widespread support. It would have been very hard for him to argue against some such extension. Indeed, on 9 March Blair and Lagos of Chile discussed a proposal for a further fifteen working days for Iraq to comply with six benchmarks or face military action. This might have led to a breach with the Americans who were no longer willing to extend the deadline because it would delay the start of fighting until the period of hot weather in Iraq. Faced with the likelihood of an even larger, and possibly fatal, revolt in the Labour Party, Blair might have had to go against all his instincts and split with Bush. That was highly improbable. But Blair's advisers were aware of the risk, which reinforced the nervousness within 10 Downing Street.

A year later, Blair raised the intriguing possibility of a way of avoiding war. In a speech in his Sedgefield constituency on 5 March 2004, he talked of going back to the UN in March 2003 to make a final ultimatum which 'we very nearly achieved'. He said: 'My view was and is that if the UN had come together and delivered a tough ultimatum to Saddam, listing clearly what he had to do, benchmarking it, he may have folded and events set in train that might just and eventually have led to his departure from power. But the Security Council didn't agree'. But would the Americans have halted their war plans at this late stage? That is a question that Blair did not address.

The Blair–Lagos compromise was publicly killed off not by the Americans but by the French. On the following evening, 10 March, President Chirac appeared on French television to state: 'My position is that, regardless of the circumstances, France will vote no because it considers this evening there are no grounds for waging war in order to achieve the goal we have set ourselves – to disarm Iraq.' Clare Short later claimed that Blair misrepresented the meaning of Chirac's words. On her view, 'this evening' referred just to the resolution proposed by Britain and still allowed scope for a different compromise resolution. Blair rang Chirac to clarify the French position. The French President made clear that he would not back any resolution setting an ultimatum which implied that if Saddam failed to take certain actions by a specified date, then military action would automatically follow. However, this would have been too imprecise for the British, let alone the Americans. Chirac – not for the first time – overplayed his hand, and missed an opportunity. He could have put Blair in a very awkward position by accepting an ultimatum and a deadline of a few weeks. But Chirac's use of the phrase 'regardless of the circumstances' let Blair off the hook. In the short term, Chirac's intervention destroyed any chance of agreeing a further resolution, not least because Mexico, Chile and the three African countries would not even risk the symbolic gesture of voting with the US in a losing cause (in the face of a French veto). Chirac's words were a relief to these countries since they did not have to take responsibility for voting on whether to go to war, thus avoiding either alienating their own publics or the United States.

Blair had been very worried by the twin pressures of American impatience and French intransigence, as well as by increasingly vocal Labour discontent. On 9 March, Clare Short had attacked Blair's approach in a Sunday evening radio interview. She warned that she would consider resigning as International Development Secretary if there was no UN mandate for action. She said 'the whole atmosphere of the current situation is deeply reckless, reckless for the world, reckless for the undermining of the UN in this disorderly world – which is wider than Iraq – reckless with our Government, reckless with his own future, position and place in history.' This was a gross breach of all the conventions of collective responsibility as well as offensively disloyal to the Prime Minister. Behind the bland official response that Tony Blair was busy trying to secure a diplomatic solution, his advisers debated how to treat Short's outburst. At a time when there were well-founded fears that Robin Cook, the Leader of the Commons and former Foreign Secretary, might resign. Blair's advisers were worried that sacking Short could fuel the already-record Labour backbench opposition to military action. Cook and Short together, joined probably by several junior ministers, would be powerful opponents, and might tip the balance so that the Government lost the support of a majority of its own backbench MPs. So Short was not sacked, though the common view at Westminster was that it was merely a stay of execution. Blair and Straw later said they considered during these mid-March days that they themselves might be forced to resign.

Donald Rumsfeld – Short's opposite in all ways except tactlessness (or candour, depending on your view) – also made life difficult for Blair. Rumsfeld insisted he was trying to be helpful but that is not how it looked at the time. Geoff Hoon, the British Defence Secretary, had phoned to warn him that Britain might not be involved militarily if the promised Commons vote went wrong. Hoon's remarks reflected an anxious debate at the top of the Blair Government about its narrowing options. At the end of the first week of March, Jack Straw had written a long memorandum for Blair (Stephens, 2004, p. 235) discussing both the probability that a second UN resolution would be lost in the Security Council, and therefore the push for one should be abandoned, and the possibility that in these circumstances a majority of Labour MPs would vote against war. If that happened,

Straw warned that the Government would not be able to commit British forces to fighting alongside the Americans, and might only be able to be involved later in helping to stabilise Iraq. This was very much a hypothetical, last resort, option.

Hoon later said about his conversation with Rumsfeld (Wintour and Kettle, 2003): 'I did not want him or anyone on the US side not to understand the significance of where we were on the importance of the parliamentary vote. The US came to understand it was about us gambling just about everything in getting this right.' At that late stage, it would have been very hard to disentangle the British forces which formed a subsidiary, but key, part of the invasion plan. By chance, immediately after the call, Rumsfeld went into a news conference and said that the US might have to invade Iraq without Britain, and could 'work around' its absence. There were then hasty transatlantic phone calls, leading to what one senior American diplomat has said is the only known instance of Rumsfeld making an apology or retraction.

The noises off from Short and Rumsfeld did not make any difference to what happened but they vividly illustrated the febrile mood in London during the second week of March. A further Populus poll for *The Times* showed that, by a two-to-one margin, the public did not believe the British and American Governments had put forward a convincing case for war. The Bush administration was now following political developments at Westminster very closely. The President had 'complete confidence in Blair but was worried about whether he would be able to deliver', according to a senior US diplomat. As Bob Woodward discloses (2004, p. 338), Bush was increasingly worried by Blair's political problems and phoned him on

9 March to offer Britain the chance of dropping out of the military action and coming in later as peacekeepers. Blair declined this option and repeated that he would be 'there to the end'.

The American Embassy in London – with very good political contacts below the level of the figurehead ambassador – was keeping Washington informed on a daily basis. Embassy officials were talking to Labour whips and as many advisers in 10 Downing Street as possible, 'every single day, sometimes two or three times a day'. Washington wanted to know what was going on. A senior Embassy official concedes that their reports may have magnified the risks to Blair. The Bush team also talked to senior Tories to make sure that they were not suddenly going to shift course to take advantage of the deepening divisions within the Labour Party.

The British Government pursued a twin-track approach. New diplomatic moves were considered – for instance, by publishing the benchmarks or tests for Iraqi compliance, as discussed earlier with Hans Blix – but these attracted little support, even from the Americans. The second resolution was going nowhere. But it was agreed to keep going at the UN until at least the following Monday, 17 March, the day after a hastily arranged summit in the Azores, hosted by the Portuguese Prime Minister and attended by Bush, Blair and Aznar. But both Washington and London were coming to the view that it would be better to base any military action on Resolution 1441 rather than press for a vote, risking a virtually certain veto by France and Russia. At the same time, ministers, particularly Straw, used Chirac's 'regardless of the circumstances' phrase to put the blame on the French for preventing agreement on a further UN resolution. This would obviously not convince the outright opponents of war, but it was intended to rally the waverers on the Labour back-benchers. There were signs on that Wednesday and Thursday that some Labour MPs were beginning to shift behind the Government, not least because they were reacting against calls by some hard-left MPs for Blair's resignation. This French-bashing – amplified in the more jingoistic tabloids – served a short-term political necessity but merely underlined the depth of the divisions within Europe, and particularly across the Atlantic.

The brief Azores summit proved to be an anticlimax. There was nothing fresh to discuss and Bush gave the impression of not really wanting to be here, as he did not. But there was a renewed American promise to press ahead with the 'road map' on the Middle East peace process once the new Palestinian Prime Minister took office and an acknowledgement by President Bush of a UN role in post-war Iraq. The Azores statement included pledges to 'work in close partnership with international institutions, including the UN' and to a new UN Security Council resolution that would 'endorse an appropriate post-conflict administration for Iraq'. As it turned out, this statement begged a lot of questions about the precise role for the UN, but the words helped the British Prime Minister in trying to make the case that America and Britain had not completely turned their backs on the UN.

The next day, Monday 17 March, Sir Jeremy Greenstock briefly announced the end of months of diplomacy at the UN. The British and the Americans withdrew their draft resolution. Everyone had made mistakes over the preceding weeks, and months: the Americans, the French, the Germans, and Saddam himself. But the outcome was a defeat for Britain since Blair had invested so much politically in obtaining a further UN resolution. For once, his optimism had not been justified. Blair and his advisers had misread the intentions of the French in particular, however convenient it was to blame them for the diplomatic breakdown. As a result, the Prime Minister was now very exposed politically. The action had moved elsewhere, initially and dramatically, to Westminster, and then to Iraq.

10. Shock and Awe

To fall back into the lassitude of the last twelve years, to talk, to discuss, to debate but never act: to declare our will but not enforce it; to combine strong language with weak intentions, a worse outcome then never speaking at all.

Tony Blair, opening debate on Iraq, House of Commons,

Tuesday 18 March 2003

One country alone cannot take the burden of the world and one country cannot deal with reconstruction.

Dominique de Villepin, French Foreign Minister, lecture at the

International Institute for Strategic Studies, London,

Thursday 27 March 2003

I believe that the Prime Minister must have concluded that it was honourable and desirable to back the US in going for military action in Iraq and it was, therefore, honourable for him to persuade us through the various ruses and devices he used to get us there. So I presume that he saw it as an honourable deception.

Clare Short, in evidence to the Foreign Affairs Committee of

the Commons, Tuesday 17 June 2003

Tony Blair was on his own. The collapse of weeks of diplomacy meant that he would now have to seek the approval of the House of

Commons for military action without a further United Nations resolution. Robin Cook had already told 10 Downing Street that he would be resigning as Leader of the Commons on Monday 17 March, after signalling his doubts at earlier Cabinet discussions.

Blair was never in any doubt that what he was doing was right. As earlier chapters have shown, he had been concerned for a long time about Saddam Hussein and weapons of mass destruction, while he believed it was not in Britain's or anyone else's interest for America to be left to act on its own. But for both political and legal reasons, Blair could not make getting rid of Saddam an explicit objective. Hence, his emphasis on Iraq's weapons of mass destruction and on Saddam's refusal to comply with repeated UN resolutions. So Blair's immediate task was to show that Saddam posed a serious enough threat to justify, both legally and politically, going to war.

The Government had always left itself a let-out clause over a further UN resolution if there was an 'unreasonable' veto, a subjective rather than a legal definition. Nonetheless, ministers always insisted that they would act within international law. After the war, there was controversy over the legal basis for the military action. Sir Michael (later Lord) Boyce, the Chief of Defence Staff, confirmed that he had sought clear guidance that what British troops were being asked to do was legal. There was concern both because the action was pre-emptive, rather than in response to an invasion (as in the first Gulf War in 1990–1), and because of fears that British troops might be taken to the International Criminal Court. This legal reassurance was provided. After the breakdown at the UN, a statement was issued by Lord Goldsmith, the Attorney General, setting out the legal basis for military action. The essence of his opinion was that a series of previous

UN resolutions on Iraq dating back to 1990 allowed 'the use of force for the express purpose of restoring international peace and security'. He said it was 'plain that Iraq has failed to comply' and 'continues to be in material breach'. Thus 'the authority to use force under resolution 678 [of November 1990 authorising force to eject Iraq from Kuwait] has revived and so continues today.' He added, somewhat disingenuously, that 'resolution 1441 [of 8 November 2002] would in terms have provided that a further decision of the Security Council to sanction force was required if that had been intended. Thus, all that resolution 1441 requires is reporting to, and discussion, by the Security Council of Iraq's failures, but not an express further decision to authorise force.' Lord Goldsmith sounded like a magician pulling a rabbit out of a hat to the familiar exclamation of 'Hey presto!' The real reason why Resolution 1441 did not contain any reference to the need for a further decision sanctioning force was, of course, that this was politically unacceptable to the United States. The Bush administration no longer accepted the legal constraints of the UN Charter on its ability to use force. This had been true for some time – as in the Kosovo conflict – but was more explicit over Iraq. Several leading lawyers challenged Lord Goldsmith's interpretation. Lord Archer of Sandwell, a former Labour Solicitor General, argued that: 'The Government has produced a resolution from ten years ago, ignoring all debate since. If the Security Council had wanted to authorise military action, it had every opportunity to say so and it never once did.' Rabinder Singh QC and Lord Goodhart, a leading Liberal Democrat lawyer, argued (in Rozenberg, 2003) that the original authorisation of force under Resolution 678 had been terminated once the ceasefire in the first Gulf war had come into operation in spring 1991. Any further decisions on the use of force required a fresh resolution by the Security Council, and could not be revived unilaterally by member states. But the Government's case was undermined by the resignation on the eve of the war of Elizabeth Wilmhurst, the highly respected deputy legal adviser at the Foreign Office, because she believed that the proposed military action was not justified legally. She knew far more about international law than even so experienced a barrister as Lord Goldsmith. But the Attorney General trumps all other lawyers. And, despite the legal disputes, Lord Goldsmith's brief statement provided sufficient – if not universally accepted – legal cover for British participation. But his backing for military action was explicitly related to the existence of Iraq's weapons of mass destruction. This became an important point in the later debate over the existence of such weapons.

More important politically, however, was convincing the Commons and the British public that Saddam's weapons of mass destruction were a serious threat. It was not enough to say that Saddam was an evil man who was guilty of appalling crimes, and that both Iraq and the world would be better off without him. That was essentially America's case. But Blair had to be more specific, as Robin Cook argued in a powerful resignation statement delivered at a quarter to ten in the evening on Monday 17 March to a packed Commons chamber. Cook had been fully involved in policy towards Iraq until less than two years before as Foreign Secretary. This prompted some Government loyalists to contrast his past support for military action against Saddam in 1998 with his opposition now – though the proposed invasion of Iraq was on a wholly different scale from the earlier, brief attacks. Cook put his finger on the core issue:

> *Iraq probably has no weapons of mass destruction in the commonly understood sense of the term – namely a credible device capable of being delivered against a strategic city target. It probably has biological toxins and battlefield chemical munitions, but it has had them since the 1980s when US companies sold Saddam anthrax agents and the then British Government approved chemical and munitions factories. Why is it now so urgent that we should take military action to disarm a military capacity that has been there for twenty years, and which we helped to create? Why is it necessary to resort to war this week, while Saddam's ambition to complete his weapons programme is blocked by the presence of UN inspectors?*

Cook argued that the credibility of the British case was not helped 'by the appearance that our partners in Washington are less interested in disarmament than they are in regime change in Iraq'. He concluded by appealing to MPs to demonstrate in their votes the following evening that the Commons still occupied a central role in British politics by stopping 'the commitment of troops in a war that has neither international agreement nor domestic support'. It was an electrifying occasion. Cook was applauded by many Labour and other MPs as he sat down. Tony Blair was lucky that Cook's statement was late in the evening, rather than just before his own speech opening the main debate the following day. If Cook had delivered his statement on Tuesday lunchtime, just before the debate, he could have made Blair's task much harder and the vote against war could have been even larger.

Tony Blair made the most powerful Commons speech of his nearly six years as Prime Minister, and twenty years as an MP. His case was both specific, pointing to Saddam's defiance of the UN over his programme to develop weapons of mass destruction, and general, stressing the importance of a firm line now to stop the spread of such weapons. He blamed the French and their allies on the Security Council for saying 'no to any ultimatum; no to any resolution that stipulates that failure to comply will lead to military action'. He directly addressed the argument that more time was needed:

> *What would any tyrannical regime possessing WMD think viewing the history of the world's diplomatic dance with Saddam? That our capacity to pass firm resolutions is only matched by our feebleness in implementing them. That is why this indulgence has to stop. Because it is dangerous. It is dangerous if such regimes disbelieve us.*

Blair accepted that the association between regimes with WMD and extreme terrorist groups was loose. But it was hardening. 'And the possibility of the two coming together – of terrorist groups in possession of WMD, even of a so-called dirty radiological bomb is now, in my judgement, a real and present danger.' Hence the need for action. He warned that failure to enforce resolution 1441 risked 'forcing nations down the very unilateralist path we wish to avoid'. To retreat now from military action would 'put at hazard all that we hold dearest' and tell allies 'that at the very moment of action, at the very moment they need our determination, that Britain faltered'. He added, 'I will not be a party to that.' The implication was clear:

without the backing of the Commons, and particularly of his own party, he would resign. This was not a vain threat. Jack Straw said in an interview with *The Times* in late April – admittedly with the safety of the main war over – that: 'There were very big political risks. I was simply conscious of the fact that if it went wrong – if we did not get the support we needed in the Commons – he (the Prime Minister) would almost certainly go and I would go with him. I did give it quite a bit of thought.' However, in practice, Blair strengthened his authority as a national leader for the period of the war, if not for much longer. Parliament had its say but, despite the nervousness both in Downing Street and the White House over the preceding few days, the Prime Minister was always likely to get his way.

The outcome was an even larger rebellion than on 26 February. The number of Labour MPs voting for an amendment saying the case for war had not been made was 139, against 121 previously, along with fifteen Conservatives and all the Liberal Democrats and nationalists. (Thirteen Labour MPs who had rebelled in February either voted with the Government or abstained. But this was more than offset by thirty new Labour rebels.) The overall vote against war was 217, against 396. So the Government passed its self-imposed test of winning the support of a narrow majority of its own backbenchers. Labour's party managers were relieved that the revolt was not much larger. MPs rallied to the Government both because war was now inevitable and because of the strength of the Prime Minister's assurances about the threat from Saddam.

The mere holding of the vote was significant, and answered the frequent charges that the Prime Minister ignored Parliament. In practice, ever since the 11 September attacks, Tony Blair – as well as

Jack Straw and Geoff Hoon – had been assiduous in reporting to the Commons about developments in the war on terrorism and over Iraq. There had been frequent statements and debates. Moreover, while there had often been Commons votes at the start of wars, and during them, Prime Ministers do not have to obtain parliamentary approval to send troops into action. This is a prerogative power, exercised by ministers in the name of the crown. But the deliberate decision by the Government to seek the approval of the Commons on 18 March – at the insistence of both Robin Cook and Jack Straw – was not just a response to the political pressures of a deeply divided Labour Party. It also established a constitutional precedent. It would be very hard, if not impossible, to go to war in future without the specific approval of the Commons – though this was only a precedent, not a legal requirement like the War Powers Act in the US.

Moreover, the Prime Minister observed the constitutional proprieties in ensuring that the full Cabinet held lengthy discussions in the run-up to the war. This was contrary both to the widely held belief that the Cabinet was largely irrelevant and to the specific charges made by Clare Short after she eventually left the Cabinet on 12 May. She claimed in her Commons resignation statement that afternoon:

> *In the second term, the problem is the centralisation of power into the hands of the Prime Minister and an increasingly small number of advisers who make decisions in private without proper discussion. It is increasingly clear that the Cabinet has become, in Bagehot's phrase, a dignified part of the constitution – joining the Privy Council. There is no real collective responsibility because there is no collective; just*

> *diktats in favour of increasingly badly thought through policy*
> *initiatives that come from on high.*

Short resigned on the grounds that the sidelining of the UN in the running of post-war Iraq betrayed understandings made to her by the Prime Minister before the war. This was widely seen more as a pretext than a cause. Her resignation statement to the Commons revealed her deep disillusion with the Government's whole approach to Iraq dating from well before the war and covering several months when she remained in the Cabinet. In her later evidence to the inquiry by the Foreign Affairs Committee (Ninth Report, 2002–3, p. 43), she alleged that a small group of officials based at Number 10 had effective control of policy on Iraq. These were, she said, 'Alastair Campbell, Jonathan Powell, Baroness Morgan, Sir David Manning, that close entourage. That was the team, they were the ones who moved together all the time. They attended the daily "War Cabinet". That was the in group, that was the group in charge of policy.'

There is an element of truth in Clare Short's claims, but they confuse two distinct elements: the hour-by-hour way in which 10 Downing Street works, and has always worked, and the taking of big decisions. Blair operates with a close group of civil and political advisers on a daily basis. They work with him and travel with him, as Peter Stothard vividly depicts in *30 Days*, his fly-on-the-wall account of life with Blair's inner circle from 10 March until the fall of Baghdad on 9 April. What Short describes as the 'in group' have considerable influence merely because they are with Blair most of the time. But the same is true of all modern Prime Ministers. They all work with entourages or 'in groups.' But elected politicians still

matter. Tony Blair has to work with ministers in charge of departments, notably with Gordon Brown who has wide control over much
of the domestic agenda.

Moreover, Clare Short is wrong to imply that the key decisions on
Iraq were taken by this 'in group'. While several key initiatives in the
first term – for instance, making the Bank of England responsible for
setting interest rates – were taken by Blair and Brown without even
consulting the Cabinet, this was not true over Iraq. As Jack Straw
pointed out in evidence to the Foreign Affairs Committee, Iraq was
discussed at every Cabinet meeting between 23 September 2002 and
22 May 2003. That amounted to twenty-eight meetings. And the
discussions became longer and more specific during February and
March 2003. Indeed, Robin Cook raised a number of questions and
doubts at these meetings, which first indicated to his Cabinet
colleagues that he was considering resignation.

Clare Short's real complaint is that she was excluded from
meetings of the key ministerial groups. The Cabinet's Defence and
Overseas Policy Committee did not meet at all during this period.
Instead of setting up a formal War Cabinet, Tony Blair preferred to
operate more informally, through an *ad hoc* committee of relevant
ministers. This involved Blair, Straw, Hoon, Sir Michael Boyce (then
Chief of the Defence Staff), John Scarlett (chairman of the Joint
Intelligence Committee) and, sometimes, the heads of other intelli-
gence agencies. John Prescott, Deputy Prime Minister; David
Blunkett, the Home Secretary; Gordon Brown, the Chancellor; and
John Reid, chairman of the Labour Party (and then, briefly, Leader of
the Commons) were also closely involved on a daily basis, as Peter
Stothard's book makes clear. Short was on the periphery, attending

some meetings, but not all the key ones. Sometimes, the main ministers held talks before the meeting of a wider committee including her. She was not present at some important discussions on the conduct of the war because, as someone closely involved in the decisions said, she was no longer trusted after her remark that Blair's attitude to the war was 'reckless'. Her loyalty to Blair was in doubt and she was seen as too garrulous.

Discussing Short's complaints, Jack Straw told the Foreign Affairs Committee (Ninth Report, 2002–3, p. 44) in diplomatic, round-about language that 'some of these decisions and discussions had to be very tightly held. There was a reason for that, which is that we were involved in very intense diplomatic activity throughout the period from the middle of July, with our partners in the United States and with other partners in the Security Council. You have to ensure that these discussions are tightly held.'

By providing ample opportunity for discussion before the start of fighting, Tony Blair ensured the support of most of his Cabinet both for the decision to go to war and for its conduct. Whatever the arguments about the legality, or broader strategic results of going to war, the Prime Minister allowed both the Cabinet and Parliament a full chance to have their say before the start of military action. Blair suffered Cook's resignation from the Cabinet (and Short's after the end of the conflict), as well as the departure of two other ministers, including John Denham, the respected Home Office Minister of State, as well as a number of parliamentary private secretaries. This was bad but no worse than other departures from the Cabinet over the 2002–3 period of loyal Blairities, such as Stephen Byers, Estelle Morris (though she came back later as a Minister of State) and Alan

Milburn. Moreover, after the first big backbench revolt in February, Gordon Brown and John Prescott, the two senior members of the Cabinet after Blair, publicly went on the offensive in support of the Prime Minister. Brown's involvement was highly significant since, as noted in Chapter 1, he had taken a low profile during both the Kosovo and Afghanistan conflicts. The stakes were obviously higher this time and Brown decided that his public support was needed and would help Blair. As usual with the Blair–Brown relationship, there was much speculation then, and later, about whether there had been a 'deal', linking Brown's support for Blair over Iraq to the later decision, announced on 9 June, to delay entry into the euro. What mattered at the time, however, was Brown's public support for Blair.

After all the political manoeuvrings at Westminster, there was a curious sense of anticlimax. The dye had been cast. Politicians and most of the public rallied to support the British forces. There were some noisy demonstrations in Parliament Square, but on nothing like the scale of the mid-February march, and the polls quickly showed a big shift in public opinion to support military action. The focus would now move to Iraq. The roughly 40,000 British forces in the region were to have an important role operating in their own area in the south of Iraq, but it was primarily an American operation fought on American terms and run by General Tommy Franks of Centcom.

For Tony Blair, the key factors now were the length of the fighting; the number of coalition military casualties; the scale of destruction in Iraq and the number of civilians killed and wounded; and whether there would be instability in the rest of the Middle East. In short, would the war be brief and decisive enough to win over many, if not all of the previous opponents? The short-term answers were reasonably favourable for Blair, though the longer-term ones have been less favourable and much trickier.

The time between the start of fighting – a failed attempt to kill Saddam Hussein and the Iraqi leadership – and the fall of Baghdad was only three weeks. Despite the relative brevity of the campaign, the course was not smooth: wars seldom are. The initial onslaught – quickly dubbed 'shock and awe' – involved both air and missile strikes and a land invasion. American marines and troops from the US 3rd Infantry Division advanced rapidly, coming within 100 miles of Baghdad within three days. At the same time, British forces advanced to secure the oil fields in the south and to surround, and then capture, the city of Basra.

After these advances, the ground campaign slowed for nearly a week. The rapid advance had strained supply lines. Moreover, Iraqi paramilitary and guerrilla forces were attacking unprotected units, prompting Lieutenant General William Wallace, Commander of the US V Corps, to comment that: 'The enemy we're fighting is a bit different than the one we war-gamed against, because of these para-military forces.' While the ground forces regrouped and dealt with fierce opposition in some places, particularly Nasiriya, air attacks continued on Iraqi forces around Baghdad. Then, in early April, the ground advances resumed. On 4 April, US forces occupied Baghdad airport and over the next few days made increasingly large incursions into the city. Instead of a full-scale confrontation with Saddam's elite troops, there were a series of smaller-scale engagements with small units. On 9 April, Saddam's statue was toppled with the help of American troops – providing a memorable picture around the world for that day's television news bulletins and the next day's papers. It was a universally shared image like the collapse of the World Trade Center towers nineteen months earlier. The fall of Baghdad was seen as the end of the war in the world's media – though it took several days more before Tikrit, Saddam's home town, was captured. As military resistance subsided, American and British troops had to cope with looting and disorder. On 1 May, President Bush used the backdrop of the aircraft carrier USS *Abraham Lincoln* to announce that the main military operation was at an end. A banner behind the President on the carrier's bridge proclaimed 'Mission Accomplished'. But, despite the striking pictures at the time, this photo opportunity backfired on the President as the violence in Iraq, and against US forces, continued.

Television viewers around the world had seen the war develop on an hour-by-hour basis. This was thanks both to the large number of journalists accompanying the forces ('embedded' correspondents in the jargon) and to developments in telecommunications which allowed instant pictures and reports to be sent back. It was 'war in your living room'. That made for excitement, immediacy and human drama. But it did not provide a balanced overall picture of what has happening. Minor engagements were presented as major battles. The bland – and largely correct – assurances coming out from Centcom headquarters in Qatar and from the Pentagon that everything was going according to plan failed to provide sufficient detail to offset the patchy and partial reports from the 'embedded' correspondents. So the 'pause' in late March, while officially denied, was presented as a serious setback in parts of the media. The words 'quagmire' and 'Vietnam' predictably appeared. Instant news often leads to mistaken judgements and a loss of balance and proportion. The political impact can be seen in the pages of Peter Stothard's *30 Days*, where Alastair Campbell, John Prescott and John Reid vie with each other in their complaints about the BBC's bias, obsession with 'friendly fire' casualties and alleged unbalanced coverage. These concerns formed the backdrop to the bitter BBC–Downing Street row of the summer of 2003. The timescale of war is incompatible with the demands of the twenty-four-hour news cycle.

If the war was brief – at least in retrospect – the level of casualties on the coalition side was also relatively low. Around 120 American servicemen died and 34 British, of whom only ten were killed as a result of enemy action. Indeed, a series of accidents and friendly fire incidents (including the shooting down of a British plane by a US missile battery) cast a shadow over the first few days of the war. Civilian Iraqi deaths are estimated at between 5,400 and 7,000. There is no reliable estimate of Iraqi military casualties, both because of the collapse of the Iraqi military command structure and because it was not in the interests of the coalition forces to collect figures. But anecdotal reports of the scale of destruction of forces by coalition air and armoured power means that the total certainly amounted to many, many thousands and could easily have been tens of thousands.

The fall of Baghdad was a memorable event. An evil dictator had been ousted. The dash, bravery and skill of the coalition forces were widely praised. It was a skilful military operation where air power and a rapid land advance disrupted Iraq's command structure. However, the war was one-sided. The Saddam regime collapsed almost from the start. Individual Iraqi units and groups of paramilitaries put up a fight, but there was no sense of co-ordinated opposition. Yet the ease of military victory was deceptive. Many of the most serious problems appeared afterwards. As Sir Timothy Garden (2003) has written from a military perspective: 'While smaller troop numbers may be right for manoeuvre warfare, they may be insufficient for securing the peace at the end of hostilities . . . This war may be the time to extend the military doctrine from fighting to rebuilding the nation.'

Moreover, despite fears that war in Iraq would cause instability in the rest of the Middle East, this did not happen. There were some anti-US and anti-British demonstrations and widespread protests, but nothing resembling the feared chaos. Towards the end of the war, there was some anxiety about whether America would turn next to Syria or Iran, after senior American officials issued a strong warning to Syria against helping Saddam. But the warning worked and the tough words were not a prelude to further military action. Jack Straw made plain that Britain would have nothing to do with military action against Syria and Iran. Indeed, Straw had taken political risks in trying to build up discussions with the Tehran Government, which he continued with a visit after the war, and, later in the year, in a joint mission with the French and German foreign ministers to discuss Iran's nuclear programme.

The main focus was on what would happen in post-Saddam Iraq and whether President Bush lived up to his promises of pressing ahead with the Middle East peace process. The appointment, and eventual ratification, of Mahmoud Abbas as Palestinian Prime Minister led to the publication at the end of April of the 'road map', laying out steps for producing a long-term settlement of the Israel–Palestine dispute. President Bush became closely involved, both visiting the region for the first time in early June and seeing both Mahmoud Abbas and Ariel Sharon in Washington in July. At one of the Prime Minister's meetings with the President in the White House before the war, one of Blair's senior advisers was struck when Bush demonstrated his seriousness about tackling the Middle East peace process by saying that 'the thing with building up political capital is to spend political capital.' The adviser later said he had been pleasantly surprised by how Bush had become so personally involved. But this proved to be a brief interlude of hope in the Middle East as Mahmoud Abbas soon resigned, and the bloody exchanges of suicide bombings and Israeli reprisals resumed. Peace seemed further away than ever.

The aftermath in Iraq has been messy and bloody, and raised questions about the political strategy which led to the war. The looting and disorder, particularly in Baghdad, in the following days and weeks could not have been entirely avoided, and largely reflected the absence of the normal institutions of civil order and policing following the collapse of the Saddam regime. Yet the occupying American forces were very slow to impose order and stamp down on looting. They appeared alternately impotent and inept in face of this disorder – partly reflecting the nature of their training, which concentrated on war fighting rather than peacekeeping. This was in marked contrast to the different approach and training of the British forces around Basra, many with experience of peacekeeping duties in Northern Ireland and the Balkans.

But these problems reflected a deeper failure in Washington both to plan properly for a post-war Iraq, and, as noted by the comments of Michael Ignatieff in Chapter 7, to understand the consequences of its military action, and what was needed to create a stable country after such a conflict. In part, there was an excessive optimism that, once military victory had been achieved, most of the Iraqi people would greet the American and British troops as liberators rather than occupiers. This was linked to an exaggerated faith in the Pentagon in some of the disputatious Iraqi exile groups, notably Ahmed Chalabi of the Iraqi National Congress. Moreover, US officials said later that the Saddam regime had collapsed faster than they had expected so that American forces were not ready, or in sufficient numbers, to handle the scale of the problems they found.

Indeed, in late July 2003, after a visit to Iraq, Paul Wolfowitz, Deputy Secretary of Defense, admitted that some of the key assumptions underlying the occupation had been wrong. This was significant since he had been one of the main architects of the political strategy behind the war. He said (see Slevin and Priest, 2003) that officials had underestimated the problems, starting with the belief that removing Saddam from power would also remove the threat posed by his Ba'ath Party. In addition, the US was wrong in assuming that large numbers of Iraqi soldiers and police would quickly join the US in rebuilding the country. The British felt that one of the big mistakes had been the rapid disbanding of the Iraqi army, given the time and difficulty of then new creating new Iraqi security forces.

Before the war, the Pentagon established an Office of Reconstruction and Humanitarian Assistance (ORHA) to run Iraq on an interim basis and to provide humanitarian aid, rebuild damaged infrastructure and help set up a representative government. This was a 'shambles', in the words of a senior British minister, the result of both poor planning beforehand and poor execution after the end of the war. Few Americans spoke Arabic and they had little contact with ordinary Iraqis. The extent of the difficulties was shown by the replacement of the first head of ORHA, retired Lieutenant General Jay Garner, within three weeks of his arrival in Iraq, and also by the removal of Barbara Bodine, a State Department official appointed to run Baghdad, less than a month after her arrival. Paul Bremer, a senior State official with an eye for public relations, took over from Garner and showed a much surer touch. The British did not hide their dissatisfaction with the initial American approach. Sir Jeremy Greenstock, the outgoing British Ambassador to the UN, had said in early May that: 'If the Pentagon runs the peace, we're in trouble.' Over the course of 2003–4, there was growing criticism of the American approach: for the failure to plan adequately for post-war Iraq; for having insufficient troops on the ground; for heavy-handed tactics by American forces and for having prematurely disbanded the old Iraqi army. This was contrasted with the lower key British approach in the southern area around Basra.

Even a year after the fall of Baghdad, American servicemen, Iraqi security forces and foreign civilian workers were being killed daily. Iraq proved to be a magnet for terrorist groups, both domestic and non-Iraqi, including associates of al-Qa'eda, keen to undermine the coalition forces and the emerging Iraqi interim administration. During the summer of 2003, acts of sabotage hindered reconstruction and there was widespread dissatisfaction, particularly around Baghdad, with the slow pace of involving Iraqis themselves in running their own country. In mitigation, the Americans and the British could fairly point out that the instability was restricted to limited areas surrounding Baghdad where the Ba'ath Party had previously been strong; that it had taken a long time to restore order and normal services in Germany and Japan in 1945; and that many of the problems with water, power and other utilities were because of sabotage, not a slow coalition response. A governing council of twenty-five Iraqis began sharing limited power with the US authorities in mid-July 2003. Moreover, the poor public health conditions and the rundown state of the infrastructure reflected a decade or more of low investment by Saddam's regime rather than damage caused during the war. Over the winter of 2002–3, conditions slowly improved, but armed bodyguards and security personnel were everywhere, particularly in the majority Sunni areas around Baghdad.

A linked argument developed over the role of the UN. As noted at the end of the previous chapter, the Azores statement on 16 March, just before the start of fighting, had referred to the involvement of the UN in humanitarian assistance and reconstruction. In his speech to the Commons on 18 March, Tony Blair had said: 'There should be a new UN resolution following any conflict providing not just for humanitarian help but also for the administration and governance of Iraq. That must now be done under proper authorisation.'

The Bush administration, however, wanted any UN role to be minimal. These tensions emerged during the two meetings between Bush and Blair during the war – at Camp David on 26–27 March, and at Hillsborough Castle in Northern Ireland on 7–8 April. At Camp David, Blair had been keen to discuss why so many long-term US allies, like Mexico, Chile, Canada and Turkey, had not joined the coalition and to examine the lessons, especially the need for a central UN role after the war. (He flew up to New York afterwards to see Kofi Annan, the UN Secretary General.) But Bush wanted to concentrate on the war, rather than the trickier questions of what happened afterwards. Peter Stothard records (2003, pp. 226–8) how, at the

Hillsborough meeting, the British pressed for the closing statement to include words about a 'vital role' for the UN in post-war Iraq. The President duly uses the key phrase:

> *Condoleezza Rice does not look so happy. Someone behind her genuinely has been counting: 'Vital role. Fine. But did he need to say it eight times?' Rice begins gently to suggest to her boss that some of their colleagues back in Washington might not be best pleased. Bush then calms her down and she is reported on the phone to Washington, to make sure that the Pentagon 'doesn't say anything wrong about this'.*

The dispute continued after the war. The Bush administration wanted to keep control in the hands of the US and the British. The anti-war countries were reluctant to be seen to be legitimising an operation with which they disagreed. But eventually a compromise was reached and the Security Council adopted a new resolution, 1483, effectively recognising the role of the US and Britain as occupying powers, known as the Coalition Provisional Authority, and supporting the formation of an interim Iraqi administration in the transition until an internationally recognised representative government established by the Iraqi people could take over. This ended the previous sanctions and the food-for-oil programme and clarified the legal position, more of a concern for the British than the Americans. But this was a weaker, advisory and supportive, role for the UN than the British had been urging during the war. Britain had originally wanted greater powers for a UN co-ordinator and a continuing role for UN inspectors.

The dilemma remained that, in order to involve a wider range of countries, a greater role for the UN was essential. Dominique de Villepin, the French Foreign Minister, highlighted the contrasting views in an interview with *Le Monde* on 13 May 2003: 'Some people think that America, because of her power, is capable of acting more effectively than an international community deemed indecisive, or even impotent. We firmly believe that the UN embodies a universal conscience transcending states.' But the US was hostile to internationalising the reconstruction of Iraq and giving the UN executive responsibilities. This reflected the Bush administration's desire to make its own rules for the international system without external constraints. As the difficulties in Iraq grew, US officials stressed that Iraq was now the key to transforming the Middle East and reducing the terrorist threat to America itself. Paul Wolfowitz said in a television interview on 27 July that 'the battle to secure the peace in Iraq is now the central battle in the global war on terror, and those sacrifices are going to make not just the Middle East more stable, but our country safer.'

The situation gradually began to change over the winter of 2003–4. While the US supplied the bulk of the occupying forces, there were British and Polish run areas with contributions from countries which had backed the war. But there were no troops from France and Germany, who wanted an explicit UN mandate and control and Spain quickly withdrew its forces in spring 2004 after the election of the new socialist government in Madrid. American policy also began to change – both in setting a timetable for the transfer of sovereignty at the end of June 2004 to the Iraqis and in trying to involve the UN more. Indeed, the UN was wary of returning – not least after the bomb attack on its headquarters in August 2003 which killed its senior representative. However, in early 2004, Paul Bremer urged the Iraqi Governing Council, and the leading Shia groups, to accept the involvement of Lakhdar Brahimi, the main troubleshooter of Kofi Annan, the UN Secretary General. There were serious doubts about how far the new Iraqi Government would exercise real control, especially over the security situation.

The turmoil in post-war Iraq showed the limitations of the neo-conservative strategy for remaking the world in the American image without involving other countries and international organisations. While, contrary to the Bush team's campaign rhetoric of 2000 about disdaining 'nation building', that is just what the US was doing on a massive scale. But the experience of both Afghanisatan and Iraq showed that America could not do this on its own. The US needed other countries and the UN, both for legitimacy and in supplying forces and resources. Moreover, while the Iraqis were grateful for the removal of Saddam and wanted to have freedom and democracy, they did not see their future as part of an American occupied fiefdom.

If the reconstruction of Iraq was the primary test of the outcome of the war, there was also a growing and intense debate about the arguments used by George W. Bush and Tony Blair justifying military action. But the failure to find either physical evidence of weapons of mass destruction or details of plans led to claims, initially in Britain, and then in the US, that Bush and Blair had misled their publics by exaggerating the threat from Saddam.

The British and American Governments remained adamant that their intelligence claims were well-founded. On 28 April, 2003, Jack Straw told MPs: 'I am absolutely certain Iraq had illegal possession of weapons of mass destruction and had those recently and therefore there is every reason why those ought to be found.' This confidence disappeared over time and the debate shifted to whether the American and British Governments had acted in bad faith by exaggerating or distorting the threat from Saddam or whether the intelligence had been faulty. As I argue in early chapters, while President Bush, and, to a slightly lesser extent, Tony Blair exaggerated the immediacy of the threat from Saddam, and hence the urgency of military action, they accurately reflected the assessments of their and other intelligence agencies in believing that such WMD existed.

A crucial intervention came at the end of January 2004 from David Kay, the former head of the Iraq Survey Group which had been looking for banned weapons since the fall of Baghdad. In evidence to the Senate Armed Services Committee on 28 January, the same day as the Hutton report was published in Britain, Mr Kay said about the pre-war belief that Iraq had WMD: 'It turns out that we were all wrong . . . and that is most disturbing'. He did not think that analysts had been 'pressured to reach conclusions that would fit the political agenda of one or another administration'. He pointed to inadequate US human intelligence and to the failure on 9 April, 2003, to 'establish immediately physical security in Iraq – the unparalleled looting and destruction, a lot of which was directly intentional, designed by the security services to cover the tracks of the Iraq WMD programme and their other programmes as well, and a lot of which was what we simply called Ali Baba looting. "It had been the regime's. The regime is gone. I'm going to go take the gold toilet fixtures and everything else imaginable".' However, Dr Kay still acceped that Iraq was in breach of successive UN resolutions, including 1441, by not disclosing laboratories and facilities as it should have.

It is still premature to reach a firm verdict on what had happened to Saddam's previous arsenal of weapons of mass destruction: how much had been hidden or destroyed before the return of the UN inspectors under Dr Blix in November 2002? And what were Saddam's plans for developing chemical, biological and nuclear weapons? Or did the Prime Minister, in Clare Short's bitterly sarcastic phrase, engage in 'honourable deception' to gain support for going to war? Tony Blair has made much of Saddam's failure to explain what had happened to past WMD stocks and facilities. However, Hans Blix, the head of the UN inspectors ahead of the war, argues (2004, p. 265) that it is probable that 'no weapons were hidden and those that had been deemed "unaccounted for" had either never existed or been largely destroyed as early as 1991'. He points to doubts in the Iraqi regime as to whether co-operation with the inspectors would lead to a lifting of sanctions, a sense of humiliation among the Iraqis, and a desire by the regime to inspire in others 'the thought that it had weapons of mass destruction and was still dangerous'.

These disputes have cast a shadow over the whole Iraqi operation. Any Baghdad bounce for Tony Blair in the polls was not only short-lived in April 2003, but quickly went into reverse. Blair's personal ratings suffered. The divisions on Iraq fuelled general discontent with Blair's leadership, while there was a growing concern over the treatment of British citizens suspected of being al-Qa'eda members who were held without trial by the US military at Guantanomo Bay – even after five were eventually returned to Britain in March 2004. Robin Cook and

Clare Short continued to challenge the Prime Minister's handling of the war – Cook forensically, particularly in his book published in late October 2003, and Short more emotionally and stridently. Blair's relations with many Labour MPs remained strained. As Philip Cowley of Nottingham University, the leading academic chronicler of recent Commons revolts, has noted, rebellions become habit-forming and rebels often become recidivists. The Iraq revolts were followed by further large Commons rebellions in the July and November 2003 over the bill setting up foundation hospitals and by the wafer thin five vote majority in late January 2004 for the second reading of the bill on tuition fees and university funding in late January 2004.

Internationally, also, the wounds from the Iraq war did not heal quickly. As the previous chapter amply demonstrates, all sides made serious diplomatic mistakes. But few were willing to admit to their errors. 'Forgive and forget' is not in President Bush's nature, nor is it in President Chirac's. As Condoleezza Rice, Bush's National Security Adviser, was reported as saying at the end of the war (in Hoagland, 2003): 'Punish France, ignore Germany, and forgive Russia.' That is, more or less, what happened, and the pre-war alliance between the three countries did not last long, much to the satisfaction, and relief, of America and Britain.

The diplomatic formalities were observed at the G8 summit in Evian in France at the beginning of June 2003, which was hosted by President Chirac, and in the preceding two days when the leaders met in St Petersburg for the city's 300th anniversary celebrations. President Bush talked in conciliatory terms when he visited Cracow in Poland in late May (the choice of country reflecting his thanks for Polish participation in the war). He said: 'The US is committed to a strong Atlantic alliance. This is no time to stir up divisions in a great alliance.' There were references to 'the wisdom of our European friends and allies'. But the remark was clearly selective. There was no warmth. Disagreements remained over trade and development issues, including genetically modified foods, as well as over the Iraq war. Greater efforts were made in late June, when EU leaders came to Washington for their regular summit with the President, where agreement was reached on several issues including non-proliferation, aviation, extradition and mutual legal assistance in tackling terrorism. In later months, President Bush did have contact with both President Chirac and Chancellor Schröder. French forces also worked closely with American troops in trying to bring order to Haiti in early 2004, while German troops continued to serve in Afghanistan and in helping to train Iraqi police (though outside the country). But they was no meeting of minds.

On the European side, French diplomats continued to challenge the US over Iraq, and Bush and Blair remained unpopular in many European countries. Iraq continued to be a factor in domestic politics, being probably a significant influence on the unexpected victory of the socialists in the Spanish general election on 14 March 2004, though turnout and the outcome were also probably affected by the bomb attacks at Madrid railway stations which killed 190 people three days earlier. The defeat of the ruling Popular Party was widely seen as a big blow for President Bush since José María Aznar, the outgoing Prime Minister, had been one of the few leaders of a major European country to back the war. The outcome even further undermined the attempt by many in Washington to divide Europe into old and new. Moreover, the socialists had promised during the election to withdraw the 1,300 strong Spanish contingent from Iraq, undermining US efforts to build an international coalition there. José Luis Rodriguez Zapatero, the new Prime Minister, had been outspokenly critical of the war. On the day after his triumph, he publicly distanced himself from both Bush and Blair, whom, he said, had lied over the war. But many other European countries were strongly critical of the Spanish pull out from Iraq.

Chancellor Schröder has been keen to rebuild relations with Washington – talking of the need for stronger 'transatlantic co-operation' in the wake of the Madrid bombings. He has been wary of French attempts to create a European pillar of power in competition, rather than in partnership, with America. Such an ambition is anyway fruitless when most European nations remain unwilling to spend more money on defence and create mobile and deployable forces. A meeting between the leaders of France, Germany, Belgium and Luxembourg in Brussels in late April 2003 to discuss setting up a separate defence organisation with its own headquarters was widely seen as anti-US, as well as anti-NATO – though the main hostility came from excluded countries, notably Spain and Italy. In London, the meeting was derided as the 'chocolate summit'. The real test of Europe's military capability is its willingness to increase defence spending and to shift the balance of its budgets to enable more forces to be deployed rapidly. But, in a significant shift of attitudes as a result of the war, the EU summit at Salonika on 20 June did adopt a tough and surprisingly pro-American security statement put forward by Javier Solana, the EU High Representative for the Common Foreign and Security Policy. This addressed, much more explicitly than before, the threats from proliferation and terrorism.

However, there was no real transatlantic reconciliation, except, temporarily, with Russia. That reflected the pre-Iraq, and to some extent pre-9/11, American strategy of forming alliances of convenience with European countries, headed by Britain, in coalitions of the willing, but making a partnership with Russia a top priority. Just before the Bush–Putin meeting in St Petersburg, the Russian Parliament ratified the treaty to reduce the two sides' nuclear arsenals by two-thirds over ten years. President Putin said Russia did not want Iran to obtain nuclear weapons, a previous point of difference with the US. As American officials pointed out, Russia wanted to work with America on strategic matters, while Europe was divided. However, Washington's relations with Russia cooled in early 2004 because of concerns over President Putin's authoritarian style and suppression of a free media and debate ahead of his overwhelming re-election on 14 March 2004.

Recriminations also continued between the US and Turkey after the Ankara Parliament's refusal to allow US troops to attack Iraq from Turkey. Paul Wolfowitz said the US would like to see 'a different sort of attitude in Ankara' and said the Turks should apologise for their mistake. This produced a dismissive response from Recep Tayyip Erdogan, the Turkish Prime Minister, who said: 'Turkey, from the very beginning, never made any mistakes.' Colin Powell later, rather belatedly, eased the tensions. And there was general support for Turkey after big bomb attacks in November 2003.

Tony Blair remained the eternal optimist. He was always looking for ways to rebuild his transatlantic bridge, even if many in Washington, most in Paris and some in Berlin were not interested in crossing it. He highlighted any evidence of reconciliation. There were some positive signs: not only the EU–US meeting in late June 2003 but also the Salonika summit of EU leaders (including the ten new entrants from central and eastern Europe) where, according to Blair, there was 'a very clear view that we do not want to go through this again'. That did not mean, however, any regrets for what had happened. Blair remained convinced both of the link between weapons of mass destruction and terrorism and that getting rid of Saddam's regime was 'morally justified in its own terms'. As he said in an impassioned defence of his actions in a speech in his Sedgefield constituency on 5 March 2004 about the decision he faced:

> *Do we want to take the risk? That is the judgement. And my judgement then and now is that the risk of this new global terrorism and its interaction with states or organisations or individuals proliferating WMD, is one I simply am not prepared to run.*

11. History Will Forgive

> *Can we be sure that terrorism and WMD will join together? Let us say one thing. If we are wrong, we will have destroyed a threat that, at its least is responsible for inhuman carnage and suffering. That is something I am confident history will forgive.*
>
> Tony Blair, speech to Joint Session of US Congress,
> Washington, Thursday 17 July 2003

> *If they [the Americans] see an integrated Europe as a threat then they must be nuts. I think that they do not think it produces very much in the way of value for them at the moment. It is up to the Europeans to demonstrate that they can produce some value added.*
>
> Robert Cooper, Director General, European Council
> Secretariat, in evidence to the European Union Committee of
> the House of Lords, 8 May 2003

> *There is a good deal less to the special relationship between Britain and the US than meets the eye. For the British, it is an emotional comfort blanket for a declining power.*
>
> Sir Rodric Braithwaite, *Prospect*, May 2003

The Iraq war was not inevitable. Few wars are. At various stages over the preceding year or two, different decisions by the key players could have produced a peaceful outcome, though possibly only delaying war for a few months, or years. The transatlantic split, and the divisions within Europe, might not have occurred, or at least been less damaging. Similarly, now, the main leaders, in both the United States and Europe, have choices over future relations. Britain and Tony Blair face the biggest decisions in this post-war reassessment.

The main determinant of the Iraq war was, of course, Saddam Hussein himself. His appalling regime had a brutal record towards both the Iraqi people and neighbouring countries, and Iraq had defied the UN for more than a decade over weapons of mass destruction (as recognised in Resolution 1441). That was the prime reason for the war, but not for its timing. The main factor here was the Bush administration's decision to deploy America's overwhelming military power against security threats, whether or not other countries or the UN agreed. This policy of assertive nationalism initially only showed itself in a dismissive attitude towards international agreements such as the Kyoto Climate Change Treaty or the International Criminal Court. Despite the desire of many in the administration to get rid of Saddam, the US President's early policy was to strengthen 'smart sanctions' rather than to take military action.

The 11 September attacks changed all that. They starkly exposed America's vulnerability and made the Bush administration determined to use American military power to remove terrorism, and its sponsors, wherever they appeared. The use of the word 'crusade' in the days after 9/11 was maladroit, but it was also revealing. The campaign against terrorism – always described as a war by the Bush team – was seen in religious terms. Born-again Christianity was the prevailing tone at the Bush White House. The language used was stark: 'with us or against us' (as much as about supposed allies as enemies), 'axis of evil' and 'rogue states'. This at times intolerant absolutism explains much of the hostility to Bush in Europe, including Britain. Javier Solana, the Europeans' foreign policy representative has noted (quoted in Dempsey, 2003) that for the White House, 'It is all or nothing. For us Europeans, it is difficult to deal with because we are secular. We do not see the world in such black and white terms.'

So once the Taliban and al-Qa'eda had been dealt with in Afghanistan, if not elsewhere, Iraq was always going to be next in the view of President Bush and his advisers. That made war probable from early 2002 onwards, but not certain. Saddam could still have backed down and accepted full international dismantling of his weapons of mass destruction. This happened with South Africa's nuclear weapons programme, with the full consent and involvement of its Government at the end of the apartheid regime. Such compliance would have annoyed the Washington hawks who wanted to get rid of Saddam. But, as Tony Blair said, such co-operation by Baghdad would have involved such a change in Saddam's method of governing as almost to amount to regime change. But the Americans never believed that Saddam would comply and were determined to force the issue, sooner rather than later. Creating an international coalition and working through the UN were secondary.

Britain, and Tony Blair, had a choice, or rather choices. At one extreme, Blair could have behaved like France or Germany and expressed hostility to any military action against Iraq in early 2003, saying the UN inspectors should be given longer. He could have threatened otherwise to use Britain's Security Council veto, as

President Chirac did on 10 March. Such outright hostility was inconceivable. It would have meant reversing the 60-year-old foundations of British foreign policy, as well as endangering American co-operation which was vital for the operations of Britain's Trident submarines and for satellite intelligence. Such opposition would have been akin to the diplomatic earthquake which would have followed the election of Labour in 1983, with its commitment to get rid of nuclear weapons unilaterally. There is a parallel with Chancellor Schröder's decision to abandon Germany's long post-war support for America and to oppose the Iraq war. But Washington has never seen Germany as an active military ally in offensive operations outside Europe, as Britain has been several times. Even so, Schröder was almost completely frozen out by Bush after the German elections.

An alternative might have been to follow Edward Heath's approach in 1973 during the Yom Kippur War and to adopt a policy of detached neutrality, declining to provide military help or the use of British bases for any attack on Iraq. A variant might have been the Harold Wilson option: backing the American action, even if in a lukewarm form, but resisting any commitment of British troops, as in Vietnam, despite repeated pleas from Lyndon Johnson. As Steven Philip Kramer has argued (2003): 'The United Kingdom could have publicly supported the American position on the war while avoiding military involvement, or it could have provided only token military support.' After all, both José María Aznar and Silvio Berlusconi did the former during the Iraq war, in the face of overwhelming public opposition in Spain and Italy. (As Blair once joked in a conversation with Aznar, fewer Spaniards supported the war than believed that Elvis Presley was still alive.) This approach would have caused less political trouble for Blair in Britain. Indeed, as Donald Rumsfeld tactlessly said when the political arithmetic in the Commons looked uncertain for Blair, the US might have to manage without British troops.

The demand by Downing Street for an instant 'clarification' by Rumsfeld showed why this approach was never acceptable to the Blair Government – though, as Jack Straw's memorandum showed, this option was certainly considered, given the uncertainties over domestic, and particularly Labour parliamentary, support for military action. But such a course would have been very much a last resort, an admission of defeat possibly involving the resignation of Tony Blair and other senior ministers. It was not just that around 40,000 British troops were in the region and pulling them out at such a late stage would have been a humiliation. Committing British troops in such crises has been at the heart of Britain's relationship with America, dating back to Washington's request in 1950 for a token ground force in Korea (much smaller than in Iraq) which was initially resisted by Chiefs of Staff in London (as discussed in Chapter 2).

In reality, none of these options would ever remotely have appealed to Blair. His decision to go to war had longstanding roots – both in his policy towards Iraq and weapons of mass destruction and in his 'hug them close' approach to working with America. As earlier chapters make clear, his concern about Saddam's regime and weapons of mass destruction long pre-dated either the arrival in the White House of George W. Bush or the 11 September attacks. He used exactly the same language in the 1997–8 confrontation with Saddam as in justifying the Iraq war in early 2003. He authorised British involvement in the Operation Desert Fox attacks on Iraq in

December 1998 and the continuing patrols between 1998 and 2003 by the Royal Air Force in enforcing the no-fly zones over northern and southern Iraq. Blair needed no persuading to take a tough line against Saddam.

Blair's approach has partly been defensive, an attempt to contain the only remaining superpower. As he has often said, the US should not be left to tackle the tricky issues alone. His fear has been that if Britain and other European allies do not stand by Washington on major issues, then the unilateralist forces in Washington will be strengthened and the world will be worse off. This view has been reinforced by his insight into the significance of 9/11. Unlike many other European leaders, he has grasped how the US feels threatened. While many Europeans, like Solana, have been aghast at the quasi-religious absolutism of Washington's response, Blair has understood it, partly because he takes a moralistic approach himself. That does not make Blair a neo-conservative. His doctrine of humanitarian intervention is rooted in liberal values, international treaties and institutions, not American hegemony. In Robert Kagan's Venus–Mars antithesis of Europeans and Americans, Blair is a Venusian in Martian clothes.

Like Jacques Chirac, and unlike Donald Rumsfeld or the various varieties of neo-conservatives, Blair wants America to be part of the international community, accepting its rules, constraints and conventions. But, unlike Chirac and some other Europeans, he rejects a competitive, multipolar view. As he said in his speech to a Joint Session of Congress on 17 July 2003:

> *There is no more dangerous theory in international politics*
> *today than that we need to balance the power of America*

with other competitor powers, different poles around which nations gather . . . It is dangerous because it is not rivalry but partnership we need; a common will and a shared purpose in the face of a common threat. An alliance must start with America and Europe. Believe me, if Europe and America are together, the others will work with us. But if we split, all the rest will play around, play us off and nothing but mischief will be the result of it.

That in essence is why Blair backed the Iraq war. Not only did he genuinely believe that Saddam and his programme of weapons of mass destruction were a threat, particularly if used by terrorists, but he also recognised, at least from spring 2002 onwards, that America was going to confront and probably attack the Iraqi dictator. And since it was in the interests of neither Britain nor the world for the US to act alone, Blair would be together with America in backing a war and in committing troops. It was not an instant or an unconditional commitment at the Crawford summit in April 2002. The conditions were that Saddam had to be given one final chance via a further UN resolution. There were always potential let-out clauses if Saddam complied over weapons of mass destruction. Even in March 2003, Blair could have been put in a very awkward political position if France had been willing to back a resolution with some kind of time-limited ultimatum. He would have been squeezed between his support for the UN inspectors and the growing impatience of the Pentagon to get on with the war. However, stage by stage during 2002, Blair became more committed in practice, even if no final, irrevocable decision was taken until March 2003.

If, in Robin Cook's phrase, there was a 'Faustian bargain', it was a lopsided one. The Bush administration would have gone ahead in Iraq with or without Britain's support and forces. Bush would always have preferred to have Blair with him, both for the value of British troops and to demonstrate that the war was not a unilateral operation. Yet Blair also recognised that the war was fought on American terms and for American reasons. As Chapter 8 shows, from the Crawford summit in April 2002 onwards, there was a contradiction in Blair's public statements. The Bush administration's overriding goal was regime change; weapons of mass destruction were secondary. As Paul Wolfowitz candidly said after the war (in Tanenhaus, 2003): 'For bureaucratic reasons we settled on one issue, weapons of mass destruction, because it was the one reason everyone could agree on.' Wolfowitz referred to other reasons: in particular, 'almost unnoticed but huge', removing Saddam would allow the US to take its troops out of Saudi Arabia, which would remove a major cause of resentment and would open the way to a more peaceful Middle East.

Blair sympathised with the goal of removing Saddam. But he could not himself make regime change his public reason for going to war. That was unacceptable legally, and diplomatically since Blair wanted, if possible, to work through the UN. Thomas Friedman, the *New York Times* columnist, put the point succinctly (2003): Blair could not make the case for getting rid of Saddam as a genocidal dictator and to 'help tilt the Middle East onto a more progressive political track . . . because the British public had not gone through 9/11 and did not really feel threatened, because it demanded a UN legal cover for any war and because it didn't like or trust Bush.' So

Blair's longstanding concern with Iraq's weapons of mass destruction and the link with terrorism became the key issue. That created all sorts of problems. There was no dispute that Saddam had, in the past, had a programme to develop biological, chemical and nuclear weapons, as well as unaccounted stocks of chemicals. That was the reason for sending the inspectors back. But that was not sufficient for military action. Hence the search by Downing Street for evidence of an existing, as opposed to a past, threat. That led to all the subsequent controversy about 'sexing up' the September dossier.

The central question is not whether the evidence presented by the intelligence agencies was genuine but whether it amounted to such an immediate threat that pre-emptive military action was necessary in mid-March 2003. This was the dilemma addressed in Jonathan Powell's e-mail of 17 September 2002. The charge is that, knowing that America was going to war anyway in March, the Prime Minister and others exaggerated the immediacy of the threat from Saddam. As the Intelligence and Security Committee said in its September 2003 report (p. 31): 'Saddam was not considered a current or imminent threat to mainland UK'. However, as both the intelligence agencies and the ISC report recognised, Saddam was unquestionably a potential threat, both through his intent to develop weapons of mass destruction, and through possible, disastrous links with terrorist groups. But the urgency of Blair's language was not the result of Saddam's current actions or even his defiance of UN resolutions, but because of the American military timetable. That was the other, unspoken, but central part of the Blair strategy, a determination to work alongside Washington. However, containment and inspections could have continued for a few more weeks and months without a greatly increased risk of action by Saddam. That meant that Blair's talk about the threat was partly an act of faith, even of political necessity. In his speech to the Joint Session of Congress, he addressed the risks that terrorism and states developing weapons of mass destruction might come together:

> *Can we be sure that terrorism and WMD will join together? Let us say one thing. If we are wrong, we will have destroyed a threat that, at its least is responsible for inhuman carnage and suffering. That is something I am confident history will forgive. But if our critics are wrong, if we are right, as I believe with every fibre of instinct and conviction I have that we are, and we do not act, then we will have hesitated in face of this menace, when we should have given leadership. That is something history will not forgive.*

The evidence for Blair's restraining influence over Bush on Iraq is limited, partly because the Prime Minister largely agreed with the direction in which the President was going. To adapt Donald Rumsfeld's phrase, the coalition, in the form of Blair, did not determine the mission, but he may have affected how it was implemented. Blair can be credited with helping to persuade Bush to obtain a UN resolution in autumn 2002, and, more reluctantly and half-heartedly, for seeking a further resolution in February and March 2002. The latter turned out to be a mixed blessing which may have aggravated, rather than reduced, transatlantic divisions. But the attempt was vital in view of Blair's domestic political pressures. Blair may have had a role – if only by sheer persistence – in helping to persuade Bush to become more personally involved in tackling the Israel–Palestine dispute. The changes to the Palestinian Authority and the publication of the road map were along the lines that Blair had long been advocating. But progress was short-lived, both because of the resumption of suicide bombings and the killing of some leaders of Hamas and other terrorist groups by Israel, and because of Bush's backing of the Sharon Government's imposed solution (in which Blair seemed to acquiesce, to the anger of many British diplomats, let alone Arab states).

Since the end of the war, there have been some positive developments on proliferation, Partly thanks to the work of the Secret Intelligence Service (MI6) in uncovering the links to Pakistan and elsewhere, Libya has admitted not just to a nuclear weapons programme, now under international surveillance, but also to having chemical weapons, now being destroyed. North Korea and Iran have been in talks over their nuclear programmes.

However, critics like former Conservative Foreign Minister Lord Howe of Aberavon have been scathing (2003):

> *It is hard now to identify any decision of substance, as opposed to process, on which Britain's Prime Minister secured any real change in American plans. By contrast, the down-side consequences for Britain's other foreign policy objectives have become ever more evident. We have seen serious damage to the effectiveness and credibility of NATO, the United Nations and the European Union – the three institutions which have in the past enabled us to*

> *amplify our international leverage, well beyond our basic*
> *strength.*

Blair did not find it easy to convince the Bush administration to listen to the rest of the world and to involve these international institutions. NATO has been sidelined despite fine words and despite its valuable work in running peacekeeping in the Balkans, and, recently, in Afghanistan. NATO is regarded by many in the Pentagon as a 'tool kit', whose resources can be drawn upon, as, and when, needed, rather than an alliance to be consulted and involved. Blair's efforts as marriage counsellor to heal the rifts with Paris and Berlin were largely unrewarded. Even before the war, in his speech to British diplomats in early January, Blair had warned that the problem people have with the US is that they 'want the US to listen back'. More than six months later, in his Washington speech in July 2003, Blair returned to the same theme, in relation to climate change as well as to weapons of mass destruction: 'The world's security cannot be protected without the world's heart being won. So America must listen as well as lead'. In remarks partly aimed at Rumsfeld in the audience: 'Let us start preferring a coalition and acting alone if we have to; not the other way round. True, winning wars is not easier that way. But winning the peace is.' The British were frustrated with America's handling of post-war Iraq and its reluctance to allow a larger role for the UN.

Blair's decision not to allow America to go to war on its own meant a split with France and Germany. It is true that a majority of European countries backed a tough line against Saddam, but only Britain and Poland, with a contingent of 200 special forces, joined in militarily. These divisions undoubtedly weakened Europe's voice and influence with Washington, in Blair's sense as a partner rather than as a rival. Blair and José María Aznar were listened to by Bush, but as members of a coalition of the willing – in Aznar's case a non-playing one – rather than as voices for Europe. And Blair looked even more isolated in March 2004 after Aznar's party lost the Spanish general election. Could this split have been avoided? In his speech on 18 March 2003 opening the Commons debate on whether to go to war, Blair raised an intriguing possibility:

> *I tell you what Europe should have said last September to the US. With one voice it should have said: We understand your strategic anxiety over terrorism and WMD and we will help you meet it. We will mean what we say in any UN resolution we pass and will back it with action if Saddam fails to disarm voluntarily; but in return we ask two things of you: that the US should choose the UN path and you should recognise the fundamental importance of re-starting the Middle East peace process, which we will hold you to.*

That was probably always a remote possibility, but was doomed by four factors.

First, the curious twists of the French Presidential election – in which Jean Marie Le Pen of the far-right had eliminated Lionel Jospin in the first round – had given President Chirac an overwhelming victory, and, for the first time in his long career, unchallenged authority. He had the domestic freedom to operate on the global stage.

Second, Gerhard Schröder had played the anti-war and anti-American cards as the only way to win the German elections in September and his very narrow victory prevented him from then being more sympathetic to Washington.

Third, Blair himself was much more concerned with opinion in Washington than in Paris or Berlin. 'The US had the power, and that is where Blair turned his attention', in the words of one of his close advisers. Even though Blair spent a lot of time on the phone with, and visiting, Schröder and Chirac (at least until early 2003), reaching agreement with them seemed a lower priority.

Fourth, by autumn 2002, many European leaders were already suspicious of American unilateralism after the rows over Kyoto and the 'axis of evil' speech. They were also bruised by high-handed American behaviour. France, Russia and, in a different way, Germany were worried about the Bush administration's attempt to operate and take military action outside international organisations and treaties. US officials showed little interest in the views of allies. Their attitude seemed often to be: 'Take it or leave it, we are going to do what we want anyway.' It was not just Donald Rumsfeld and the Pentagon. There was also a major failure of diplomacy by the State Department, notably by Colin Powell. This may have made all the difference to the breakdown of negotiations with Turkey about allowing access to US land forces for the invasion of Iraq. European foreign ministers liked Powell and regarded him as sympathetic to their worries. But Powell made little direct effort to improve relations. As Ivo Daalder has pointed out (2003), Powell travelled to Europe just six times in 2001, and only three times in 2002. By contrast, James Baker was constantly travelling to Europe before the 1991 Gulf War and this helped to shore up the European side of the wide-ranging coalition then. Daalder comments about Powell's failure to travel around the capitals of allies: 'The unwillingness to engage in this kind of personal give-and-take underscores the declining importance of Europe to Washington policymakers, and raises questions in Europe about whether the US is more interested in stating firm American convictions than forging common positions.'

For all these reasons, there was probably little or no chance in autumn 2002 of reaching the kind of deal between Europe and America which Blair later described, desirable though it would have been. Thereafter, relations got steadily worse as each side annoyed the other. The first three months of 2003 were a textbook case in how not to conduct diplomacy. In themselves, the various incidents described in Chapter 9 probably made war neither more nor less likely, but they made the resulting divisions and recriminations worse.

So how much damage was done? The domestic impact has been most obvious in the fall in Tony Blair's popularity. Discontent with his handling of Iraq fed into a sharp drop in trust in him generally. A decline in the credibility of the Government has affected its ability to persuade voters that public services are improving, as well as fuelling opposition within the Labour Party to controversial policies such as foundation hospitals and tuition fees. A year after the fall of Baghdad, Tony Blair's authority remained weakened by his handling of the Iraq war and by the revelations about the operations of 10 Downing Street at Lord Hutton's inquiry. This may just be temporary. But once trust is lost, it is hard to rebuild.

This decline in Blair's standing made it inevitable that a referendum on entry into the euro would not be held before the next general election, likely at some time in 2005. The consistently better performance of Britain than the main eurozone economies had anyway made a referendum unlikely and a 'not yet' verdict the result of Gordon Brown's comprehensive assessment in June 2003. But the political results of the war removed even the slim hopes of the pro-euro campaign of a later referendum. So it was a mere formality when Brown announced in his budget speech on 17 March, 2004, that he would not be undertaking another euro assessment. The euro was effectively off the political agenda for the foreseeable future.

Nearly a year before the war, Robin Cook, then Leader of the Commons, had warned Blair that he could not both commit Britain to a war in Iraq and win a referendum on the euro. As Cook later wrote (2003, p. 357): Blair has 'exhausted his stock of credibility and trust in delivering Bush's strategic designs on Iraq, and has none left to secure Britain's interest in membership of the euro'. It is arguable that the failure to join the euro has had as much impact on Britain's standing within the EU as the strains over the Iraq war. As Blair has acknowledged, 'it is a statement of the obvious that if we are outside the single currency we have less of an influence on it.'

Both the euro non-decision and the divisions with France and Germany have revived the old questions about Britain as a nation apart, the perpetual awkward partner. These qualify Blair's talk about a 'transformation' in Britain's position in Europe since 1997. 'A constructive role', certainly, and progress, but not quite the 'substantial progress' which Blair claims. Admittedly, the Prime Minister can point to the British influence on the economic reform agenda (though the results have so far been limited). The Foreign Office has argued, with evident relief, that the divisions over Iraq did not prevent agreement at the Convention on the Future of Europe on proposals for the future government of the EU which are a good deal for Britain. This may be more because the Convention's proposals – under the guiding hand of former French President Valery Giscard d'Estaing – have been favourable to big countries generally, including France as well as Britain. However, the continuing ambiguities in Britain's relations with Europe were underlined in April 2004 when Blair announced – to the surprise of many of his Cabinet colleagues and to the dismay of other EU leaders – that a referendum would be held on any EU constitutional treaty. This was further evidence of his political weakness, another price of the Iraq war.

Tony Blair has been, however, characteristically optimistic that the wounds caused by the Iraq war will quickly heal. At his end-of-term press conference on 30 July 2003, when asked whether his 1997 objective of Britain playing a leading role had been set back, he replied:

> *In respect of Iraq, this may seem a slightly counter-intuitive thing for me to say, I think in a curious way, after the disagreement on Iraq, having been through that experience, all of us, there is a genuine desire not to repeat it if at all possible. And I would say that our relationship with France and Germany at the moment is strong, and it is accepted that we had a disagreement over Iraq, and that we took different positions. But what was interesting was that both at the most recent European Council, where Javier Solana presented a paper on European security which was very pro-transatlantic alliance, and when I was*

> *over in Congress recently where I thought, I won't say I was*
> *surprised, but on the other hand I was pleased to find that*
> *a statement that we had to work with Europe was well*
> *received. On both sides of the Atlantic there is a recogni-*
> *tion that this alliance is necessary. Provided we can create*
> *a sense of partnership, rather than rival poles of power, if*
> *we can create a genuine sense of partnership than that is*
> *ground upon which France, Germany and Britain can*
> *congregate in the same place.*

I have quoted these remarks at length because they are quintessentially Blair – reflecting his belief that, with a bit of goodwill and
common sense, differences can be reconciled and the transatlantic
bridge rebuilt. But he cannot simply regard the breakdown in
diplomacy and the European divisions of spring 2003 as an unfortu-
nate incident best forgotten. It was not just President Chirac's
intransigence or Chancellor Schröder's weakness. It is also no good
pointing to the support of Spain, Italy and the new entrants to the EU
in central and eastern Europe as proof of a shift in European thinking
– not least when Spain shifted to a more hostile view of the US after
its election in March 2004. France and Germany matter. President
Chirac may not have spoken for a majority of European countries,
but he did reflect the views of a majority of individual Europeans.

Aware of these tensions, Blair has taken some risks to demonstate
his pro-European credentials – particularly in pushing defence co-
operation in the EU (as discussed later in this chapter). He has also
fostered talk of tripartite leadership involving Germany, France and
Britain in the new expanded European Union, up to twenty-five

members after 1 May 2004. Foreign ministers of the three worked closely together in going to Tehran in October 2003 to try and defuse tensions over Iran's nuclear programme. This led to a less aggressive approach than many in Washington would have preferred. This was seen as the power of the three being greater either than Britain on its own dealing with Washington or the probably ineffective approach of all twenty-five, if they could agree. But this Iran initiative has not worked so far, Iran's nuclear programme continues. This initiative excluded Javier Solana, who was supposed to be the EU's main representative in foreign affairs. Moreover, smaller countries have resented this tripartism, particularly after Blair, Schröder and Chirac held a well-publicised meeting in Berlin in Feburary 2004. However, Chirac's typically blunt remarks then about the depth of the Franco–German alliance exposed the limits of any British role and of the tripartite approach generally.

Relations have remained correct and cool between Washington and both Paris and Berlin. There has been no meeting of minds between American unilateralists and European multilateralists, particularly when President Chirac has repeated his talk about a multipolar world. At the annual Munich conference of defence ministers and experts – the scene of an open confrontation between Donald Rumsfeld and Joschka Fischer in February 2003 ahead of the Iraq war – relations were not much improved a year later. Everyone agrees about the need to win the peace together, but the mutual suspicions remain great. There is little sense of a conversation, as opposed to talking past each other. Despite all the obvious problems in Iraq, particularly after the formal end of US occupation, France and Germany are still deeply sceptical about becoming more directly involved. Moreover, as the comprehensive survey published by the Pew Research Center in March 2004 shows, opinions towards America in France and Germany are at least as negative as at the end of the Iraq war, and are more critical in Britain. Large majorities in Germany, France and Russia still believe that their countries made the right decision in not taking part in the war. And there is broad agreement in all the main countries, apart from the US, that the war in Iraq hurt, rather than helped, the war on terrorism.

Admittedly, France, Russia and other countries backed UN Resolution 1483 in late May 2003 legitimising the occupation, but the US opposed giving the UN responsibility for the future of Iraq over the head of Paul Bremer. Bush's unilateralist instincts were not tempered by the experience of war and by transatlantic splits. Yet the Bush doctrine of pre-emptive action and coalitions of the willing rather than alliances is unsustainable in the long term, even in Iraq. Over the course of 2003–4, there was a shift towards accepting a greater role for the UN in Iraq and for the involvement of other countries. But this was the result of necessity, not conviction. The judgement of Ivo Daalder and James Lindsay in the autumn of 2003 (p. 195) still stands:

> *The deeper problem was that the fundamental premise of the Bush revolution – that America's security rested on an America unbound – was mistaken. This premise would have been right if the unilateral exercise of American power could have achieved America's major foreign policy goals. But the most important foreign policy challenges America faced – whether defeating terrorism, reversing*

weapons proliferation, promoting economic prosperity,
safeguarding political liberty, sustaining the global envi-
ronment, or halting the spread of killer diseases – could not
be solved by Washington alone. They required the active
co-operation of others.

'Never again' requires more than just good intentions – though avoiding the type of mutual invective seen in early 2003 would obviously help. Robert Cooper (2003, p. 172) has argued that if Europe wants to influence these developments, 'we shall need more power, both military power and multilateral legitimacy'. Charles Grant of the Centre for European Reform proposed in the summer of 2003 a series of steps to bring Americans and Europeans back together, most of which come down to considering the other sides' views and interests, rather than thinking and behaving unilaterally. For America, they included being aware that unilateral actions carry costs, that the style of diplomacy affects outcomes, and that the reconstruction of Iraq is an opportunity to revive transatlantic co-operation. For the Europeans, the steps involve adopting new economic policies to boost growth and therefore to permit a stronger foreign and security policy, enhancing military capabilities, improving decision-making on foreign policy and trying to overcome divisions between 'new' and 'old' Europe. For both, he suggested insulating the Doha trade round from security issues, working out a common approach to Iran, reaching an understanding on weapons of mass destruction and discussing principles of intervention. By spring 2004, there were few signs of progress on most of these steps.

From an American internationalist standpoint, James Steinberg, formerly a senior adviser in the Clinton White House, argued in an article for *Survival* in summer 2003:

> *Developing a new, sustainable transatlantic relationship will require a series of deliberate decisions on both sides of the Atlantic – a partnership of choice, not necessity. For the US, this means avoiding the temptation, offered by our unprecedented strength, to go it alone in pursuit of narrowly defined national interests. For Europe, the new partnership will require a willingness to accept that the US plays a uniquely valuable role as a leader in a world where power still matters, and that a commitment to a rule-based international order does not obviate the need to act decisively against those who do not share that vision.*

These questions have been endlessly discussed since the fall of Baghdad at a series of conferences of the transatlantic great and the glib. Most of the internationalist foreign policy elite agree on what should be done. Their suggestions are generally all sensible, and desirable. Many of the earlier suggestions were echoed in the spring of 2004 by a high-powered report from a task force sponsored by the Council on Foreign Relations, comprising leading Europeans and Americans, chaired by Henry Kissinger and Lawrence Summers, the former Treasury Secretary in the Clinton administation. Their report (2004, p. vii) stressed the compatible interests and complementary capabilities of the US and Europe and recommended that both sides 'should reassess existing principles governing the use of military force and seek to reach agreement on new "rules of the road". Similarly, it argues that America and Europe should develop a common policy towards states that possess or seek to possess weapons of mass destruction or that support terrorism in any way'. However, it may suit Washington for Europe to remain divided – and indeed to encourage such divisions as the US picks and chooses allies for coalitions of the willing. But such divisions should not suit Britain, nor should they suit Washington in the long term. As Charles Grant rightly argues (2003, pp. 56–7):

> *Even if US policy succeeded in keeping the wound open, the consequences would be bad for America. For if one group of states supports the US, the opposing group, with real economic and diplomatic clout, will be actively hostile. That would make it much harder for the US to build alliances and gain the support of international organisations – without which it cannot tackle a host of global problems. In a divided Europe, Britain, its best friend in the EU, would suffer a loss of influence. The British cannot achieve their objectives – such as radical reform of the Common Agricultural Policy, structural economic reform across the EU, or effective institutions which respect the role of national governments – without the co-operation of the French and the Germans.*

One of the Blair Government's prime foreign policy objectives, like its predecessors, has been to avoid choosing between Europe and America – as both euro-sceptics and euro-enthusiasts would like.

American conservatives and anti-Europeans in London who urge that Britain should turn from the EU to the US are living in a fantasy world. Of course, many of Britain's interests in fighting terrorism and weapons of mass destruction coincide with America's and the close military and intelligence links should be preserved. But an even closer relationship with America, at arm's length from Europe, as some Conservatives want, would undermine British independence and sovereignty just as much as becoming part of some European super-state. A British prime minister has influence because he or she represents a country sympathetic to US values, which also has a leading role in Europe. Britain is a European power with global interests, not an adjunct of the US. Equally, Britain cannot, and should not, turn its back on Washington. That would negate its history, instincts and interests. Britain is always likely to be closer to the US than most, if not all, other EU members.

In the aftermath of the Iraq war, there has been pressure for a reassessment of transatlantic links. These have ranged from claims on the left (for instance by David Leigh and Richard Norton-Taylor of the *Guardian*) that 'Britain has by now lost its sovereignty to the United States and has become a client state' and, intriguingly, on the right, by former Foreign Secretaries like Lords Howe and Hurd, and Sir Malcolm Rifkind. After the war, Sir Malcolm argued (2003) that: 'British interests are best served by a close relationship with the United States, but Blair has yet to learn that unqualified endorsement of US policy is a bridge too far.' The qualifications were there in private, as is clear from conversations with Blair's advisers, but his public style of wanting to please and agree with those he meets gives the impression that Sir Malcolm notes – particularly when he has so little apparently to show for the 'hug them close' approach. Even more startling, the whole basis of the 'special relationship' was questioned by Sir Rodric Braithwaite, a former British Ambassador in Moscow and one-time chairman of the Joint Intelligence Committee. In an article in *Prospect*, Sir Rodric stripped away what he called 'an emotional blanket for a declining power'. He said the traffic was one-way, as the Americans have rarely adapted to accommodate the British, while the close links in nuclear defence and communications intelligence in reality involve British dependence on the US. Moreover, as Robin Cook has argued (2004), while Blair was 'right to try to influence Bush and correct to recognise the trade off between being given private access in return for public support', the Prime Minister has been 'short changed in the trade off' and a relationship 'which under Bush has become a one-way street'.

But if the balancing act is to continue, the Blair Government needs to be more independent of the US. Independent need not mean hostile. Tony Blair is right that Europe, including Britain, should seek to be partners of the United States on security issues, notably terrorism, however much we are competitors economically. But being an effective partner – rather than a US satellite or opponent – means at least a greater effort at establishing joint European positions, where possible. In practice, there are major areas of agreement, not least between Britain and France, over the Balkans, Afghanistan and much of the Middle East, apart from Iraq. No one is seriously talking about a single European foreign policy. But there is more scope to develop a common policy over a wide range of issues. Javier Solana's security paper, mentioned by Blair, is a big step forward, towards what its main author has called 'effective multilateralism'. This means engaging with the US on proliferation and terrorism: in the immediate future particularly on Iran. The aim is to show that the EU can be effective on issues of interest to Washington, so that the US finds it difficult to turn Europe down, and, in turn, adopts a more multilateral approach.

The main test is defence. Since the St Malo summit in December 1998, the Blair Government has backed closer European defence links, allowing the EU to run its own military missions, as in the French-led operation in the Congo in June 2003. But how far does this commitment go? There has been a running tension within the British foreign and defence establishment between Europeans and Atlanticists. The 1991 Gulf War, Kosovo, Afghanistan and, now, Iraq have all reinforced the natural tendency of the Ministry of Defence to work alongside the Americans. Geoff Hoon, the Defence Secretary, said after the war (2003) that 'it is highly unlikely that the UK would be engaged in large-scale combat operations without the United States, a judgement born of past experience, shared interest and our assessment of strategic trends'. That has big implications for the pattern of defence spending and commitments. As Geoff Hoon pointed out, the issue is not whether 'the US decides to develop a unilateral or a multilateral approach over the long term.' That will depend on 'the role, persuasiveness and capabilities of its allies'. The entrance ticket to playing on the same team as the Americans is high and Britain is at present the only European country realistically in a position to do so. The key features are lift (aircraft to transport forces rapidly around the world), intelligence, special forces, smart precision guided weapons, an ability to fight at night and sufficiently advanced technology to work as part of the US's integrated 'network-centric capabilities.' In political terms, however, Hoon's candour about fighting alongside the Americans may encourage some EU countries to develop a core European alternative, along the lines of the four-country summit in Brussels in late April. This is, in practice, impracticable given that any credible EU defence operation has to involve Britain, Yet when Britain took further steps with France and Germany in autumn 2003 towards developing defence co-operation in an EU context, the immediate response from Washington was open hostility and the summoning of NATO ambassadors to demand an explanation. This was only partly offset by President Bush's qualified response that he trusted Tony Blair's personal assurance that such a European defence initiative would not undermine NATO.

America remains wedded to creating more coalitions of the willing rather than trying to work with Europe collectively. The key is a *rapprochement* between Britain and France. They need each other. Britain needs France if Europe is ever to speak with one voice, while France needs Britain if Europe is not constantly to be at odds with America.

If Tony Blair should be more consistent in his European aspira-tions, he should also ensure that being a candid friend to Washington involves candour as much as friendship. That means pointing to the virtues of listening to other countries and international organisations. It also means acknowledging differences with Washington: on, for example, climate change, the International Criminal Court and, at times, the Middle East peace process. However, Europe and other countries will have to recognise how much the world has changed. To persuade America to participate positively in the UN will mean a new international consensus on intervention in response to the new threats from terrorist groups and weapons of mass destruction. This may involve pre-emptive action in extreme circumstances.

The need for reform of the UN, 'to construct a consensus behind a broad agenda of justice and security and the means of enforcing it', was one of the main themes of Blair's speech on 'The Threat of Global Terrorism' in his Sedgefield constituency in March 2004. This was a deliberate attempt to take forward his Chicago speech in April 1999, during the Kosovo conflict, on the doctrine of international community. As he argued in Sedgefield:

> *So, for me, before 11 September, I was already reaching for a different philosophy in international relations from a traditional one that has held sway since the treaty of Westphalia in 1648; namely that a country's internal affairs for it and you don't interfere unless it threatens you, or breaches a treaty, or triggers and obligation of alliance. I did not consider Iraq fitted into this philosophy, though I could see the horrible injustice done to its people by Saddam.*

Blair linked this shift with his concern about Islamic extremists and attempts by often unstable states to develop chemical, biological and nuclear programmes. He has a strong case that these developments do require a new approach by the UN if it is not to be paralysed by disagreement. Yet a new international approach also requires a shift by the US to answer what Blair described as 'worries that the US and its allies will by sheer force of their military might, do whatever they want, unilaterally and without recourse to any rule-based code or doctine'.

There is no possibility of going back to the Cold War type of relationship between Britain and America, or between Europe and America. Even the uneasy post-Cold War relations of the 1990s have been left behind. The Iraq war both reflected and reinforced big shifts of view on both sides of the Atlantic. As Ivo Daalder has argued (2003): 'What is no longer possible is for the relationship to continue to drift. There is too much resentment, and too many are becoming alienated, for the drifting apart to continue indefinitely.'

America and Europe could easily diverge, with Britain awkwardly in the middle. As Lord Hurd of Westwell vividly wrote in the *Financial Times* (2003): 'Mr Blair has been the farthing in the penny-farthing bicycle of the Anglo–American alliance. This makes hard going for the farthing.' 'Hug them close' has produced few benefits, but plenty of pain, for Blair. A year on from the Iraq war, the danger for Tony Blair remains that his views will be ignored in much of Europe and taken for granted in Washington.

Bibliography

Ashdown, Paddy, *The Ashdown Diaries: Volume One, 1988–1997*, London, Allen Lane, Penguin, 2000.
Ashdown, Paddy, *The Ashdown Diaries: Volume Two, 1997–1999*, London, Allen Lane, Penguin, 2001.
Baker, Gerard, 'A testing time for the special relationship', *Financial Times*, 22 February 2001.
Baker, James A. III, 'The right way to change a regime', *New York Times*, 25 August 2002.
Balz, Dan, and Woodward, Bob, 'Ten days in September', *Washington Post* series on 'America's chaotic road to war', 27 January 2002 until 3 February 2002.
BBC News, *The Battle for Iraq: BBC News Correspondents on the War against Saddam and a New World Agenda*, edited by Sara Beck and Malcolm Downing, BBC, 2003.
Blair, Tony, speech at the Lord Mayor's Banquet, London, 10 November 1997.
Blair, Tony, speech to the French National Assembly, Paris, 24 March 1998.
Blair, Tony, 'Doctrine of the International Community', speech in Chicago, 22 April 1999.
Blair, Tony, statement to the House of Commons, 14 September 2001.
Blair, Tony, interview with CNN, 16 September 2001.
Blair, Tony, speech to the Labour Party conference, 2 October 2001.
Blair, Tony, speech to the Lord Mayor's Banquet, London, 12 November 2001.
Blair, Tony, speech at the George Bush Senior Presidential Library, College Station, Texas, 7 April 2002.
Blair, Tony, interview with Robert Thomson and Bronwen Maddox, *The Times*, 21 May 2002.
Blair, Tony, interview with David Goodhart, *Prospect*, August 2002.
Blair, Tony, *Iraq's Weapons of Mass Destruction: The Assessment of the British Government*, 24 September 2002.
Blair, Tony, statement to the House of Commons on Iraq and terrorism, 15 October 2002.
Blair, Tony, speech to the Foreign and Commonwealth Office Leadership Conference, Queen Elizabeth II Conference Centre, London, 7 January 2003.
Blair, Tony, statement to the House of Commons on Iraq, 25 February 2003.
Blair, Tony, speech to the House of Commons in debate authorising military action against Iraq, 18 March 2003.
Blair, Tony, speech to Joint Session of the US Congress, Washington, 17 July 2003.
Blair, Tony, statement to the House of Commons on the Hutton report, 28 January 2004.
Blair, Tony, speech on The Threat of Global Terrorism, Sedgefield, 5 March 2004.
Blix, Hans, *Disarming Iraq, The Search for Weapons of Mass Destruction*, London, Bloomsbury, 2004.
Blumenthal, Sidney, *The Clinton Wars*, London, Viking, 2003.
Braithwaite, Sir Rodric, 'End of the affair', *Prospect*, May 2003.
Burk, Kathleen, and Cairncross, Alec, *Goodbye Great Britain: The 1976 IMF crisis*, New Haven and London, Yale University Press, 1992.
Burk, Kathleen, 'We Are Down On Our Knees to the Americans': Anglo–American Relations in the Twentieth Century, Inaugural Lecture at University College, London, 8 October 1996.
Bush, George W., 'A distinctly American internationalism', speech at the Ronald Reagan Presidential Library, 19 November 1999.
Bush, George, W., speech to a Joint Session of the US Congress, 20 September 2001.
Bush, George, W., State of the Union address to a Joint Session of the US Congress, 29 January 2002.
Bush, George W., Graduation speech at US Military Academy, 1 June 2002.
Bush, George W., 'National Security strategy of the United States', 20 September 2002.
Chirac, President Jacques, interview with the *New York Times*, 8 September 2002.
Clark, General Wesley K., *Waging modern war*, New York, *Public Affairs*, 2001.
Clarke, Richard A., *Against All Enemies – Inside America's War on Terror*, New York, Free Press, 2004.
Clinton, Hillary Rodham, *Living History: Memoirs*, London, Headline, 2003.
Cook, Robin, Personal Statement on Resignation from the Cabinet, House of Commons, 17 March 2003.
Cook, Robin, evidence to the Foreign Affairs Committee of the House of Commons, Tuesday, 17 June 2003.
Cook, Robin, *The Point of Departure*, London, Simon and Schuster, 2003.
Cook, Robin, 'The diplomats are right: Blair has been short-changed by the Bush administration', *The Independent*, 28 April 2004.
Cooper, Robert, 'In the name of the law', *New Statesman*, 9 September 2002.
Cooper, Robert, *The Breaking of Nations – Order and Chaos in The Twenty-First Century*, London, Atlantic Books, 2003.
Cradock, Sir Percy, *In Pursuit of British Interests: Reflections on foreign policy under Margaret Thatcher and John Major*, London, John Murray, 1997.
Cradock, Sir Percy, *Know Your Enemy: How the Joint Intelligence Committee saw the world*, London, John Murray, 2002.

Daalder, Ivo, and O'Hanlon, Michael E., *Winning Ugly: NATO's war to save Kosovo*, Brookings Institution, Washington DC, 2000.

Daalder, Ivo, and Lindsay, James, *America Unbound – The Bush Revolution in Foreign Policy*, Washington DC, The Brookings Institution, 2003.

Daalder, Ivo, 'The end of Atlanticism', *Survival*, International Institute for Strategic Studies, volume 45, number 2, summer 2003.

Danchev, Alex, *Oliver Franks, Founding Father*, Oxford, Clarendon Press, 1993.

Danchev, Alex, *On Specialness: Essays in Anglo–American Relations*, London, Macmillan Press, 1998.

Defence Committee of the House of Commons, *Lessons of Kosovo*, Fourteenth Report of Session 1999–2000, Volume 1, House of Commons Paper 347–1.

de Gaulle, Charles, *War Memoirs: Unity 1942–44*, London, Weidenfeld and Nicolson, 1959.

Dempsey, Judy, 'Europe's foreign policy chief sees widening gulf with US', *Financial Times*, 8 January 2003.

Denman, Sir Roy, *Missed Chances: Britain and Europe in the twentieth century*, London, Cassell, 1996.

de Villepin, Dominique, lecture at the International Institute for Strategic Studies, London, 27 March 2003.

de Villepin, Dominique, interview with *Le Monde*, 13 May 2003.

Dimbleby, David, and Reynolds, David, *An Ocean Apart: The relationship between Britain and America in the twentieth century*, London, BBC Books/Hodder and Stoughton, 1988.

Dumbrell, John, *A Special Relationship: Anglo–American relations in the Cold War and after*, London, Macmillan Press, 2001.

European Union Committee of the House of Lords, *A Fractured Partnership? Relations between the European Union and the United States of America*, Thirtieth Report of Session, 2002–3, House of Lords paper 134.

Ferguson, Niall, *Empire: How Britain made the modern world*, London, Allen Lane, Penguin, 2003.

Financial Times, 'The divided West', four-part series, 27–30 May 2003.

Foreign Affairs Committee of the House of Commons, *Foreign Policy Aspects of the War Against Terrorism*, Second Report of Session 2002–3, House of Commons Paper 196.

Foreign Affairs Committee of the House of Commons, *The Decision to go to War in Iraq*, Ninth Report of Session 2002–3, House of Commons paper 813.

Foreign Affairs Committee of the House of Commons, *Foreign Policy Aspects of the War Against Terrorism*, Tenth Report of Session 2002–3, House of Commons paper 405.

Friedman, Thomas, 'The war over the war', *New York Times*, 3 August 2003.

Garden, Sir Timothy, 'Iraq: the military campaign', *International Affairs*, volume 79, number 4, July 2003.

Goldsmith, Lord, Attorney General, Statement on the Legal Basis for Military Action, 17 March 2003.

Gould, Philip, *The Unfinished Revolution: How the modernisers saved the Labour Party*, London, Little, Brown and Company, 1998.

Grant, Charles, *Transatlantic Rift: How to bring the two sides together*, London, Centre for European Reform, 2003.

Henderson, Sir Nicholas, *Mandarin: The diaries of an ambassador, 1966–82*, London, Weidenfeld and Nicolson, 1994.

Hennessy, Peter, *The Secret State: Whitehall and the Cold War*, London, Allen Lane, Penguin, 2002.

Hoagland, Jim, 'Blair in the middle', *Washington Post*, 16 April 2000.

Hoagland, Jim, 'Three miscreants', *Washington Post*, 13 April 2003.

Holbrooke, Richard, *To End a War*, New York, Random House, 1998.

Hoon, Geoff, speech to the Royal United Services Institute, 30 June 2003.

Horne, Alistair, *Macmillan, 1957–86, Volume II of the Official Biography*, London, Macmillan, 1989.

Howe, Lord, of Aberavon, Madron Seligman Memorial Lecture, London, 16 July 2003.

Hurd, Lord, of Westwell, speech to the Royal United Services Institute, 27 January 2003.

Hurd, Lord, of Westwell, 'The penny-farthing's little wheel', *Financial Times*, 16 April 2003.

Hutton, Lord, Statement on 28 January 2004, and *Report of the Inquiry into the Circumstances Surrounding the Death of Dr David Kelly C.M.G.*, House of Commons paper 247.

Ignatieff, Michael, *Empire Lite: Nation-building in Bosnia, Kosovo and Afghanistan*, London, Vintage, 2003.

Ignatieff, Micahel, 'The Way We Live Now', *New York Times*, Sunday 14 March 2004.

Intelligence and Security Committee, *Iraqi Weapons of Mass Destruction – Intelligence and Assessments*, September 2003, Command 5972.

Jenkins, Lord, of Hillhead, interview with Donald Macintyre, *Independent*, 23 September 2002.

Jenkins, Lord, of Hillhead, speech in the House of Lords, 2 September 2002.

Kagan, Robert, *Paradise and Power: America and Europe in the new world order*, London, Atlantic Books, 2003.

Kampfner, John, *Blair's Wars*, London, Free Press, 2003.

Kaplan, Lawrence F., and Kristol, William, *The War over Iraq: Saddam's tyranny and America's mission*, San Francisco, Encounter Books, 2003.

Kay, David, testimony to US Senate Armed Services Committee, about search for weapons of mass destruction in Iraq, 28 January 2004.

Kissinger, Henry, *The White House Years*, Boston, Little, Brown and Company, 1979.

Kissinger, Henry, *Diplomacy*, London, Simon and Schuster, 1994.

317

Kissinger, Henry, *Does America Need a Foreign Policy?: Towards a diplomacy for the twenty-first century*, London, Simon and Schuster, 2001.

Kissinger, Henry, 'The US must help craft a new international order', *New York Post*, 11 August 2002.

Kissinger, Henry, and Summer, Lawrence H., co-chairs, Independent Task Force – *Renewing the Atlantic Partnership*, Council on Foreign Relations, March 2004.

Klein, Joe, *The Natural: The misunderstood presidency of Bill Clinton*, New York, Doubleday, 2002.

Kramer, Steven Philip, 'Blair's Britain after Iraq', *Foreign Affairs*, volume 82, number 4, July/August 2003.

Leigh, David, and Norton-Taylor, Richard, 'We are now a client state', *Guardian*, 17 July 2003.

Lemann, Nicholas, 'The next world order', *New Yorker*, 1 April 2002.

Little, Richard, and Wickham-Jones, Mark, *New Labour's Foreign Policy: A new moral crusade*, Manchester, Manchester University Press, 2000.

Lloyd, John, *Iraq and World Order*, Foreign Policy Centre, 2003.

Ludlam, Steve, and Smith, Martin J. (editors), *New Labour in Government*, London, Macmillan, St Martin's Press, 2001.

Major, John, *John Major: The autobiography*, London, HarperCollins, 1999.

Meyer, Sir Christopher, interview for 'Frontline', American Public Television, 18 March 2003.

Milbank, Dana, 'White House didn't gain CIA nod for claim on Iraqi strikes', *Washington Post*, 20 July 2003.

Milward, Alan S., 'The Rise and Fall of a National Strategy 1945–63', *The United Kingdom and the European Community: Volume I*, London, Whitehall History Publishing in association with Frank Cass, 2002.

Naughtie, James, *The Rivals: The intimate story of a political marriage*, London, Fourth Estate, 2001.

Neustadt, Richard E., *Report to JFK: The Skybolt case in perspective*, Ithaca and London, Cornell University Press, 1999.

Nye, Joseph S., *The Paradox of American Power*, Oxford, Oxford University Press, 2002.

Patten, Chistopher, 'America and Europe: an essential partnership', speech to the Chicago Council on Foreign Relations, Chicago, 3 October 2002.

Patten, Christopher, interviewed for 'United but falling apart?', BBC Radio 4 *Analysis* programme on US and European relations, 29 October 2002.

Patten, Christopher, interview with Peter Riddell, *The Times*, 19 November 2002.

Quinlan, Sir Michael, 'War on Iraq: a blunder and a crime', *Financial Times*, 7 August 2002.

Rashid, Ahmed, *Taliban: Islam, oil and the new great game in Central Asia*, London and New York, I. B. Tauris, 2000.

Rawnsley, Andrew, *Servants of the People: The inside story of New Labour*, London, Penguin Books, 2001.

Rentoul, John, *Tony Blair – Prime Minister*, London, Little, Brown and Company, 2001.

Renwick, Sir Robin, *Fighting with Allies: American and Britain in peace and war*, New York, Times Books, Random House, 1996.

Rice, Condoleezza, 'Promoting the national interest', *Foreign Affairs*, volume 79, number 1, January/February 2000.

Riddell, Peter, 'The dangers in being close to Uncle Sam', *The Times*, 4 November 2002.

Riddell, Peter, 'Blair hasn't even won the Establishment round to war', *The Times*, 20 February 2003.

Rifkind, Sir Malcolm, 'That's enough grovelling, PM', *Spectator*, 10 May 2003.

Rogers, Simon (editor), *The Hutton Inquiry and Its Impact*, Politico's/Guardian Books, 2004.

Rozenberg, Joshua, 'How one word made the Iraq war legal', *Daily Telegraph*, 20 March 2003.

Seitz, Raymond, *Over Here*, London, Weidenfeld and Nicolson, 1998.

Short, Clare, Personal Statement on Resignation from the Cabinet, House of Commons, 12 May 2003.

Short, Clare, evidence to the Foreign Affairs Committee of the House of Commons, 17 June 2003.

Sifry, Micah, and Cerf, Christopher, *The Iraq War Reader: History, documents, opinions*, New York and London, Touchstone/Simon and Schuster, 2003.

Skidelsky, Robert, *John Maynard Keynes: Fighting for Britain, 1937–46*, London, Macmillan, 2000.

Slevin, Peter, and Priest, Dana, 'Wolfowitz concedes Iraq errors', *Washington Post*, 24 July 2003.

Solana, Javier, 'A secure Europe in a better world', European Council, Salonika, 20 June 2003.

Steinberg, James B., 'An elective partnership: salvaging transatlantic relations', *Survival*, International Institute for Strategic Studies, volume 45, number 2, summer 2003.

Stephens, Philip, 'Married man seeks friendship', *Financial Times*, 16 February 2001.

Stephens, Philip, *Tony Blair – The Making of a World Leader*, New York, Viking, 2004.

Stothard, Peter, *30 Days: A month at the heart of Blair's war*, London, HarperCollins, 2003.

Straw, Jack, interview with Richard Beeston and Philip Webster, *The Times*, 6 November 2001.

Straw, Jack, interview with Philip Webster, *The Times*, 1 January 2002.

Straw, Jack, speech in House of Commons debate on Iraq, 25 November 2002.

Straw, Jack, interview with Peter Riddell and Philip Webster, *The Times*, 28 February 2003.

Straw, Jack, interview with Tom Baldwin and Philip Webster, *The Times*, 26 April 2003.

Tanenhaus, Sam, 'Bush's Brains Trust', *Vanity Fair*, July 2003.

Talbott, Strobe, *The Russia Hand: A memoir of presidential diplomacy*, London, Random House, 2002.

Thatcher, Margaret, *The Downing Street Years*, London, HarperCollins, 1993.

Thatcher, Margaret, *The Path to Power*, London, HarperCollins, 1995.

Tyrie, Andrew, 'Axis of Anarchy: Britain, America and the new world order after Iraq', Bow Group and the Foreign Policy Centre, 2003.

Webster, Philip, 'Blair–Bush ties will bring future trouble', *The Times*, 26 February 2001.

Wilson, Sir Richard, 'How I helped the Government to come of age', interview on his retirement as Cabinet Secretary with Peter Riddell, *The Times*, 31 July 2002.

Wintour, Patrick, and Kettle, Martin, 'Blair's road to war', *Guardian*, 26 April 2003.

Woodward, Bob, *Bush at war*, New York and London, Simon and Schuster, 2002.

Woodward, Bon, *Plan of Attack*, New York and London, Simon and Schuster, 2004.c

Index